BELLES & WHISTLES

ALSO BY ANDREW MARTIN

NOVELS
Bilton
The Bobby Dazzlers

The Jim Stringer Series:
The Necropolis Railway
The Blackpool Highflyer
The Lost Luggage Porter
Murder at Deviation Junction
Death on a Branch Line
The Last Train to Scarborough
The Somme Stations
The Baghdad Railway Club
Night Train to Jamalpur

NON-FICTION
Underground Overground:
A Passenger's History of the Tube
Funny You Should Say That: Amusing Remarks from Cicero
to The Simpsons (editor)
How To Get Things Really Flat: A Man's Guide to Ironing,
Dusting and other Household Arts
Ghoul Britannia: Notes From a Haunted Isle

BELLES & WHISTLES

Five Journeys Through Time on Britain's Trains

ANDREW MARTIN

P
PROFILE BOOKS

PICTURE CREDITS

The author and publisher would like to thank the following for their kind permission to reproduce the images in this book: Illustration 5, photograph by Ian Britton/ Freefoto.com; Illustration 7 and Plate 6 © Belle Gateway 5BEL Trust Collection; Illustration 8 © John Bird, of Southern Images. All other images reproduced with permission ©National Railway Museum/Science & Society Picture Library.

First published in Great Britain in 2014 by
PROFILE BOOKS LTD
3. Exmouth House
Pine Street
London 201? 075
www.profilebooks.com

Typeset in Quadraat by MacGuru Ltd
info@macguru.org.uk

Printed and bound in Great Britain by
Clays, Bungay, Suffolk

ISBN 978 1 78125 212 3
eISBN 978 1 78283 025 2

CONTENTS

INTRODUCTION

THE RAILWAY PLAYER

I practically grew up on a train, but my nominal base, in between journeys, was the city of York. York is still an important railway junction. About six thousand people work on the railways there, more than anywhere outside London, but a tourist arriving by car could spend a whole day in the city without really noticing the trains. When I was born in York, in 1962, twenty thousand people worked on its railways, which were rather less discreet in the way they conducted their business.

As we were regularly told at school, York has always been a major centre for communications. As Eboracum it was a kind of Roman roundabout, with roads coming in from all directions, and then there were the two rivers, the Ouse and the Foss. In the 1830s and 1840s George Hudson, the 'Railway King' (and crook), made York the spider in the web of his York & North Midland Railway. This connected to London Euston via Normanton, which was – and is – east and south of Leeds. He then persuaded the Great North of England Railway to bring its line from Newcastle to York rather than Leeds. In short, Hudson put York on what would become the East Coast Main Line, instead of the perhaps more deserving candidate, Leeds. York was rivalled only by Crewe as a northern railway junction. It took up thirty pages of *Bradshaw*, which was the principal railway timetable until 1961. As the fulcrum of the East Coast route to Scotland, it was the place where passengers stopped to take lunch in the mid-Victorian days before restaurant cars. They had twenty minutes. It is said the soup was deliberately served boiling, so that it would not cool down to a drinkable temperature in time. It was then poured back into the pot and served to the next lot. York was the place where the 'grass-green' Great Northern engines were taken off, and the 'light green' North Eastern engines put on. It had been the headquarters of the North Eastern Railway (1854–1923), and as a boy I would contemplate the beautiful tile map in the station circulating area showing the North Eastern territory. It was an impressively dense network, and yet my father explained that it had been necessary for reasons of space to leave off some of the mineral lines, which carried ironstone or coal.

With the railway grouping of 1923, and the creation of the Big Four, York became headquarters of one of the four: the London & North Eastern Railway. (The others were the Great Western, the London, Midland & Scottish and the Southern.) In 1947 the railways were nationalised, and York eventually became the headquarters of the North Eastern Region of British Rail.

North Eastern ... London and North Eastern ... North Eastern Region ... All these concerns were headquartered in an elegant neo-Georgian building that had been erected just inside the city walls in 1906. The building's sootier counterpart, the station itself, was required to be just *outside* the city walls, but if any station could be said to be beautiful, then York fitted the bill, with its elegant curvature, soaring iron and glass roof spreading from decorated columns as gracefully as the leaf canopy from forest trees. The station sat in the centre of the 'railway lands'. In my lifetime these included 'down yard', 'up yard', numerous sidings (exotically extending to 'banana sidings'), coal plant, water tower, goods station, goods warehouse, Railway Institute. Until 1903 locomotives were built on the railway lands; carriage building continued until 2002.

Goods operations were mainly conducted outside the decorous station. But sometimes, while waiting for a train, I'd watch a fascinating freight come rumbling through: say thirty wagons of coal. It was like seeing a gardener tramping through the living-room of a grand house.

My father worked in the above-mentioned railway headquarters, which he always called 'Head Office', very definitely with capital letters. I was never allowed in. I had to wait for him outside, but I knew that it contained the largest boardroom table in Britain. There was a seven-foot-long gilded weathervane on the roof, in the profile of an NER locomotive with steam streaming out behind. During my boyhood a giant radio mast was erected beside the weathervane. This enabled Head Office to keep in touch with Doncaster, Darlington and Newcastle by microwave radio telephone – to command the prime industrial territory in Britain. In those days, the north-east could still look London in the eye, because we had the iron and we had the coal.

By virtue of my father's job, I had free first-class train travel. I would irritate pinstriped businessmen by settling into first-class compartments in my jeans and trainers, and reading the *New Musical Express* while eating a bag of smoky

1. York Station, c. 1906, before the arrival of Burger King.

bacon crisps. After smouldering for a while, one of them might say: 'Are you aware this is a first-class compartment, young man?' 'Yep,' I would say, and I would hope the ticket collector would come along, knowing I would only have to flash my 'Priv' pass at him, whereas the businessmen's tickets might be subjected to longer and more suspicious scrutiny. I once went to Aberdeen and back in a single day, just because I could. Because it was *there*. My schedule allowed a full twenty minutes on the platform at Aberdeen before setting off back.

Every summer we holidayed on what was archly called 'the Continent' with the British Rail Touring Club, whose members were just as keen on foreign trains as they were on British ones, no doubt because they were allowed to use them for free as well. I parked my bike in the hollowed-out interior of the smaller, early Victorian Old Station (in whose dining-room the hot soup had been served), where it was overseen by a railway security guard, so that I never needed a bike lock. I played snooker with train drivers in the Railway Institute and attended gym classes in what had been the loco erecting shop, which explained the generally cavernous size of the building and the six-foot-diameter clock at one end. I assisted backstage with the Railway Players (all railway employees), whose theatre was above the Institute, and perilously close to the station, so the heartfelt soliloquies of the actors had to contend with the tannoy and 'Platform 9 for the 20.15 service to Scarborough, calling at Malton, Seamer and Scarborough'.

Lying in bed in the small hours, I was lulled to sleep – or kept awake – by the ghostly clanking from Dringhouses Marshalling Yard, where about a thousand wagons a night were sorted into perhaps forty trains for the distribution of coal and other freight across the north. One of my early ambitions was to be the man who supervised this proceeding from the elevated control tower. His job seemed like a giant game of solitaire, which he could make 'come out' by having no spare wagons left at the end of the sorting.

THE POST-IMPERIAL MID-LIFE CRISIS

But this railway world was doomed, as I think I knew from an early age, and my loyalty to the railways was born out of sympathy for the underdog, just as Charles Dickens's affection for the stage-coach, expressed in *Pickwick Papers*, was forged by resentment of the *arriviste* railways.

British Railways had been born under a shadow. At the time of its creation 3 million cars were licensed in Britain; by 1974 the figure was 13 million. At the time of BR's demise in 1994 the figure was 25 million. (Today it's 36 million.) The annual number of railway journeys was well over 1 billion in 1910. It was down to about 800 million in the late 1950s.

In 1959 Ernest Marples, owner of a road construction business, became the Minister for Transport under the Conservative government of Harold Macmillan, which was like making Richard Dawkins Archbishop of Canterbury. Marples appointed his close personal friend Dr Richard Beeching as chairman of BR, and in 1963 Beeching published his report, *The Reshaping of British Railways*, which advocated cutting the network by about a third, and was implemented almost in full. Beeching's idea was to eliminate 'bad traffics', mainly rural branch lines, while promoting the trunk network, which became known as Inter-City. The idea was that people would drive to the Inter-City network, then board a train. In practice, they just drove all the way. Those few railway professionals who have any time for Beeching point to his progressive ideas about freight. In place of the shuffling of small wagons at numerous yards, he promoted containerisation: larger wagons, longer trains and fewer 'concentration points'. But you couldn't see what these new containers were carrying, which (if you were a fourteen-year-old boy) was the whole point of freight trains.

Romanticism as an intellectual movement was rooted in the appreciation of nature. By killing country railways, Beeching killed railway romance. As David St John Thomas wrote in *The Country Railway*:

> Except where they helped develop suburbs on the edges of great cities, railways did not urbanise the countryside but became part of it ... The railways were liked – by virtually everyone. Archaeologists welcomed the opportunities for discoveries of fossils and Roman remains ... Geologists excitedly studied rock faults laid bare by tunnels and embankments. Naturalists noted how different vegetation grew on new ground and quickly appreciated that a 300-ton train disturbed wildlife less than a man on foot. Above all, the railways brought a new realisation of the beauty and variety of the British Isles ...

In the early twentieth century the railway companies produced numerous guides to what could be seen from the window of a railway carriage. They were in harmony with the countryside, and with the town. For example, a London & North Eastern poster captioned 'York, It's Quicker By Rail' showed a painting of York Minster by Fred Taylor. Only when competition with the car became acute did railways start to boast about the speed and comfort of trains per se.

As a boy, I felt besieged by Beeching-ites. My uncle Peter was one. He didn't get on with his brother-in-law: my dad. When he came to our house, he might deign to remove his string-backed driving gloves, but he wouldn't take off his car coat. 'We're not staying, thanks.' It's possible he kept the engine of his beloved Ford Capri (or whatever was that year's model) running outside while he grudgingly accepted a cup of tea. He was an adherent of the sinister 'Rail Replacement' philosophy, which had a vogue in the '70s. All railways, even the trunk routes, would be replaced by roads. My dad once scored a rhetorical coup by asking, 'And would you run fast coaches along these roads?'

'We certainly would,' replied Uncle Peter.

'And would these coaches follow one another in quick succession?'

'Absolutely.'

'So there would be hardly any gaps between them?'

'That's right.'

'Then that,' said my dad, 'is called a train.'

Looking back, I think Uncle Peter was drawn into the pre-vailing, glib neophilia: the idea that said Britain, having lost its empire and been outstripped by America, must get 'with it', even if that meant middle-aged men like him wearing flares and long hair, even if they didn't really have any hair, even if this meant wrecking the countryside with motorways and the towns with car-oriented 'redevelopment', and aban-doning British industry. But Uncle Peter did seem to be on the winning side, and I think of my childhood as one long railway decline.

Steam traction faded, and in 1963 the steam locomotive weathervane on Head Office came close to being replaced by a diesel. Yes, relatively glamorous Deltic diesel-electrics appeared on the East Coast Main Line. Their cab windows made them look as though they were wearing wrap-around shades, and they were the only engines I 'spotted', partly because they had names not just numbers. They were called after racehorses or regiments, and I never knew which of the two the Deltic called 'Royal Scots Grey' was named after. But the only reason we had the Deltics was that there wasn't the money to electrify the line.

In 1965 British Railways became British Rail, in much the same ingratiating way that Anthony Wedgwood Benn became Tony Benn. A new, dour and depressed livery was introduced: blue and off-white, known as 'blue and dirt'. In 1960 BR had introduced a series of luxury trains called the Blue Pullman. They had full air-conditioning and an intercom, enabling on-board announcements. Both innovations soon became standard on ordinary BR carriages. So that was the end of peace and quiet on a train, and the pleasure of sticking your head out of the window, or opening the window when you got too hot. (The greater speed of trains also did for those pleasures. You can't stick your head out at 125m.p.h.)

In the early '70s the coaling plant and the water tower on the York railway lands were demolished (with some difficulty), and by now the lustre was going out of our continental railway holidays. Freddie Laker was a celebrity with his charter plane business, and Hughie Green hosted a game show called *The Sky's the Limit*, which began with an exciting shot of an aeroplane taking off and featured prizes in the form of what would now be called air miles. (Not that Hughie Green was anti-train. He lived in Chiltern Court, which sat above Baker Street station, and he had a big model railway in his living-room.)

In 1976 the Intercity 125, or HST (High Speed Train), was introduced. This – still ubiquitous – could do 125 m.p.h. and had pleasingly streamlined front and back ends, but it was another stopgap diesel in the absence of electrification, and when you'd seen one you'd seen them all. The carriages associated with the HSTs were called British Rail Mark 3, and it was with these that BR 'standardised on open', partly

2. The Intercity 125 (or HST); exciting in 1976.

in emulation of aeroplanes. The seating was open-plan: no compartments. Before then, compartments had been the norm, echoing the seating arrangement of stage-coaches. You sat opposite your fellow traveller in fairly intimate circumstances. I grew up on the first-class compartment stock of British Rail Mark 2 Carriages. Michael Caine sits in one of these on his way to Newcastle at the start of *Get Carter*. The appeal of the compartment was that it was cosy – a room of one's own, and if you did have one to yourself, it was heaven. There were so many slightly decadent things you could do: put your feet up on the opposite seat, stretch out and sleep, scatter your papers all over the opposite seat, move about according to the direction of the sun or the best view. You can fit more people in without compartments, but their removal seemed to be the snatching away of my childhood, and ever since then I have felt exiled from my true home. I have also been placed at the mercy of whoever is the worst – that is, loudest – person in the entire carriage. In a full compartment only six people had to behave. In a full open-plan carriage, eighty have to, and you are never free of the sound of pop music leaking from earphones, the railway tinnitus of today.

In the early '80s, when the number of journeys had reached the all-time low point of 700 million per year, the tile map on the York concourse was covered up for a while, perhaps by the same BR executive who wanted to rename Edinburgh Waverley station 'Edinburgh'. Rationalisation – that was the name of the game, and York station was re-signalled, which involved removing most of the tracks. The station signal box became a Costa Coffee, part of the old booking office a Burger King. In 1996 Dringhouses Marshalling Yard closed.

Two years earlier, the railways had been privatised. I didn't believe that thirty train operating companies could be more efficient than one, and I still don't. They are supposed to bring innovation, but, given that they operate under tight government contracts, don't build their own trains or maintain the tracks over which they run (the infrastructure is managed by Network Rail, which is effectively government-owned), this innovation comes down to new sandwich fillings, or overcomplicated 'marketisation' of tickets. A nation's railway ought to be too important to privatise. Gladstone, Lloyd-George and Churchill were all sympathetic to state ownership. It has been argued that we are only able to contemplate having a fragmented railway because we never had a standing army, and so lacked the sense of strategic imperative.

Anyone attempting to write a book about modern railways soon finds out about fragmentisation. You never know whether to speak to a train operator, the association of operators, Network Rail or perhaps something called the Office of Rail Regulation. It is hard to warm to a railway that has no voice; and it has been said we have no longer have a 'railway mind'.

Under privatisation, railway use has increased to the highest level since the 1920s, and the privatised companies claim credit for this. But it's road congestion that has boosted railway use, with the expense of car insurance for young people (who no longer buy cars as a rite of passage) and the death of the 'company car' as contributory factors. Also, we as a society seem to have been travelling more – by whatever means – ever since journey indices began to be collected.

In 2010 Head Office at York became the Cedar Court Grand, the city's only five-star hotel. The golden locomotive remains on the roof. My dad's old office is the whisky bar, where, as he was told on a guided tour, 'more than a hundred single malts are available'. Guests taking beauty treatments in the basement spa, or swimming in the adjacent pool, might wonder at the six-inch-thick steel doors. Well, it was

3. Head Office. The author's father, J. B. Martin, worked here when it was the HQ of BR North Eastern Region. It had been built in 1906 for the North Eastern Railway. Today it is the Cedar Court Grand Hotel, and J. B. Martin's office is the whiskey bar.

in the basement that the money earned by the company was stowed. That money gave the whole city a prestige that no amount of modern tourism will recapture.

FAMOUS ENGINES AND FAMOUS TRAINS

No matter how much I rummage through the drawer marked 'memory', or turn it upside down and shake it, I have no recollection of steam days. But as I began to read railway history I became doubly nostalgic: for the denuded railways of my childhood, and also for the un-rationalised railways beforehand. It is debatable whether the steam-age railways provided a better service than the present one, but it was more variegated and interesting. There was the contrast between the solidity of the engine itself and its swirling, ever-changing penumbra of steam – that quality of literal atmosphere that so entranced the Post-Impressionist painters who brought their easels to the great Gare St-Lazare terminus in Paris.

There were longer trains back then (fourteen carriages not unusual), and also shorter ones. Steam locomotives might be seen passing one's train completely unencumbered by carriages, like a child let off school with a sick note but nothing really wrong with them. And sometimes they'd be doing this backwards, but then it was actually easier to drive the smaller type of engine – a tank engine – backwards than forwards because there were porthole windows to the rear and no tender to peer over. Trains could be observed performing tricks while moving: collecting water, collecting or depositing mail bags, slipping carriages like a magician palming a card. And there was much greater line-side drama, in the form of marshalling yards, sidings of all kinds and manned signal boxes, like elevated cottages, that controlled semaphore signals: wooden arms that clunked up and down with pleasing decisiveness.

In the Edwardian period railways were at their bustling height. The peak was the network as captured by the Bradshaw of 1909. That particular edition was republished in 1968 by the railway publishers David & Charles, and it sold 25,000 copies. Another firm attempted to republish it in the late '90s, but (I was told) 'the computer crashed'. It couldn't handle the density of text and figures – all the footnotes running up the side of the page or along the bottom, denoted by little pointing finger icons and reading things like 'but not on Tuesdays', 'Market Days only', 'Change here for the Loch Lomond Steamer'.

Back then, railways seemed a protean force. Half a million people worked on them, as against ninety thousand today. Even a basic country train of five coaches and perhaps a couple of freight vans would have two guards, and these have been poetically described as 'the captains of land ships'. Railwaymen liked their jobs, even if they weren't well paid, and they formed strong bonds of loyalty with the companies, which in turn promoted the areas they served, making it seem as if they were graciously on the side of the *people* they served. In 1906 the Great Northern paid John Hassall 12 guineas to design a poster promoting Skegness. He came up with a fat fisherman skipping along the beach, and the slogan 'Skegness is SO Bracing', while the artwork and literature of the Great Western did its best to install the Cornish Riviera as the Riviera.

But it was in the inter-war period, after the grouping, that railway advertising consciously promoted railway glamour. This was the time of the best posters: for example, the little boy looking up reverently to the engine driver, who beams down from his footplate as the boy says, 'For holidays, I always go SOUTHERN, cos it's the Sunshine Line!' Later, the London & North Eastern parodied this, with a bigger engine, a frightening, black futuristic thing whose driver has to lean down with an ear trumpet as the boy pipes up, 'Take Me by The Flying Scotsman.' It was the time of the streamlined locomotives, depicted like colourful missiles in railway art. The most famous of these was Mallard, driven at 126 m.p.h. down Stoke Bank by Joe Duddington, who wore his flat cap back to front, as though to make himself streamlined.

This was the time of the famous engines and famous trains that are the focus of this book. It sounds like a heroic era, but it was a rearguard action against the challenge of the automobile and the aeroplane. Railway PR had to be invented, and brought to bear. The first Briton to be designated a Public Relations Officer was John Elliot, a former guards officer and *Evening Standard* journalist. He had been sacked from the *Standard* for printing a too graphic account of a murder on the front page, but he always maintained that he'd been asked to do so by the paper's proprietor, Lord Beaverbrook. He then applied to the Southern Railway. In his autobiography, *On and Off the Rails*, Elliot recalls how, in 1925, he was recruited by Sir Herbert Walker, General Manager of the Southern, to improve the public profile of the company. The Southern, as the main commuter railway, catered to bristling businessmen who wouldn't stand a minute's delay and did not think it a reasonable excuse that the Southern was electrifying its network. Walker asked Elliot what he would like as a job title. Elliot replied, 'Well, sir, when I was on the *New York Times* in 1921, there was a man called Ivy Lee who called himself "public relations consultant" to the underground system of New York. So why not call me Public Relations Assistant?' Walker agreed, because 'No one will understand what it means and none of my railway officers will be upset.'

Elliot was unsure whether, in becoming Britain's first PR man, he 'ought to have a statue in Parliament Square or should have been publicly hanged on Waterloo Bridge'. It was 'probably the latter', he decided.

Elliot (who commissioned the boy-and-train poster mentioned above) gave names to express locomotives on the Southern because the naming of engines was proven to generate goodwill at little cost. The Southern, like the Great Western, ran into Cornwall – in its case, north Cornwall. The line ran near Tintagel, and Elliot suggested the Southern should 'cash in' on the proximity to Arthurian legend by naming a new batch of locos after characters and places from the Knights of the Round Table. The extreme whimsicality of this did draw some flak. ASLEF, the train drivers' union, objected to the engine called *Joyous Garde*, asking, 'What about the bleedin' driver?' and Sir Charles Morgan, a director of the Southern, raised an eyebrow at *Morgan le Fay*.

I once attended a talk given by Michael Palin about his love of railways, and he said that, as a boy, he'd been fascinated by such poetic/bloody silly locomotive names as *Sir Ontzlake*, *Sir Meliot de Logres*, or *Sir Dodinas le Savage*. Here, clearly, was one of the brains behind the Knights who 'eat ham and jam and spam a lot'.

There followed on the Southern the Lord Nelson class of engines, the Schools class, the Merchant Navy, West Country and Battle of Britain classes (the latter two the same except for the name). 'Having got over the locomotive hurdle,' Elliot wrote, 'naming expresses [express *trains*, that is] followed naturally, starting with the eleven o'clock to Exeter and all points west, which we called the *Atlantic Coast Express*, or *ACE*, as it became popularly known. The *Bournemouth Belle Pullman* followed a little later ...'

In fact, the naming of engines and trains long pre-dated

this time of conscious railway glamour. It seems more natural for men to give names to fast vehicles than not to do
so. In *All about Our British Railways*, a book of 1922 aimed at
children, and poignantly dedicated 'to Gerald, a young but
keen railwayist (1902–1909)', G. G. Jackson explains 'Why
Some of Our Locomotives are Named'. He begins by men-
tioning that, if you'd been walking around London 'just a
hundred years ago', you would have seen placards such as
'The *Lightning* coach will set out at 10 a.m. prompt for Birmingham', followed by small print boasting that the coach
maintained an average speed of 10 m.p.h. He adds that, in
the locomotive competition of 1829 the Rainhill Trials, three
of the five competitors were named after stage-coaches: *Sans
Pareil*, *Novelty* and *Rocket*. The last of these – the winner – was
designed by George and Robert Stephenson, and George's
earlier engine, *Locomotion*, was also named after a stage-
coach. The railway pioneers, writes Jackson, 'hoped for an
easy transition from road to rail' by naming their locos after
stage-coaches.

Train *and* locomotive names were pioneered on the pre-
grouping Great Western (the only company to keep the
name *after* the grouping). In 1879 a Paddington-to-Didcot
service was called *The Zulu*, and for its onward journey, from
Didcot to Wolverhampton, it was known as the *Northern Zulu*,
the *Wolverhampton Zulu* presumably being considered slightly
ridiculous. (This is probably the only train that changed its
name half-way through its journey.)

All these names suggested manly power, the Anglo-Zulu
War being then under way. Later, the Great Western would try
to embed itself into British history with a mellower nomen-
clature, as applied to its locomotives. The Star class of locos
comprised sixty express passenger engines built between
1907 and 1923. They were named after stars, knights,

abbeys, kings and queens, and the Star-class engine called *Knight of the Bath* was nicknamed 'Friday Night' by its drivers and firemen. (Here are some of the other 'F's from the exhaustive *Dictionary of Steam Locomotive Nicknames* by Thomas Middlemass: *Fat Nancies, Flat Irons, The Fish, Floating Batteries, Folkestone Tanks, Footballers, Fowler's Ghost, Freaks, Frothblowers*.)

The Stars were succeeded by the larger Castle class – 171 engines named after West Country castles. You wouldn't have thought there were enough West Country castles to go round, but that would be to forget Usk Castle, Ogmore Castle, Eastnor Castle and other baronial obscurities. Then came the King Class on the same railway, the engines named after kings, starting with George V and working backwards. But it's as if this theme wasn't sufficiently challenging for the men of the GWR because they then – like nerdy pub quiz entrants – set themselves the challenge of naming locomotives after *halls* of the West Country. Required to come up with a hall in the West Country, I would probably say 'Baskerville Hall', but that's fictional. The GWR blokes came up with about a hundred and fifty, including Kinlet Hall, Hinderton Hall, Cogan Hall and Rood Ashton Hall; but eventually they did have to range beyond the West Country.

The men who named those engines may have been trying to refute the words of Dr Arnold, headmaster of Rugby School, who, seeing a train go past Rugby in 1832, remarked that 'feudality had gone for ever'. The very early railways incurred the hostility of the landed interest and were deemed to promote a dangerous social mixing. By the inter-war years they had ceased to be the brash newcomers. Whatever social storm they brought about had been weathered. They had all but ceased knocking down houses and digging up the countryside.

Fashions in names came and went. The trains called

'flyers' were born between the late nineteenth century and
the 1920s: the *Flying Welshman* (1897), the *Scarborough Flyer*
(1923), the *Flying Scotsman* (1927). I don't believe that any railway company was so naive as to call a train a flyer once those
things that could really fly started to compete with trains.
The suffix 'Limited' also belongs to the early days. The word
imported the glamour of exclusivity: the train was limited to
a certain destination, and seats on it were limited (so you had
to book), an echo of the early use of 'express', which meant
a messenger, stagecoach or train existing expressly for the
purpose of travelling to wherever it was going.

The Belles belonged to the cloche-hatted 1930s – the
Southern Belle, *Brighton Belle*, *Bournemouth Belle* – although the
Kentish Belle did not have her coming-out party until 1951,
with BR the proud parents. From the modern, globalised
and London-centric angle the names often seem charming
for the way they bring provincial England into the spotlight:
the *Devonian*, *Mancunian*, *Bristolian*, *Northumbrian*, *Midlander*.
But from that same modern perspective such names often
seem framed in a gratuitously sexist way: the *Cornishman*, the
Man of Kent, the *Norfolkman*. The electrification of the West
Coast Main Line in the 1960s triggered a new genre. A service
called the *Executive* tried to entice businessmen to commute
between Wolverhampton and London. It was followed by the
Leeds Executive, the *Bradford Executive*, the *Glasgow Executive* and
the *Hull Executive* (which survives). It's as if the BR publicity men who named these trains had never read John Betjeman's damning poem 'Executive', beginning: 'I am a young
executive. No cuffs than mine are cleaner;/I have a Slimline
briefcase and I use the firm's Cortina.' Or perhaps they had
read it, and they were trying to get him out of his Cortina and
onto the train.

WHERE DID THE TRAIN NAMES APPEAR?

Usually – from the late 1920s – on crescent-shaped boards
fixed on the smoke-box door: the very front of the engine.
At the National Rail Museum in York a wall is given over to
displaying fifty of these headboards. The names might also
appear on roof boards, fixed on to the sides of carriages
above the windows. Roof boards were about five feet long
and four inches high. If you turned up early for your named
express, you might see a porter pushing a barrow filled with
these, like so many sticks of firewood. He might have a step-
ladder over his shoulder. He would stop at every carriage and
fix on the board. The story is told of a young boy in the 1930s
whose mother put him onto the *Cornish Riviera Express* at Paddington, entrusting him to the care of the guard. A few minutes before departure time, the boy leaned out of a carriage
window to say goodbye to his mother. She asked, 'Now,
you've got your ticket safe, haven't you?' As he brandished
the ticket to reassure her, he dropped it, and it fell between
the platform and the train. His mother summoned a porter
who, after swiftly assessing the situation, took down the
nearest roofboard and carried it into the train's WC, where
he dabbed a bit of soap on to the end. He then picked up the
ticket from the track ballast by prodding it with the soapy
end, which caused it to stick. One of the reasons named
trains faded away was that it was very labour-intensive to fix
on the roof boards or headboards; and sleeker post-war rolling stock offered no place to fix them at all.

The named trains advertised themselves not just to their
passengers but to anyone along the line who might be interested. They were like beacons of glamour. Farmers in the
Lake District might set their pocket watches at the sight
of the *Royal Scot*, highly noticeable against the hills in LMS
maroon. Children playing in sight of the South East main

line in Kent would pause the game as the *Golden Arrow* hurtled past. The harried commuter at Victoria, scurrying towards the ticket gate and day's work, might glimpse the rumpled red blankets inside a compartment of the *Night Ferry*, and wonder whether he was living his life the right way.

The names also appeared in the timetables, written sideways down the vertical columns, in the white space afforded by the fact that the train was usually an express, so not many departure and arrival times had to be written in the column. Part of the commercial logic of the named trains was that they stood out easily in the timetable.

I have just walked past my local Oxfam bookshop, where I saw in the window a pasteboard railway book for very young children, probably dating from the early 1960s. There are six pages in the book, and the only words are the names of the engines or trains depicted. The cover shows the *Golden Arrow*, and I suppose they might have been the first words that some child learned to spell.

A train with a name would justify a book devoted entirely to it. There were also many books about named trains collectively. In *Titled Trains of Great Britain* (1946) Cecil J. Allen supplies page-long accounts of seventy of them, largely concentrating on details of their exact timing and (an obsession of Allen's) their weight. We will be seeing more of Cecil Allen. He was an engineer who had been employed on the Great Eastern Railway as 'Inspector of Materials', which sounds like a trainspotter's ideal job. Allen's autobiography was called *Two Million Miles of Rail Travel*, and he computed that he had travelled forty thousand miles a year by train. All his work seems afflicted by arithmomania, whereas I think the appeal of the famous trains lies in their transcendence of numbers.

Another railway PR man, Frank Ferneyhough, wrote an

autobiography called *Steam Up! A Railwayman Remembers*: 'Undoubtedly a train with a name', he wrote, 'is a public attraction and acquires an aura of romance such as that which made the steam railways so fascinating. For the passenger there is something of a secret pride, or at least a pleasure, when he tells a friend, I went on the Royal Scot, rather than "I travelled on the 10.45 from Euston."'

NAMED TRAINS OF TODAY

A couple of years ago *The Railway Magazine* published *The Encyclopaedia of Titled Trains*. It is a historical document rather than a snapshot of the contemporary scene. Of the 350 trains listed, the vast majority no longer exist as named, or even un-named, services. Here are some of my favourite of the historical names (and, by the way, the definite article was usually not regarded as part of the name): the *Afternoon Talisman* (1957–9), the *Cambridge Buffet Express* (1932–64), the *Easterling* (1950–58), the *Flushing Continental* (1927–47), the *Mid-Day Scot* (1932–65), the *Night Limited* (1966–85), the *Norwegian Boat Express* (1928–31), the *Shakespeare Express* (1928–31), the *Sunny South Express* (1905–39), the *Welsh Dragon* or *Y Ddraig Gymreig* (1950–70), the *Yorkshireman* (1925–77).

A clue to the fate of the named trains lies in the fact that their names were suspended for the duration of the Second World War. It wouldn't do to promote certain elite, luxury trains when the nation was supposed to be pulling together. In the demotic '60s this prejudice became entrenched. To vaunt a few services was to imply the rest were inferior. In 1971 Frank Ferneyhough wrote: 'Modern trends require high-quality services in terms of speed and comfort for all trains, making it less easy to pick out trains of a much superior quality to justify a title.'

Some of the old names survive. I have just returned from
a journey on the *Flying Scotsman*, the name now designating
the 5.40 a.m. departure from Edinburgh Waverley to London King's Cross, as opposed to the 10 a.m. services from
King's Cross and Edinburgh Waverley, as used to be the case.
Most of those on board did not seem to know it *was* the *Flying Scotsman*, not having noticed the microscopic initials 'FS'
denoting the train on the pocket timetables. Several of the
old names, including the *Cornish Riviera Express* and the *Night
Riviera*, are retained by the operator called First Great Western, which is in fact successor to the *real* first Great Western,
which inaugurated those trains.

Some trains and some engines, or 'power cars' as they
tend to be today, are still named. But this is done in the way
that park benches are named: with a note of sentimentality
or moral worthiness. A power car might be named 'Driver
Mick Smith' after a late railwayman, or given the name of
a local school or hospital. That engaging railway academic
Paul Salveson ('the railway professor') wrote the policy on
train names when he worked for Northern Rail. 'I called a
150 Power Car *Benny Rothman*, after the communist leader
of the Kinder Scout trespass. I was particularly pleased to
get that past the commercial team ... not that it's expensive
to put a name on. It's just a twenty-five quid transfer.' Other
Salveson names are *Alderman J. Arthur Godwin* (first mayor of
Bradford), *Barbara Castle* (Labour transport minister) and *Jane
Tomlinson* (Wakefield-born athlete and charity fundraiser).
These last, says Salveson, 'were to get a better gender balance ... Most locomotive names were always male, weren't
they?'

In this book, I wanted to concentrate on named *trains*
rather than engines. I travelled the routes of four of the most
historically famous named trains, and for my final journey I

travelled on what is perhaps the most famous of them, even if this train is part of a faded genre: the sleeper service.

This is not a 'view from the window' book – a detailed account of how the passing landscape has changed. There is an element of that, but the book is mainly about changing railway experiences over time. It could be argued that, in choosing named trains as my point of comparison, I am setting the bar too high. The modern railway is bound to lose out when compared to the high points of the Golden Age. I admit that part of my aim is to show up the modern railway for lacking romance and style, with its crammed-in 'airline' seats, vacuous and paranoid announcements, and ugly liveries and train interiors. Let's face it: to travel in most of the carriages on British railways is to be trapped in a noisy hell of shuddering grey plastic.

But I will try to put some nuance into my nostalgia. I do not want this to be 'chocolate box' so much as bitter-sweet. Modern-day trains are faster and safer than ever; there are also more of them, albeit running over a smaller network. The passenger waiting for a train on the platform of a country station might have been in pretty surroundings, whether in the 1890s or the 1950s, with the stationmaster tending his garden, the amusing little tank engine playing about with coal wagons in the siding like a puppy with a rubber ball ... but that passenger might have been waiting for one of just two trains a day from that station. The surviving country stations have more frequent services than in the past, even if the platform is now concrete rather than wooden; the waiting-room fire (if the waiting-room survives) long since boarded over; the stationmaster deceased, his house demolished, his garden a car park, his role usurped by a CCTV camera.

Between 1904 and the start of the Second World War the *Cornish Rivera Express* began its journey to Cornwall by running non-stop from Paddington to Plymouth. No modern train does that, and for a commendable reason. Whereas in Edwardian days the *Riviera* was one of a couple of trains a day from Paddington to Plymouth, there are about a dozen today. They stop at several places on the way. A service going directly to Plymouth without stopping would be almost empty, the passengers wanting to go there having so many trains to choose from.

Any passenger boarding the *Riviera* in 1904, especially any first-class passenger, would have had his or her bags lifted up by a porter. Somewhere around Exeter he or she would have been summoned to the dining car by an attendant, handed a menu by another attendant and perhaps served an aperitif by another one again. This was because labour was cheap, and these attendants were dependent on tips to bring their income up to a tolerable level. Cheap labour also helps explain the bustling, communitarian nature of Golden Age stations, and the fine workmanship of railway carriages.

Which brings me to the question of elitism. Isn't it pure snobbery to invoke the named trains? Yes, they were usually expensive. It is said that we in Britain today have the highest rail fares in Europe, and the government admits that it is making the passenger pay for the investment programme belatedly under way (thus making users of the most civilised and environmentally friendly form of travel pay disproportionately for it). But train travel in the past was more expensive. In the late nineteenth and early twentieth century it was an almost exclusively middle-class affair, so that some companies were required by government to introduce special cheap 'working men's fares' for journeys to and from work, and these were among the few concessionary fares until the 'Cheap Day Returns' of the 1940s. Our leading fares expert, Barry Doe, whose column in *Rail* magazine is called *Fare Dealer*, says 'I can remember my father looking at rail fares between London and Edinburgh in the 1950s: five pounds for a return. He said "I can't possibly afford that, it's a week's wages."'

Then again, there was a certain magnanimity about the famous trains. They were usually expresses, but they were not generally more expensive than slower trains serving the same destinations, and they usually admitted second- or third-class passengers. In this, Britain was unusual. Expresses were first-class-only on the continent. The railway historian Jack Simmons has written that Britain's policy on expresses was 'a quiet, firm assertion of a sensible kind of democracy'. But we needn't get too dewy-eyed about our spirit of fair play, because this encomium does not seem to apply to Pullman expresses. These charged an (admittedly usually modest) supplementary fare, and they might be first-class only. Let's look a bit more closely at this question of elitism.

A NOTE ON CLASSES

On the very early railway there was first, second and third class, the terminology borrowed from university degrees. Third-class carriages were open-air, and some people – probably not regular users of third-class – said this might actually be preferable in good weather. By the 1860s third-class was usually enclosed, so it became more popular. Observing this trend, the canny Midland Railway (always looking for a customer service angle, since it had come late to the Anglo-Scottish business) abolished second-class in 1872. Specifically, it made its second-class less luxurious and its third-class more so, and called the merged accommodation third. Other railways followed suit, but slowly in the case of the railways operating south of London, which served class-conscious commuters, who appreciated social distinctions. The three classes also lingered on the boat-train services, which mainly ran south of London, but second-class was mainly gone by 1930, and this is why railway historians speak of first and third in an apparently elliptical way.

Since then the trend towards egalitarianism has continued. In 1940 wartime exigencies prompted a government ban on railway class distinctions within London, and that has remained ever since. Today some operators over crowded routes extending well beyond London have no firsts.

In the mid-'50s, first and third became first and second, in an attempt to make the gulf seem smaller. In 1987 'second' became 'standard' for the same reason. As from 2009, MPs and other public officials have been reimbursed for standard-class only, not first, and for a while first-class travel declined. But in 2013 the Association of Train Operating Companies reported: 'Demand for First Class Travel Hits Ten Year High.' This is accounted for by refined ticket pricing. When the first, and cheapest, tranche of advance standard-class tickets has sold out, the cheapest tranche of advance firsts may cost less than the next-most-expensive standards. Also the demise of the dining car has been compensated for – the railway companies say – by a better 'at seat offer' offer for first-class passengers. More coffee is offered in first than you could ever drink. There is usually also complimentary food, and this has increased the attraction of first.

My own attitude towards first-class is that I'm in favour of it when I'm in it, against it when I'm not. I recently had an argument about Virgin Trains with a successful businessman. He liked their Pendolino rolling stock. I don't, because the seats are frequently not aligned to windows; leg room is cramped; the 'shop', with its 'Grab Bags' of crisps, Danielle

Steel novels and copies of OK magazine, is tacky. It became apparent that, whereas I usually went standard on Virgin, he always went first, and so had more legroom, a guaranteed window, and he didn't need to visit the 'shop' ... at which point I became resentful and truculent.

It is hard to defend class divisions, especially with a railway as overcrowded as ours, and I have seen other examples of class war. A couple of years ago I did happen to be in a first-class carriage on a Virgin service on the East Coast Main Line. The train in front failed, and all its passengers boarded ours, sprawling – with the guard's permission – into first as well as standard. A first-class ticket-holder sitting near me called the guard over and said he assumed he'd be entitled to a refund, since he'd paid not to be in the company of standard-class passengers. The guard reassured the man that he, unlike the interlopers, was still entitled to free hot drinks, or at least he would be except that the water heater wasn't working. I reprehended the man's snobbery while admiring his bravery, but I believed that he was on to a loser. It is well established in railway by-laws – has been, I think you'll find, since Jones v. Great Northern Railway (1918) – that there is no compensation for a 'second-class irruption' caused by an operating emergency.

What *can* be said in favour of first is that helps maintain the glamour of railways in their battle with the airlines.

A NOTE ON PULLMANS

George Mortimer Pullman was born in New York in 1831. In the US his name is synonymous with luxury train travel and social changes progressive in their results if not intention. In Britain his name is connected only with luxury train travel.

At the age of seventeen he went into business with his

brother, a cabinetmaker. This involved Pullman in a lot of train travel, which he usually found uncomfortable. In the winter of 1853 he travelled overnight in a train from Buffalo to Westfield. There was no heating, and lighting was by candles. He didn't get any sleep. Being equipped with a tape measure, he began to measure the carriage, thinking how it might be redesigned. But he kept his ideas to himself for a while, because he first set up as an engineering contractor specialising in the movement of entire buildings. In Chicago he jacked up the Tremont House Hotel, a four-storey building that had been sinking into a swamp. It was said that the connection between this feat and the cultured railway catering he would go on to pioneer lay in the fact that no glass or crockery was broken, and not a drop of beer spilt.

Pullman persuaded the Chicago & Alton Railroad to loan him two carriages. He installed new seats that could be converted into beds. They were upholstered in plush; there were washrooms and oil lighting, and other luxury trappings. The beds, incidentally, were aligned longitudinally, like a coffin in a hearse. In 1864 Pullman built another luxury carriage, called *Pioneer*. The next year he offered it to Mrs Lincoln, for the transportation of her assassinated husband's body. This publicity coup ensured the success of what became the Pullman Palace Car Company, which built and operated what were considered hotels – indeed palaces – on wheels. A train of Pullmans might include, besides sleeping and dining cars, a car with an organ, a hairdresser or a library. One French observer spoke of 'rolling villages'. Henry James spoke of Pullman 'making mobile what ought, by its sumptuousness and solidity to be stationary'.

The attendants in the cars were black, often emancipated domestic slaves. They were relatively well paid, and Pullman jobs were considered prestigious among those aspiring to

them. Pullman's rationale was that former slaves would
have the right quality of deference for dealing with rich passengers, and he became the biggest employer of African-
Americans after the Civil War. In 1880 he built a factory with
adjacent housing south of Chicago. The settlement was itself
called Pullman. You could say it was a model village run on
paternalistic lines, with healthy conditions and many munic-
ipal facilities. Or it was a pool of labour run along feudal
lines, with the extremely fastidious George Pullman control-
ling every aspect of life. This bred resentment, which was
fuelled by wage and job cuts at the factory in 1894. A strike,
and violent protests, had to be put down by the army. When
George Pullman died, in 1897, his body was buried in a lead-
lined coffin sealed inside a block of concrete, to prevent it
from being disinterred by his opponents.

In 1873 he had brought the Pullman concept to Britain.
He would contract with railway companies to build, supply and operate luxury carriages, for admission to which
passengers would be charged a special supplement. Most
companies took him up on this. The first Pullman service in
Britain ran over the metals of the Midland Railway between
St Pancras and Bradford on 1 June 1874. The very early Pullmans were luxury carriages without kitchens, so food had
to be prepared outside. The first proper dining-car-with-
kitchen was operated by Pullman for the Great Northern in
1879, but Pullmans would become particularly closely associated with the boat-train services of southern England. The
first Pullman car on a boat train was called *Jupiter*, and it ran
from 1882 to 1884 under contract with the London, Chatham
& Dover Railway on a Victoria–Dover service. (Pullman provided some sleeping car services in Britain, but only up to
1907, when an Inverness–Glasgow Pullman sleeper was
withdrawn.)

British Pullman cars were built at Birmingham or Brighton, and they always *were* 'cars', reflecting their American origins, in the same way that carriages on London Underground – largely funded by American capital – are cars. ('Move down inside the cars.') Some Pullman cars incorporated two compartments, called *coupés*, at either end, but most seating on Pullmans was 'open' – that is, like the seating on a bus. Open seating was the favoured layout in America. Think of any cowboy film in which a train appears. The passengers – who are usually being robbed – are never in compartments. Even though Pullmans were luxury trains, there might be thought something democratic about open seating, but the rationale was that it allowed a fluid at-seat waiter service (except that the waiters were always called 'attendants').

Pullman involvement in a train might be limited to supplying a single carriage, but there were also entire trains of Pullmans, such as the *Golden Arrow* and the *Brighton Belle*, the subjects of our first two chapters. A Pullman car might be classed as first, second or third. In each case it was more luxurious than the ordinary equivalent. The classic Pullman style crystallised in the inter-war period. A parlour car was a car with seats that were called 'chairs', and they were free-standing, well-upholstered armchairs. In a first-class parlour car the seating was usually '1+1': that is, one seat facing another seat across a table. There would be two rows of 1+1 either side of a central gangway. In third class, the seating might be 2+1 or 2+2. Either way, there was always a freshly laundered tablecloth on the table, and – a Pullman trademark – a lamp with a warm-coloured shade, usually of silk and resembling an inverted tulip. To oversimplify somewhat, there were also kitchen cars, which had seats as above plus a kitchen, and bar cars.

The livery of the cars was umber and cream, a colour

scheme borrowed from the London Brighton & South Coast Railway. The roofs were painted white. First-class cars had names, painted in an ornamental frame below the windows. In *Pullman Trains in Britain* R. W. Kidner writes: 'At first royal personages were used, followed by girls' names, precious stones and some romantic places.' The word 'Pullman' was written in elongated gold lettering above the windows. The interiors were panelled in exotic woods, with decorative marquetry. They were plushly curtained and carpeted, with gilt fittings. Kidner bemoans the bandying about in Pullman publicity of heady, yet vague, terms such as as 'Pergolese', 'French renaissance', 'damask silk', 'fine mohair velvet', and he sums up the overall impression as one of 'Edwardian opulence'. Keith Waterhouse said of the all-Pullman Brighton Belle, 'If you will imagine the Palace of Versailles pulled out on a string of sausages, and mounted on bogies, it was like that.' In Pullman cars electric lighting, steam heating and air-conditioning were all pioneered.

In his book *Pullman* Julian Morel – a former employee – writes:

> [The company] was a hard taskmaster demanding a certain standard of conduct, discipline and deportment. You were Pullman. You either loved or you hated Pullman, there were no half measures. The majority who served loved Pullman; it became part of their lives. Pullman staff were the *corps d'élite*. Long service was more the rule than the exception.

After the war an increasing number of women were employed as Pullman attendants, and several Pullman chefs (never 'cooks') were women. The grades were attendant, attendant-in-charge, leading attendant and conductor.

From 1954 the Pullman company began to be absorbed into BR, a process complete by 1962. BR used the Pullman brand and concept on some of its expresses, but these were debased Pullmans: the shells of ordinary BR carriages were fitted out to a higher spec, and waiter service provided. The last BR Pullman, *The Manchester Pullman*, ran in 1985.

By then, as R. W. Kidner writes, 'most of the glamour had gone; there were still privileged rail travellers but they were mostly businessmen or officials for whom speed meant more than luxury. Real prestige now lay with the private aircraft.' Pullmans had catered to the wealthy in the days when they had no option but to go by train. Pullman guaranteed the kind of exclusivity the richest travellers had sought on the very early railways, when they would travel on flat-bed trucks inside their own carriages, unhitched from their horses.

In Britain the word 'Pullman' is synonymous with luxury. It was illegal to apply it to other sorts of railway carriage, but there have been Pullman aeroplanes, cars, cinemas, mattresses, ladies' hairdressers. There is currently a chain of Pullman hotels, one of which is on Euston Road, near St Pancras International, the terminus for Eurostar, arguably the successor to the all-Pullman *Golden Arrow*. Hence the Golden Arrow Restaurant inside this hotel ... and I'm sure the food is better than the grammar of the advertising: 'Dining aboard the *Golden Arrow* was once an experience as much as reaching its destination. Today', the copy bafflingly continues, 'the journey is the destination and the *Golden Arrow* is the place to explore new flavours.'

Those words are a somewhat mangled tribute to a train made special, and memorable, by the magic touch of Pullman. Let us climb aboard that train.

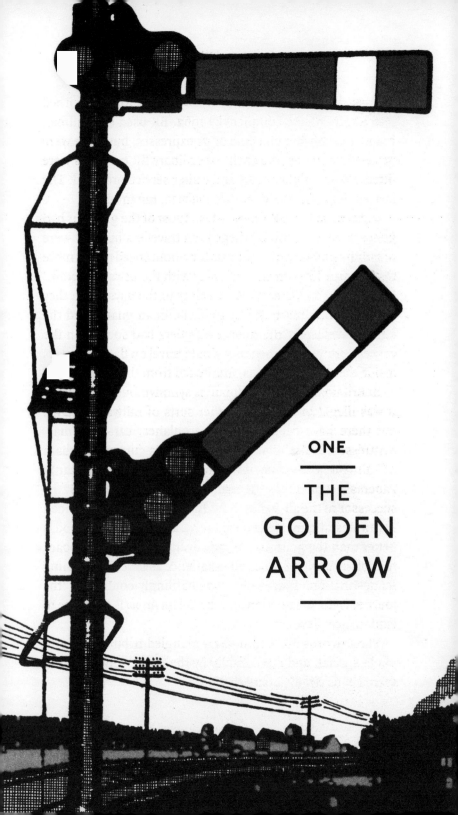

ONE

THE
GOLDEN
ARROW

THE GOLDEN ARROW

THE ABSENT SEA

The railways operating from the south London termini are disappointing to the railway romantic for many reasons. The trains are uninspiring: stubby, overlit electrical 'units' in ahistorical liveries. There are relentless, robotic announcements, and too much catering on the station concourses, where you don't want it, and not enough on the trains, where you do.

And there are no long-distance expresses. Generally speaking, there isn't room for the southern operators to stretch out, and there never has been. Yes, the London & South Western Railway did reach as far as Padstow from its base at Waterloo – much to the irritation of the Great Western, which regarded Cornwall as its own backyard – but that was a freakish bit of outreach.

There was self-consciousness about this among the southern companies, which would be amalgamated into the company *called* Southern in the railway grouping of

1923. Whether we're talking about the above-mentioned LBSCR and LSWR, the South Eastern Railway, or the London, Chatham & Dover, none dared claim the prefix 'Great', unlike the Great Western, the Great Northern or the Great Central. But while the southern trains may not have travelled over long distances, they could take a running jump at the sea. They could operate trains that connected with boats: 'boat trains' in fact, and these could be the first leg in the longest journeys of all.

By the 1840s the Channel ports were linked to London by rail, and the French ports were linked to Paris. A journey from London to Paris took eleven and a half hours in 1851. This was down to six and a half hours by 1913, when faster trains and faster steamers (propeller, as opposed to paddle-driven) had opened up the Continent. It is estimated that 150,000 Britons crossed the Channel or North Sea in 1850; in 1913 it was more like 2 million.

At Victoria today there are few signs of the days of the boat train, when the station proclaimed itself 'The Gateway to the Continent'. Yes, there is a *bureau de change*, and the left luggage office is subtitled '*consigne*', but these facilities are mainly for passengers to Gatwick Airport.

Victoria station used to bristle with inducements to foreign travel, and images of boats and the sea. Today there is only one boat at Victoria. It is on a pretty, tiled map located in an alcove off one of the entrances to the station from Victoria Place. The map is opposite a South African deli called Savanna, which is built into what used to be the booking office of the London, Brighton & South Coast Railway. Because the map is in a quiet alcove, somebody is usually making a mobile phone call right in front of it, and you have to ask them to step aside, at which point they will notice the map for the first time, and be amazed and appalled at your interest in it. At the top of the map are gold letters on a semicircular blue mosaic: 'LB & SCR Ry. Map of System.' The map shows the lines of the railway stretching south of London 'showing all important landmarks': in other words, 'Stations, Motor Halts, Golf Links, Race Courses, Harbours for Yachts, Military Stations and Castles.'

At the bottom is the sea, and dotted lines showing London, Brighton & South Coast Railway boat-train connections from Portsmouth to the Isle of Wight, and from Newhaven to Dieppe, Bordeaux, La Rochelle and St Nazaire. At the *very* bottom is a small vertical sailing ship, apparently tumbling off the edge of the world. It is odd that this one remaining ship at Victoria should be associated with the LBSCR, and for the following reason ...

Victoria used to be two stations. Anyone who doesn't know this, must think it a very bizarre design indeed, what with the two different façades and the brick wall dividing Platforms 1 to 8 from Platforms 9 to 19. One side was owned by the London, Chatham & Dover Railway, the other by the LBSCR. Older staff at the station still refer to 'the eastern side' (Platforms 1 to 8) and 'the central side' (9 to 19). The tile map is on the central, or LBSCR, side. It was put up by that company when it redeveloped its half of the station in 1906, employing a pleasing, airy Art Nouveau style. It is ironic that the one remaining ship at Victoria should be on that side because, as we will be seeing in the next chapter, the LBSCR was mainly concerned with ensnaring commuters rather than operating boat trains.

The other tenant of Victoria, the London, Chatham & Dover, was the more seagoing railway, being one of two companies (we will meet the other in a minute) serving Dover and Folkestone. In 1907 the LCDR rebuilt its own half of Victoria. In *London's Termini* Alan A. Jackson writes: 'a

handsome four-storey masonry block rose up. The style was
French Second Empire, with a maritime flavour bestowed by
four mermaids contemplating their well-parted bosoms.'
Let's get it straight about the bosoms. You can see both nip-
ples on the four mermaids on the LCDR side, whereas you
can only see half of one breast belonging to the one mermaid
on the LBSCR side.

The canopy in front of the LCDR side boasted 'Shortest and Quickest Route to Paris & Continent – Sea Passage
One Hour'. The Brighton side countered with 'To Paris and
the Continent via Newhaven and Dieppe – Shortest and
Cheapest Route'. In the case of the Brighton side, 'Shortest
Route' meant 'shortest to Dieppe' rather than Paris. But it
certainly was the cheapest route, for the very good reason
that Newhaven–Dieppe took three and a half hours – which
on the steamers of the time meant three and a half hours of
being sick – as against one hour from Dover to Calais. (Incidentally, modern ferries serving those routes take slightly
longer. Cynics say the trip is prolonged so people will spend
more in the on-board shops.)

The LCDR side boasted more numerous destinations,
ranging from Crystal Palace to (rather vaguely) 'India'.
If you go to Blackfriars – built as the City terminus of the
same company and recently rebuilt – you will see a monument resembling a wall of paving stones, each inscribed
with the name of a destination theoretically reachable by
the LCDR. Dresden jostles with Faversham, Chatham with
Lucerne, Berlin with Bickley. This sort of grandiosity had
been satirised as early as 1839 by Angus B. Reach in *A Comic
Bradshaw*. He lists the destinations of the fictional 'Eastern
Countries Line'. The train leaves Shoreditch at 6; it arrives at
Bow at half a minute past six. It then goes to Constantinople,
Aleppo, Jericho, Baghdad, Canton, Peking.

To be clear, the LCDR trains, whether from Victoria or Blackfriars, went no further south than Dover. You would have had to change several times to get to Lucerne, and many more to reach India.

France was always the main destination. Cheap excursions to France were widely available by Edwardian times, and the newly formed Workmen's Travelling Club suggested that a week in Paris could cost 'less than a week at Margate'. A weekend return ticket to Paris could be had for a pound (the weekly wage of the very lowest earners), and foreign hotels were cheaper than British ones. But there was also a big luxury market.

In 1889 both the London Chatham & Dover Railway and the South Eastern Railway – which was based at Charing Cross – put on luxury trains to Paris via Dover–Calais, to coincide with the Paris International Exhibition of that year. They were known as the Club Trains, and these two trains corresponded to a single French train – operated by the Nord company – that collected passengers from Calais and took them on to Paris. On the British side the services exemplify the absurdity of a free market in railways. The LCDR, based at Victoria, ran its Dover trains over its main line via Chatham and Canterbury. This was called going 'up Chatham'. The South Eastern, based at Charing Cross, ran its Dover trains over its own main line, via Orpington and Ashford. (The lines, and sometimes the Club Trains themselves – which left their respective stations at 4.15 p.m. – crossed at Chislehurst.) In other words, the LCDR approached Dover from the east, while the South Eastern approached it from the west, even though the point of origin of the LCDR (Victoria) was *west* of that of the South Eastern (Charing Cross).

The two lines, and the two trains, converged again on windswept Admiralty Pier at Dover. Back then, as today,

there were always plenty of bored fishermen on Admiralty
Pier, and they would make bets on which company's train
would arrive first. But it didn't really matter (except to the
fishermen), because the two sets of passengers were des-
tined to board the same steamer, which awaited, bucking
about on its moorings. As the passengers queued to board,
a boy with a barrow offered hot coffee or soup.

The club trains were not great successes and were with-
drawn in 1893, although each company continued to operate
several Paris trains a day, most including Pullman carriages.
In 1899 the South Eastern and the Chatham companies saw
sense and pooled their assets. They didn't formally merge
but began operating jointly as the South East & Chatham
Railway. Their two main lines were joined by means of the
'Chislehurst Loops' at Chislehurst, where they had crossed.
The preferred route for the boat trains was from Charing
Cross to Folkestone and Dover along the old SER main
line, via Tonbridge and Ashford. This was flatter than the
Chatham route or, as the railway surveyors say, 'less graded'.

After the First World War the old SER route remained
the preferred option for boat trains, but *Victoria* became the
favoured starting-point, since it had more and longer platforms. Charing Cross dwindled towards being a commuter-
only station, and the traditional boast of the hotel became
all too true: 'Acknowledged one of the quietest hotels in the
West End.'

In the railway grouping of 1923 the companies using
the southern termini were collected under one head as the
Southern Railway. Its boat-train services were listed in its
Continental Handbook, which began with a quotation from
Henry VI Part One, Act V, scene i: 'See them guarded and safely
brought to Dover;/Where, inshipped, commit them to the
fortunes of the sea.' The book would make a Phileas Fogg

of any reader. Hundreds of destinations were listed, and the fold-out map showed international routes such as 'London–China–Japan by the Trans-Siberian Rly'.

Here, apparently, was the high point of the boat train era, but a shadow loomed over the cross-Channel business. In 1922 the first scheduled air services between London and Paris had begun. Meanwhile there were complaints from the users of luxury boat trains that the trains weren't quite luxurious enough. The delays in the customs sheds at Dover were too long; the Channel boats were overcrowded. There was a desire for a smoother, more coherent journey.

Whereas some of the Paris-bound boat trains had incorporated one or two Pullman coaches, in 1924 the Southern met the demand for greater pampering with the first all-Pullman boat train. It ran from Victoria to Dover, and it was nicknamed 'the White Pullman'. The train ran in what had become the standard Pullman livery of umber and ivory, and 'white' referred to the ivory part. This whiteness was deemed worthy of comment because the South East, Chatham & Dover Railway (which had been operating to Dover until the grouping of the year before) had been unique in running its Pullmans in its own 'crimson-lake' livery.

In 1929 this train was formally named the *Golden Arrow*.

The inaugural run of the *Arrow* took place at eleven o'clock on 15 May 1929. The single fare, including supplement, was £6 10s., or about £260 in today's money. At the time of writing the most expensive single first-class (or 'Business Premier') fare between London and Paris on *Eurostar* is £276. After a steady decline that will be described later, the *Arrow* ran for the last time on 30 September 1972.

The train was the brainchild of Davison Dalziel, chairman of the International Sleeping Car Company, known for short as *Wagons-Lits*. This operated such famous continental

4. *The Golden Arrow* at Dover in 1948. It runs under the walkway that leads to Admiralty Pier. The Lord Warden Hotel (as was) is in the background. The engine is *Boscastle* of the West Country class.

trains as the *Train Bleu* and the *Orient Express*, and it had a close relationship with the Pullman company. John Elliot of the Southern – that pioneering PR man mentioned in the introduction – was all in favour. 'It was the number one train for us', he wrote.

Like the *White Pullman*, the *Arrow* was all first-class Pullman. It was a long steam train operating amid the many electrical pygmies of the Southern. Until 1961 it was hauled by a succession of big locomotives. From inception until 1939 these were of the King Arthur or Lord Nelson classes. After the war bigger locomotives still were used: engines of the Battle of Britain, Merchant Navy and Britannia classes. On their smoke-box doors the engines sported a golden arrow, pointing diagonally down to the right, and the *Arrow* was advertised by posters showing the train inhabiting a thunderbolt pointing in that direction.

The *Arrow* was a long-distance express, taking the record time of six hours thirty-five minutes to reach Paris. It left Victoria at 11 a.m. and arrived at Paris at 5.35 p.m. But it was a long-distance train only by virtue of its being *two* trains. You had to add together the *Golden Arrow* strictly speaking (London–Dover) with the French counterpart, which was called, with pleasing reciprocity, the *Flèche d'Or* (*Golden Arrow* in French), its own luxury carriages supplied by *Wagons-Lits*. The *Flèche d'Or* collected the passengers from Calais and took them on to Paris. In between came the steamer (never to be called a mere 'ferry'), a luxury vessel called SS *Canterbury*, whose only job was to carry *Arrow* passengers. In the pious business-speak of today, it would be called a 'dedicated service'. Other than for boarding and disembarking from the steamer, there were no stops, or no 'station stops' in the modern parlance. And the whole thing happened in reverse, the *Flèche d'Or* leaving Paris at noon, France being an hour ahead. Passports and hand luggage were examined on the train; bigger luggage was examined before it was put into the baggage wagon. So *Arrow* passengers could be 'waved through' the customs shed at Dover.

The *Arrow* was the golden train of the Golden Age. In his memoir John Elliot writes, 'I well remember the inauguration party on the day of the initial run.' He doesn't actually give much detail about it, except to say that 'Javary, Director-General of the Nord Railway' was present; also Viscount Churchill, although why *he* was there Elliot couldn't think, since he was a director of the Great Western Railway. Lord Churchill's better-known relation Winston was to become a regular on the service, and Elliot writes that in the early days, 'the *Golden Arrow* departure platform from Victoria was like a page from *Who's Who*.' A book about the *Arrow's* Channel steamer, *The Canterbury*, lists the following as regulars: Lord Birkenhead, Lloyd George, Jack Buchanan, George Bernard Shaw, Tallulah Bankhead, Gordon Selfridge, the Dolly Sisters, Maurice Chevalier, Lord Carnarvon, Prince Chula of Thailand, Sir Austen Chamberlain, the Aga Khan, the kings of Spain and Romania ... and 'indeed almost every celebrity extant at the time'.

The named trains were used to propagandise railways to children, and the best account of *Arrow* glamour that I have read comes from *The Children's Railway Book*, by Cecil J. Allen, whom I said we would be encountering again. He masquerades here as 'Uncle Allen', which sounds alarming to modern ears, but his wife, 'Auntie', is present as he escorts his 'young charges' – twins called Janet and Peter – about the network. The book is undated, but I think it's very early '30s. It contains a chapter called 'To Paris with the Golden Arrow', in which 'Uncle' and 'Auntie' take Janet and Peter to 'the land of mystery that sometimes they had seen as just a faint, faint line of cliff' – i.e., France.

Here they are arriving by taxi at Victoria:

'Golden Arrow, Sir?' asked the porter, as he flung open
the door, and was nearly knocked over by the Twins in
their excitement to get out. 'Yes,' I replied, laying a
restraining hand on my two charges. 'Some of these bags
are to be registered, and the rest we shall take in the
carriage with us.'

In those days each platform at Victoria was approached
through iron gates, like park gates. The platform number
was set into the iron arch above the gate, like a keystone. The
platform for the *Arrow* in its first thirty years was number 2.
(From the '60s it left from number 8).

On the concourse side of these gates there'd be a throng
of people who'd come to see passengers off, or just to see the
train off. You needed to show your passport to get through
the *Golden Arrow* gate, this literal 'gateway to the continent'.
Immediately on the other side there'd have been the bustle
of baggage loading, and passengers would crowd apprehen-
sively around a blackboard indicating the state of the Channel. 'Sea Slight' meant you were probably going to be sick on
the *Canterbury*, or that you'd do well to postpone lunch until
the Calais–Paris leg.

You would see the perfunctory back end of the train first.
In Uncle Allen's account Janet is intrigued by the very back
of the train. 'Oh, Uncle!' she exclaims, being only a girl, and
therefore ignorant about important matters, 'What funny little guard's vans!' Uncle Allen points out that these are the
storage boxes for the registered luggage, at which Janet asks
what 'registered' means (which I'm glad she did, because I
wasn't sure myself), to be told it means anyone who's con-
signed a bag to the van has a ticket to collect it at the other

end. Young Peter, meanwhile, is contemplating the carriages, and 'reverently' breathing the word 'Pullman', quite overawed, even though he's 'been running Pullmans on his Hornby railway at home for a year or two'.

He and Uncle walk past the carriages:

> Deep and wide glass windows showed us one charming interior after another. There were no ordinary seats; every car was like a drawing room or a lounge, with cosy armchairs scattered about on a carpeted floor, and little tables, each with its electric table-lamp and coloured shade.

They come to the business end of the train.

> One glance was sufficient for my nephew. It was clear that his study of my railway books had not been in vain. 'A Lord Nelson', he replied promptly. 'Right,' I replied. 'What's more it's Number 850, Lord Nelson himself.'

This was the kind of excitement I was hoping to kindle in myself, using the modern railway.

RAIL-SEA-RAIL

I began by attempt to replicate a journey on the *Arrow* by queuing for an advanced ticket at Victoria. Why Victoria? The *Arrow* left from there. It might be argued that I should have gone straight to St Pancras International and boarded Eurostar. Surely that is the modern equivalent of the *Arrow*, being a glamorous train that goes to Paris? There can be no doubt about that glamour. In the late '90s I wrote an article about Motor Books, a transport bookshop (now closed) in Cecil

Court, WI. The owner insisted that he catered to a new, more sophisticated sort of trainspotter: 'They're interested in the French high-speed trains, and Eurostar.' The latter was – and is – *our* only high-speed train, and its glamour was endorsed in the film *The Bourne Ultimatum*, in which Jason Bourne travels from Paris to London by Eurostar. (It must have been a toss-up between that and flying, because it is impossible to imagine Bourne, this 'psychogenic amnesiac', driving his car on to a roll-on, roll-off ferry.)

Standing in that ticket queue at Victoria, I thought back to my latest trip to Paris on Eurostar. I had been in Business Premier on a press ticket. I recalled rocketing through northern France with the sun setting, and a dinner on the table before me. This dinner had been 'designed' by the famous chef Raymond Blanc: cod fillet in sauce armoricaine. The starter had been marinated sardine fillet with cauliflower tartare and fennel.

When I accidentally dropped my napkin, an attendant immediately scooped it up, and to spare me the embarrassment of apologising offered, 'Anozzer white wine, sir?' *Wagons-Lits* (those operators of the Flèche d'Or) are involved in the catering on Eurostar. The pink-shaded table lamps that were a feature of Pullman cars appear in Eurostar Business Premier coaches, and Eurostar, like the Flèche/Arrow is a joint Anglo-French operation. But the Arrow was a boat train, and it was the advent of Eurostar in 1994 that finally killed off the boat trains.

I am glad that Eurostar now commands more of the London–Paris traffic than all of the airlines combined – that it has won London-to-Paris back for the railway – but it is more the murderer of the Arrow than its heir. The Arrow was also a 'rail-sea-rail' experience, combining boat and train, which Eurostar does not, and Eurostar runs over a new railway line, High Speed 1, that long post-dates the Arrow.

St Pancras also offers the Class 395 trains (known as Javelins) operated by Southeastern Trains. They go to Dover, but they also use High Speed 1 as far as Ashford International, and they only have one class. This is called 'Premium', whereas the few classless Pullman cars were more modestly called 'Nondescripts'. Premium is apparently 'Better than standard but not as expensive as first', which is a case of the operator having their cake and eating it: combining elitism and egalitarianism. But *any* element of egalitarianism in a train bars it from being compared with the *Arrow*.

... Which is why I was queuing at Victoria. When I reached the ticket window, I asked, 'I don't suppose you can sell me a ticket to France, can you?' That arch question deserved an arch reply, and the clerk, of Asian origin, asked, 'Do you doubt it?' He then proposed a special train and ferry package called a 'Cheap Day Return to Calais ... I will explain all about it, and if you don't buy, no hard feelings.' I told him a cheap day return would be no good; I wanted to stay overnight in France. (No one who travelled on the *Golden Arrow* came back the same day.) 'Then buy two of them,' he said. 'It's cheaper than buying separate train and ferry tickets.'

'Is first-class available on that ticket?' I asked.

'No. Standard only.'

That was no use either. I then explained that I didn't just want to go to Calais but all the way to Paris.

'In that case,' said the clerk, 'you'll need three separate tickets: train, boat, train. First, you go to Dover ...' and he printed out something headed a 'departure line-up' (such a nuisance that the word 'timetable' has fallen by the wayside). The first morning train shown was accompanied by a note 'change at Faversham'. Now that was suspiciously far east, and it occurred to me that Dover-bound trains from Victoria, operated by Southeastern Trains, had reverted to the practice of the earlier South Eastern Railway: they all went 'Up Chatham'. That was not the way the *Arrow* went. It started from Victoria, but then headed directly south via Orpington, Ashford etc. I explained it was essential that I went over this route, and the clerk – who now clearly thought I was deranged but remained forbearing – explained that trains running by that route to Dover all went from Charing Cross these days. So I had a choice between starting from the right station for the *Arrow* but going over the wrong route or starting from the wrong station but going over the right route. As I frowned over the Departure Line-Up, the clerk surreptitiously handed me a small slip of paper, about the dimensions of a cigarette paper. 'Or try these people,' he said mysteriously. The paper read: 'Golden Tours – Visitor Centre, 11(a) Charing Cross Road.' 'Do they run trains to Paris?' I asked, incredulously. 'I think they can help,' the clerk replied, continuing mysterious.

I thanked him, got on my bike and rode straight towards 11(a) Charing Cross Road. It was a very resonant address, I reflected as I pedalled with mounting excitement along Piccadilly. If any small operator was somehow providing a revived a *Golden Arrow*-type rail experience, then 11(a) Charing Cross Road would be where they would be doing it from. '11(a)', for instance was perfect, echoing the 11 a.m. departure time of the *Arrow*.

When I arrived at Charing Cross Road, I couldn't at first find 11(a), but, judging by the adjacent numbers, it seemed to denote a black door bearing a gold plaque, and promisingly located next to a *bureau de change* at the faded southern end of the street. This, too, was perfect. Behind such a door would be an antiquated clerk of cosmopolitan aspect: a shambolic old gent from the pages of a Joseph Conrad novel. I would gauchely remark, 'But I thought the *Golden Arrow* was dead and buried?' 'Yes,' he would reply, 'that is what most people think ...'

But 11(a) turned out not to be the black door. Instead it denoted a glass booth on the pavement, decorated with advertisements for London tourist attractions. A jolly-looking woman sat behind the counter. 'Can I buy a railway ticket for Paris here?' I asked, hopelessly.

'No dear, have you tried Eurostar?'

'But what is Golden Tours?'

'It's one of the firms working from here. It offers BritRail products to foreign visitors. They can't be purchased by UK residents,' she added, driving the final nail into the coffin. The decision was made. I would start from Charing Cross, as I had done in the very last days of what might have been called the last boat train ...

Charing Cross station today looks bereft, fallen not so much on hard times as small times. If you go to the ticket windows and look up, you will see a stone balcony projecting from the back of the Charing Cross Hotel. London swells used to sit here with their cigars, bought from the station tabac, their drinks and their mistresses (this hotel was traditionally louche), watching the arrival and departure of the boat trains, and contemplating a trip to the Continent themselves, where even better wine, cigars and women were reputed to be available. It has been a long time since anyone sat on that balcony. It's covered with a net to keep pigeons off, and it hasn't really been viable since 3.40 p.m. on 5 December 1905, when a defective tie-rod caused the station roof to collapse. Six people died, including an employee of the W. H. Smith's bookstall on the concourse. The new roof was built cheaper, therefore lower, and if you stood up on the balcony today, you'd hit your head against it.

Until 2007 I often used to queue up at the ticket windows

beneath the balcony in order to buy a ticket for the service that was the bathetic heir to the last boat trains: the rail–sea–rail ticket. I might be standing behind a man buying a ticket for Greenwich, and in front of a man proposing to buy a ticket for Orpington. When the man for Greenwich had finished, I would step forward and say, 'A ticket for Paris, please,' at which the man for Orpington might give a snort of amusement. But he would quickly cease to be amused when he learned that a ticket for Paris was indeed available; that the clerk would have to go off and find it and that, having found the ticket, he would have to spend five minutes filling it out.

The rail–sea–rail looked like a ticket should: flimsy, and about the size of a chequebook down to its last three cheques. The part giving authority for the ferry crossing was called a 'Sea Coupon' and embossed with an anchor. I travelled by rail–sea–rail many times. I used to enjoy looking up Paris in the later years of the National Rail timetable. (It was there, between Parbold and Park St.) The entry tried to direct me to a schedule of *Eurostar* services, but I ignored that in favour of the note reading. 'Rail–sea–rail services are offered by Southeastern Trains in partnership with P&O Ferries. Details of these may be obtained by visiting Charing Cross Station.' A footnote read: 'NB: Connections between rail–sea–rail services are not guaranteed.' In the 2005 timetable an even more ominous footnote appeared: 'The timings for this service are not known' ... not that the timings had ever been given.

A journey on the rail–sea–rail ticket – which was withdrawn in 2007, by which time the railway travel agency, Ffestiniog Rail, was selling a dozen a year, at most – worked like this. You took a train leaving Charing Cross at about seven; you transferred to a mid-morning ferry, then took a train departing Calais at about two and arriving in Paris at about five. It was clear that a journey much like this would be as near as I would get to the *Arrow*.

I called Ffestiniog Rail. Being a railway specialist, the man I spoke to betrayed no surprise when I said I wanted to duplicate the route of the *Golden Arrow*. The crucial thing, we agreed, was that I should avoid travelling on a French TGV (or high-speed) train, because although the *Arrow* had been an 'express', that meant at the time an average of 60 m.p.h. rather than the 180 of the TGVs, which in any case take a different route between Calais and Paris from that of the *Arrow*. I paid just over £100 for ferry and train on the French side. The ticket on the English side I acquired separately.

The *Arrow* permitted a civilised starting time (11 a.m.) for a cocktail-hour arrival in Paris. But that was in 1929. In 2013 you must set off at 7.10 to reach Paris for early evening.

THE ELECTROSTAR

At 6.45 a.m. at bleary Charing Cross there were no crowds of the kind that had waved off the *Golden Arrow*, but just a few rain-sodden commuters looking up at the departure board. It was late spring, but wintry. A TV screen outside the front of the station had spoken of emergency engineering works on the Dover line, so I was in need of advice. In his book of 1970, *The Golden Arrow*, Alec Hasenson writes: 'On the platform the bewildered traveller will find a good-looking BR hostess who will supply him with all up-to-date information about his journey. All the girls speak two or more foreign languages and also carry out duties on the telephone and at the counter of the Continental Enquiry Office at Victoria.' I walked up to the barrier and consulted a young female platform guard, whose personal appearance is, as we now know,

5. An Electrostar 375, heir – in a way – to *The Golden Arrow*.

completely immaterial. I asked if everything was all right on the way to Dover. 'Far as I know it is,' she said. I mentioned the screen outside. 'Oh, that dates from last week,' she said dismissively.

I could think about food. Those boarding the *Arrow* would already have eaten breakfast, probably in the Grosvenor Hotel adjacent to Victoria station, but they were offered a mid-morning snack on departure: coffee or tea and smoked salmon or chicken sandwiches. 'And', says a brochure for the *Arrow* dating from the 1940s, 'if you happen to ask for cigarettes, don't think you're dreaming when he [the attendant] answers with a smile, "Yes sir, how many would you like?" and stands by with a match.' The cigarettes served on the inter-war Pullmans were called Abdullas. The label read 'Turkish Egyptian Virginia', whatever that meant.

I walked into W. H. Smith's at Charing Cross and surveyed the elegantly named Foo Go sandwich range. No chicken or smoked salmon, but egg sandwich always feels like a railway sandwich to me, so I bought one of those. Egg and *cress*, it should really have been. (The railways put egg and cress on the map.) I bought a coffee in a cardboard cup from the chain called Délice de France – the name, for once, sort of appropriate. I went through the barrier and approached the train. Whereas I would have been greeted by an attendant at the carriage door if travelling on the *Arrow*, before being shown to my seat by another attendant, boarding the 7.10 for Dover was a lonely business. The train, operated by South-eastern, was an electric multiple unit – an Electrostar 375, if you must know. A multiple unit is a train with its motive power – its engines – distributed at intervals along the length of the train. There is no locomotive. The driver drives from a cordoned-off part of the front carriage. There are diesel and electrical multiple units. Most multiple units are about as exciting as the term suggests (but see the next chapter for an exception).

I walked to the very front, and boarded first-class: ten empty seats, insufficiently divided from standard seats in the rest of the carriage for my liking. Not that there was anyone else in the carriage. The seats were plum-coloured, with yellow dots. The only real difference between these and seats in standard was a blue antimacassar. If I'd gone into standard and a put a clean blue handkerchief between my head and the seat, I would effectively have been travelling in first. (On Pullmans the antimacassars were known as 'antis', and those on the *Arrow* were of embroidered linen.)

There was much shuffling about of cars during the first years of the *Arrow*, but for simplicity's sake let's say they were all of the Edwardian sumptuousness described in the introduction. The very first cars were inherited from the White Pullman. One of them was called *Fingall*, and it has been preserved on the Bluebell Railway. *Fingall* had (and has) a floral theme on the marquetry, dark blue carpets, armchairs of a mid-blue decorated with silver leaves. *Fingall* is a kitchen car: twenty-two places for diners, plus a kitchen. The seating is 1+1. Single men boarding a first-class Pullman might collude with the attendants to be seated opposite an attractive woman. But, since this was an open carriage, any too forward behaviour would be observed, whereas compartments were, in the words of the *Oxford Companion to Railway History*, 'convenient for sexual assaults', as we will be seeing.

The Electrostar juddered into life, and an automated announcement informed me – for the first of what would turn out to be about thirty times – that the train would be dividing at Ashford International, the rear four coaches going on to Canterbury West, the front four to Dover.

I hate train announcements, but in fact the post-war

Golden Arrow was fitted with a pioneering loudspeaker that allowed the conductor to talk to passengers 'who,' as Alec Hasenson writes, 'had become accustomed to being talked at by such means in stations, camps, ships and airports in the war ... Such a thing would have been unthinkable before the war, even on such "matey" excursions as the Eastern Belle.' The modern injunction 'Please remember to take all your personal belongings' was prefigured in that, on arrival at Dover, the conductor reminded passengers not to forget their umbrellas.

We rolled away towards the first of the fourteen stops we'd be making before Dover: London Bridge. I had a view of the misty river and Parliament. Those leaving Victoria on the *Arrow* in its first years would have seen the river and Battersea Power Station under construction.

In about 2002, when I was on one of my rail–sea–rail jaunts, a Maltese gent boarded at London Bridge and set a rail–sea–rail ticket on the table in front of him. Unable to believe he was a fellow nostalgist, I asked if he'd ever heard of *Eurostar*. 'Yes,' he said, 'but I am afraid of it. I would rather be on the sea than under it.' I thought I would give him a vicarious thrill by telling him about something that had happened to me on *Eurostar* in 1996 ...

We were proceeding towards the Chunnel in a heavy snowstorm. We entered the tunnel so tentatively that I thought, 'The driver doesn't fancy this very much. Something bad's going to happen.' At the mid-point, sure enough, the train stopped abruptly. Alongside me were some men playing bridge. After half an hour the guard made an announcement: 'The driver informs me ... that this train cannot go.' 'Oh dear,' said one of bridge players. Over the next couple of hours the train began to expire. The air-conditioning and the heating stopped working. The lights would periodically flicker. I knew something really serious was amiss when the guard announced that food and drink were being given away in the buffet. I went and got a sandwich and a half-bottle of wine, feeling like the condemned man eating his last meal. In the buffet I met a German engineer, who said he was 'very interested' to see whether the train, having been stuck for so long in the same position, would crash through the bottom of the tunnel. 'I cannot see why it would not happen,' he said, smiling. An hour later, I was back at my seat when all the lights went out. The guard came into the carriage and placed a torch on one of the tables. When the torch failed, one of the bridge players said, 'This really is rather irritating.' After six hours we were pushed to Calais by another loco. A few weeks later, I was sent a full refund and vouchers entitling me to two complimentary returns. When I presented these at Waterloo (which was the Eurostar terminus in those days), the ticket clerk said, 'Wow, you must have had a really terrible delay.'

The Maltese gent had remained silent at the end of the story, and indeed all the way to Dover.

After half an hour we were at Chislehurst, in the middle of bright green woods, where, in circumstances of great complexity and apparent secrecy, the railways meet: the old South Eastern main line and that of the old London, Chatham & Dover. I was now properly on the route of the Golden Arrow and soon flashing through Petts Wood and Orpington, where I looked at commuters waiting for London-bound trains with as much arrogance laced with pity as if I'd been on the real Arrow. All the while the line was climbing. On a modern train you don't notice, but in The Children's Railway Book Uncle Allen mentions that, on reaching the end of the climb at Knockholt (17 miles from Victoria), 'the loud voice of Lord Nelson quietened, so that we could no longer hear it.'

Then it was through the mile-and-a-half Polhill Tunnel, emerging on to the North Downs under light rain. In his book *Pullman in Europe* George Behrend wrote: 'The wide view to the left hereabouts is one of the most beautiful in Britain and always seems to the author typically English as though challenging the departing traveller for leaving the country.' Yet Behrend, an expert on international luxury trains (as well as a distinguished soldier, an expert on the art of Stanley Spencer and sometime chauffeur to Benjamin Britten), often did leave the country. I spoke to him once in the mid-1990s. He was getting on by then, and he said he didn't much care to be in a world that lacked the *Golden Arrow* and its nocturnal counterpart, the *Night Ferry*.

We were approaching Sevenoaks, the right geographical point to consider the *Night Ferry*, for a reason to be revealed after a bit of history.

When I mention the *Golden Arrow*, people tend to say, 'Wasn't that the train that was put on to the boat?' No. That was the *Night Ferry*. It began operating in 1936, leaving Victoria Platform 1 at about 10 p.m. (the timings varied over the years), arriving in Paris at about 9 a.m., and vice versa. At Dover or Dunkirk the carriages were shunted on to a special 'train ferry', supposedly 'while the passengers slept'. In practice, what with the shunting, the tremendous susurration, general shouting, swearing and noises-off as the sea level was adjusted in the train ferry dock, followed by the clangourous shackling down of the carriage bogies in the echoing hold of the boat, passengers did *not* sleep. They put on their dressing gowns and padded up to the ferry's bar. It was the amphibious nature of the train that made it so famous. There was a lifebuoy in every compartment, and every compartment was a sleeper. There was also a Pullman restaurant car. It was a French train, built and operated by

6. The *Night Ferry*, leaving Victoria in December 1947. Its carriages were loaded onto a cross-channel boat, supposedly while passengers slept.

Wagons Lits, with carriages of a seductive dark blue, trimmed down slightly to the British loading gauge. ('Loading gauge' refers to the dimensions of the carriages, as opposed to the track gauge – the distance between the wheels – which is uniform throughout Europe. French carriages have bigger dimensions than British ones, which is partly why they seem more comfortable.)

The locos that drew the train bore a nameboard featuring a crescent moon. The *Night Ferry* wasn't the first train to be put on a boat. Train ferries were used to cross the Firths of Forth and Tay until the waters were bridged in 1890. There are many train ferries still operating. In his book *Italian Ways* (2013) Tim Parks describes the train ferry between Calabria and Sicily. He leaves his compartment on the train to go up on deck and take pictures of the setting sun, but then he can't find his way back: 'You would have thought it was easy to find a train in the bottom of a boat, but actually, no. There were an extraordinary number of stairways and corridors, and no signs telling passengers where to go.'

The *Night Ferry* ran for the last time on 31 October 1980, by which time electro-mechanical indicators had been installed at Victoria. On that night the indicator on Platform 1 read, 'Au revoir mon ami,' and the driver brandished a copy of the London paper, the *Evening News*, which also shut down that night.

I never went on the *Night Ferry*, but a year ago I met a man of about my own age, Dr David Haslam, whose father was a railwayman, and who also went on jaunts with the British Rail Touring Club, including one involving the *Night Ferry*. I asked him what he'd thought of it. 'In a word, cosy,' he said. 'When I got back to school after the holidays, I was asked what the French word for train was, and I got told off for saying "*Wagons-Lits*".'

As our Electrostar approached Sevenoaks, I recalled the one time the Night Ferry stopped to pick up a passenger before Paris. It was on 16 December 1951, when the Night Ferry called at Sevenoaks to collect Winston Churchill. His country seat, Chartwell Manor, was at nearby Westerham, along a branch line now closed. The Night Ferry conductor had been given orders to put a bottle of Dewar's White Label whisky, soda water and cracked ice in Churchill's compartment.

Churchill was a regular on both the Night Ferry and the Arrow. The attendants were advised not to ask him if he wanted an aperitif. 'I don't need an aperitif to have an appetite,' he would growl. Another reason he didn't need one was that he was already drinking something else. Another notable regular on the Night Ferry was the violinist Yehudi Menuhin. And in 1978 Ernest Marples, the former transport minister, builder of roads and recruiter of Dr Beeching, fled Britain for Monaco using the Night Ferry. He was avoiding a big tax bill. Many of his possessions were left at his Belgravia flat; others were loaded into tea chests and put into the baggage wagon of the Night Ferry. It was a good job for Marples that his man Beeching hadn't cut the service, as he had so many others. Marples never returned to Britain.

When our Electrostar stopped at Sevenoaks, at 7.42 a.m., a crowd of schoolchildren climbed up. They were perfectly well behaved, if noisy, but I resented these boarders. The fact that both hand luggage and passport examinations happened on the Arrow guaranteed that it would not stop to pick up or set down passengers. To do so would have created what is now called a security risk.

We buzzed (the Arrow would have roared) through the two-mile Sevenoaks Tunnel and descended towards Tonbridge, where the noisy schoolchildren got off, and some even noisier schoolchildren got on. Then came Paddock Wood, in the Weald of Kent. The Weald, as seen from windows of the *Golden Arrow* in the 1930s, would have been all fruit orchards, hop gardens and oast houses. The majority of the Kentish orchards and hop gardens have been lost, but some oast houses remain, like funny hats. The passing fields were small and – now that the rain had cleared – bright green, often with a haze of bluebells, and scruffy horses standing in them.

When we reached Marden, the day had become properly sunny. It checked my watch (whereas on the *Arrow* I would simply have looked at the clock at the end of the carriage). It was 8.04. The *Arrow* would have sped through Marden shortly after mid-day, and passengers would be thinking about walking through to the bar car. The *Arrow* had a number of bars cars down the years, and the actual bars within them were always called Trianon. The name, chosen by John Elliot, was taken from two small castles found in the grounds of the Palace of Versailles. The most famous Trianon was the one that appeared when the *Arrow* was re-launched after the wartime suspension.

In 1946 a booklet called *London to Paris, a Journey in Pictures*, was produced to mark the re-launching of the *Arrow*. It was written by someone called George C. Jury. 'It's "chic",' he writes of the new bar, 'done in pale pink and grey plastic throughout. The little lounge compartment is very cosy – plastic too, even to the curtains.'

Jury, I suspect, was chosen for his ultra-modern prose style, which is incomprehensible. Here he is (I think) defending the *Arrow* against criticism that a luxury train ought not to be revived at a time of austerity:

The voice of Austerity whispers, For Shame! That *Trianon*'s modicum of comfort should be a substantial reason for riding Parisward this way! A far, far better thing it ought to be that the *Arrow* does you Paris, or from Paris does you London, with a save of anything from four to thirteen hours, which, multiplied like the efficiency experts can't help doing it, would aggregate to something disturbingly unprogressive.

The plastic bar lasted until 1951, when it was replaced by another Trianon, fitted into a car called *Pegasus*. In 1963 this became the Nightcap Bar on the *Night Limited* (my favourite name for a train *full stop*), a sleeper service from Euston to Glasgow. In the '90s this carriage was restored and brought up to spec to run on main lines of the modern railway. It formed part of a diesel-hauled train comprising some replica Pullman cars (along with *Pegasus*) and providing a 'railway cruise'. In the year 2000 I went on this cruise. Over the course of five days we roved over the north of England and Scotland, and I sat next to a charming American called Tom Savio. Over Brut Premier Cuvée champagne, Scottish smoked salmon, caviar and scrambled eggs – in other words, breakfast on the second day – Savio explained all about our Trianon bar, which resembled a cocktail bar in a good hotel, with a marble top, a chrome rail along the front, and, behind the actual bar, an image in Lalique glass of Cupid firing an arrow from London to Paris. Savio gave me a copy of his book, *The World's Great Railway Journeys*, signing it 'Railway Dreams'. Savio is known as 'the railway baron'. Aside from writing railway books, he had been the assistant curator of California State Railway Museum, Sacramento, California, and, even better, station-master at the small town of Davis, California. He revered Britain as 'the motherland of railways'. 'With respect,' he told me, as we were rolling past a sunlit Loch Lomond, 'your country is like a model railway layout.'

... Then again, if I – as an *Arrow* passenger – couldn't be bothered to leave my seat as we ran through Marden, I might press the bell to summon the attendant. Since Paris was in the offing, I might order a quarter-bottle of champagne. Quarter-bottles were first seen in Britain on Pullman coaches. They were introduced in 1947, because passengers always seemed to want some champagne – but not too much – to fortify themselves for the Channel crossing. Quarter-bottles of red and white burgundy, red and white Bordeaux, a hock and a port were also available.

At 8.08 a.m. we stopped at Staplehurst.

At 3.13 p.m. on 9 June 1865 ten people were killed and fourteen were injured in a train crash on a viaduct near Staplehurst. One of the survivors was Charles Dickens.

The train was an express from Folkestone to London. Workmen had taken up the track in order to repair a fault in the viaduct, and they seemed to have forgotten about the 'up' train from Folkestone. The confusion arose because it was a 'tidal' train, as were most boat trains up the 1880s, before harbours were deepened to allow boats to dock at regular times irrespective of tides. Early Continental timetables showed perhaps half a dozen departure times – varying between, say, seven in the morning and two in the afternoon – for any given boat-train service, depending on the tide.

Nonetheless Dickens was a regular on the boat trains, which connected him with his mistress Ellen Ternan, whom he'd set up in a house near Boulogne. He had been 'enchanted' by getting from London to Paris in eleven hours in 1851. He blessed the South Eastern Railway Company 'for realising the Arabian Nights in these prose days'. However, he had disliked trains *other* than boat trains before the Staplehurst crash, and he disliked the *generality* of trains afterwards, always clutching the arm-rests of the seat, and feeling the carriage was 'down' on the right-hand side.

The 1860s was the worst decade for railway accidents, when train numbers and speeds were outstripping safety provision. The worst of the decade occurred at Abergele, in Wales, where runaway paraffin wagons – vehicles obviously emanating from some signalman's nightmare – collided with the Irish mail train from Euston. Thirty-three people were instantly immolated. A year after Staplehurst, Dickens wrote the best of his ghost stories, *The Signalman*, which is about a train crash in a tunnel. We will be considering this in the next chapter, since it was 'inspired' not only by Staplehurst but also by a smash that occurred on the Brighton line.

Twelve minutes after Staplehurst, we came to Pluckley. Speaking of ghosts, Pluckley has the reputation as the most haunted village in Britain. Difficult though it was to believe on this bright morning – or on *any* morning – it is on the route of a phantom coach and horses: there's an old mill haunted by an old miller, and a ghostly monk, a Red Lady, a White Lady, a poltergeist in the Black Horse inn, over the road from which the ghost of a schoolmaster who hanged himself has been seen dangling from a tree.

I would have thought that to read a ghost story, or any book, on the *Golden Arrow* would have been to miss the point. You should be looking out of the window, eyeing up your '+1' or savouring the food and drink. But in 1948 BR, W. H. Smith's and Pullman combined to institute a bookstall service on the *Arrow*. I own copy of a magazine called *The Railway Digest* from that year, and it shows a 'bookstall boy', dressed as a Victorian urchin, proffering a rack of books to languid-looking, cigarette-smoking passengers. Why the urchin get-up? I frowned over this for quite a while before reading the small print, which revealed that the whole stunt was by way of celebrating the centenary of W. H. Smith's.

At 8.30 we reached Ashford International, and here were more ghosts, in the form of the old loco and carriage works, which closed in 1962. They are now largely a retail park. Ashford is called 'International' because Eurostar calls there, but the station has been upstaged by – and lost Eurostar services to – Ebbsfleet International. Railway traditionalists consider the suffix 'International' pompous. It was never 'Victoria International', even when it was the 'gateway to the continent'.

At Ashford the train divided; our front half rolled on towards Dover. There was only one other passenger in the carriage with me: a youth who fell asleep on departure, with mouth wide open. We came to Folkestone, rumbling over the nineteen arches of the Foord Viaduct, which commands a view of the town in its entirety. (The youth was now snoring.) The Channel lay to the right, glittering and beautiful but completely empty, whereas in 1970 Alec Hasenson had written, 'The steamers are just discernible amongst the harbour cranes.' Most of the intercontinental action at Folkestone is now under the sea, because it is here, beneath Shakespeare Cliff, that the Channel Tunnel begins.

We came off the viaduct and began threading through the cliffs, the sea appearing intermittently on the right. This run is called 'the Warren', and it is the ultimate English theme ride, in that you are actually penetrating the White Cliffs of Dover. The track here has suffered many landslides, with particularly severe ones during both the First and Second World Wars, as though symptomatic of a momentary collapse of confidence. Emerging from the cliffs, we curved left, heading inland and past the remains of Dover Harbour station, which closed in 1927 but remains shockingly dead, like a corpse in the street. We were heading towards Dover Priory, the only surviving railway station in Dover. At least half a dozen others have come and gone, the result of the competition between the South Eastern and the London, Chatham & Dover.

The building that housed one of those half-dozen survives on the edge of the sea. Craning to the right, I looked at it with a certain longing, because this was once Dover Marine, where *Golden Arrow* passengers disembarked to begin their Channel crossing.

DOVER MARINE: A DETOUR

Dover Marine station was built as part of the widening of Admiralty Pier that was completed immediately before the First World War. In the Deco style, it looks somehow Egyptian, or like a giant mausoleum, its great maw facing inland to suck up incoming trains that never arrive, since all the railway approaches have been lifted and turned into a lorry park.

I formulated my plan to visit Dover Marine a few weeks before undertaking my *Golden Arrow* journey. I was at Deal with my wife. She loves looking around the antique shops there, whereas I *quite like* looking around them. 'I have an important closed-down railway station to go and see,' I told her, as she sifted through some Victorian napkin rings, and – making an arrangement to see her back in Deal for dinner – I was off, racing along the A258 to Dover docks.

In Dover the situation was much as it has been for the past twenty years: the white Georgian houses of the Marine Parade looking ghostly in the centre of the otherwise unlovely seafront; the giant car ferries coming and going metronomically from the Eastern Docks, which has been the base of all ferry activity since 1994, and a dreaming silence on the western side, where Admiralty Pier and the building formerly known as Dover Marine stand.

A towering, apparently empty, multicoloured cruise ship was tethered to Admiralty Pier, like a Eurotrash blonde on the arm of a decrepit English gentleman. Dover Marine closed as a station – and a transfer point to ferries – in 1994, when Eurostar commenced.

Today the Dover Marine building, in conjunction with the landward end of the pier, is a cruise ship terminal, and if you are the passenger on a cruise ship docked at Dover, you have a pass enabling you to come and go. But if you are a writer who's turned up on the off-chance, you can forget it. The ferry terminal is guarded by G4S staff clad in fluorescent orange. They control a barrier located two hundred yards in advance of the building. From there I could make out where the platforms had been, and I could see the iron gantries of the roof, under which, in the mid-'70s, I had watched my father carry our family's two suitcases, repeatedly stopping to set them down in order to let the blood flow back into his hands, or to check that, yes, all the passports and tickets were in his inside pocket ... because even passengers arriving on ordinary trains for ordinary ferries used to go from Dover Marine.

'Do you get many rail enthusiasts turning up?' I asked the G4S man.

'The odd one,' he said, with the emphasis on 'odd'.

'Is is still recognisably a railway station?'

'Oh yes,' he said, 'it's pretty much as was. Look, I'm sorry I can't help you, but try giving this number a call.'

The number was for the Dover Port Police, and the idea was that I would get authorisation to enter the building. I called it a couple of times, listening to a series of messages referring me to other numbers that also went unanswered. I was forced to conclude that the police at Dover port took Saturday off. But the Dover Transport Museum – a scruffy, enthralling barn of a place on the edge of town – is open on Saturdays.

A rusting hovercraft propeller is propped outside the entrance. It commemorates what was in retrospect the short-lived and eccentric heyday of the hovercrafts (if that's the plural) which operated alongside the cross-Channel ferries between 1968 and 2000. They took only thirty minutes to cross the Channel, but carried only carried about thirty cars and two hundred and fifty passengers. Not enough of either; and the end of duty-free shopping in 1999 killed them off.

A man selling tea and cakes in the Dover Museum told me his uncle had worked as a signalman at Archcliffe Junction, Dover, and sometimes he'd telephone to say, 'The *Arrow's* coming down if you want to have a look.' I talked to another man, a visitor to the museum, who said he'd spent many evenings inside the Marine station as a boy. 'I wasn't intending to go anywhere. It was just a place to hang about in the evening. It was brightly lit, warm – well, warmer than outside – and there was a bookstall and a café. The café was always full of fishermen, coming in out of the rain for a bottle of beer.' He liked the sound of the sea echoing about in the station, and the screaming of the gulls.

In the late afternoon I returned to the waterside. There was a beautiful golden haze in the air, and a new man on the G4S barrier. He blocked me, just as his colleague had, but he indicated a rusting gateway a few feet off. It gave access to a stone staircase, and a structure I had somehow overlooked among the salt-stained hangars of Dover docks: an elevated, enclosed walkway circumventing Dover Marine but running closely alongside the western side of its roof and leading to a staircase giving access to Admiralty Pier. The walkway, with its peeling blue and pink paint (a raddled remnant of Edwardian seaside gaiety) and frequent puddles of seawater, was a genuinely frightening place to walk alone, but I was consoled by the sight of an elderly red setter standing beside a ticket booth at the seaward end. From the booth the dog's master checked the permits of fishermen going on to the pier. Immediately left of this booth was a lateral extension of the walkway that had once given access to the upper regions of Dover Marine, but this was all blocked off.

I descended onto Admiralty Pier and tried, as it were, to crane around the bulk of the old Marine station to see the bit of quayside adjacent to it. Here the Arrow's own steamer, the SS Canterbury, had waited, in the very spot occupied by the garish cruise ship. A small crane winched the luggage aboard. This was done in one go, the Arrow's luggage van comprising a single container atop a flatbed truck. As the passengers walked up the gangplank, the Arrow's locomotive would have been turned on the turntable where the lorry car park now stands, and the attendants would have switched the menus around, so passengers boarding the train from the ferry (having left Paris on the Flèche d'Or) would be offered afternoon tea rather than mid-morning sandwiches or an early lunch.

On the way back to my car I stood outside what had once been the Lord Warden Hotel, a beacon of early Victorian elegance on the Dover dockside. For many years cross-Channel travellers stayed here, including Thackeray and Charles Dickens, who resented being turfed out of bed too early in the morning, before boarding the steamer on a wild and dark sea. Shivering and bilious on the Channel, Dickens would look back at the illuminated hotel. 'I know the Warden is a stationary office that never rolls or pitches, and

I object to its big outline seeming to insist upon that circumstance.' In the Second World War the hotel was known as HMS *Wasp*, HQ of the Naval Coastal Force. It later became an office of BR Southern Region. Now, although it has a closed-down air, it is something to do with Dover Port Authority. George Behrend wrote of the hotel that 'It might have been built for the railway student, with the turntable slap outside the lounge windows.'

I was now late for dinner in Deal ... but a shuttered pub close to the Lord Warden caught my eye. It was called The Golden Arrow, the name seeming burned into the panel above the boarded-up windows. I had read about this on the internet – from the archive of the *Dover Mercury*. The pub had previously been called The Terminus. It was renamed The Golden Arrow in 1962, by which time the train was hauled by an electric loco, on which it was impossible to fit the down-pointing arrow and the big, intertwined British and French flags that the *Arrow* had carried since the war. Instead, the engine carried in its front a sort of plank reading 'Golden Arrow', and two small flags, about the size of the things children stick on sandcastles. But the train's loss was the pub's gain in 1962, when the landlord, Mr P. Pettet, 'was presented with the headboard from the famous steam train of that name by railway representatives'. He was also given the old flags. The article continued: 'BR said they could think of no more suitable resting place for the *Golden Arrow* regalia, as the public house stands opposite the Marine Station and is greatly used by railwaymen.'

The pub was closed in 1987. It then became a profound contradiction in terms: The Golden Arrow Truckers' Diner. This development was also chronicled by the *Mercury*: 'Maintaining its link with the past, the diner features a specially designed board outside, recalling the days when the famous steam train, the *Golden Arrow*, called at Dover.' That has long gone. One part of the window was un-boarded up, and I squinted inside, half-hoping to see some *Golden Arrow* regalia gathering dust, but there was just a wall painted dark below and white above, with a wave effect at the top of the blue, like a primitive representation of the sea.

TO 'THE CONTINENT'

Arrow passengers arrived at Dover Marine at 12.35 and were departing on the steamer at 12.55, and if that's not integrated transport I don't know what is. By contrast, the 7.10 from Charing Cross carried me into Dover Priory at 9.02, and my ferry was not due to depart until 11.15.

After disembarking at this bland bunker of a station, I walked around the corner to where the buses leave for the Eastern Docks. There I took my place under the dispiriting sign familiar from rail–sea–rail excursions: 'Passengers are reminded that ferry operations are not train connected and we cannot guarantee the bus service will connect with either ferry or train services.' This used to be a courtesy bus, but the fare to the docks is now a pound. The implied message is clear: 'By using the ferries in the old-fashioned way – as a foot passenger – you are being a thorough nuisance, and we would rather you either drove onto a ferry or used Euro-star.' It was the French who started it, introducing a charge in 2004 for the equivalent bus on their side: the one from Calais Harbour to Calais Ville station. And the French ferries have refused to take foot passengers for years.

The bus took eight of us to the sleepy foot passenger reception for P&O Ferries. But, while sleepy, it is also friendly, and the woman at the ticket desk said I could board an earlier ferry, the 10.15. 'But what about the hour-long check-in time?' I said. She just shrugged and smiled. From there we boarded another bus that took us across a car park to a metal detector in a gloomy hangar. Our reward for passing through the detector was a small red card reading 'Bon Voyage'. This entitled us to board another bus, which carried us towards the ferry gangway. The gangway is almost entirely enclosed, but at the very top, as you pass into the ferry, you are briefly in the open air and looking down on all of Dover, with the wind in your hair and seagulls crying.

Then you are into the ferry – in this case the *Pride of Burgundy* (launched in 1992) – and all maritime sensations recede once again. Ferries are now floating shopping arcades-cum-multi-storey car parks, with stabilisers that banish almost any possibility of seasickness. When, during the safety announcements, reference is made to 'the vessel', you are surprised at the word. As a boy, I crossed the Channel on the ferries of Sealink, the seagoing arm of BR. Some were for foot passengers only; some had car-carrying capacity. Either way, you could have fitted three of them into the *Pride of Burgundy*, and you knew you were on a vessel. At any one time about a quarter of the passengers were throwing up. Some of the Sealinks were operated by the French, and I preferred these because the coffees were fascinatingly smaller and the sandwiches fascinatingly bigger: long and thin baguettes, and with simple ingredients – pâté or cheese – yet still delicious. (I speak as someone who's never been seasick.)

For those *Arrow* passengers with sea legs, the crossing was the time for lunch. For those without, it might be time for another dose of the pills – Aspros, they were called – offered for sale on the train. The *Pride of Burgundy* Food Court offered a 'meal deal: curry and beer, £7.99'. There was also the Commercial Drivers' Restaurant, for which I lacked accreditation, and the Costa Coffee outlet in the 'family lounge'. Un-tempted by these, I loitered in a gangway and went into a daydream about the *Golden Arrow*'s private steamer.

The SS *Canterbury* must be one of the very few cross-Channel steamers about which a biography has been written, and I use the word advisedly, such is the loving anthropomorphi-sation of the vessel in the 150 limited-edition pages of *The Canterbury Remembered* by Henry Maxwell, who self-published the book in 1970. 'The *Canterbury*', he begins, 'was a queen. She stood apart from the ordinary. There was regality in her every line. She was the best known, certainly the best-loved cross-channel steamer there has ever been.' He then gives her technical specifications, her vital statistics as it were. Her elegance he attributes to 'a slightly different rake here, a modified prop there, a mere gradation in scale elsewhere', and let me assure the lay reader that in any picture book of cross-Channel ferries the *Canterbury* does look the slimmest and sleekest.

One of many curious things about Henry Maxwell is that he was not an expert on shipping. He worked in the offices of ICI, and his introduction to the *Canterbury* was through the *Evening Standard*: 'I was turning the pages idly and sud-denly there it was, and I became immediately excited: a new cross-Channel steamer for the Dover–Calais service.' It is difficult to know whether this points to the peculiar obsession of Mr Maxwell, or the fame of the *Golden Arrow*. Maxwell goes on to say that 'The *Golden Arrow* steamer was "news". She need only to be delayed to find herself upon the front page of the evening newspapers ... What was new and distinctive about her', he gushes, 'was the unwonted spaciousness and luxury of her passenger accommodation and furnishings.'

The Canterbury could accommodate 1,700 passengers, but the 300 stepping aboard from the Arrow had her all to themselves. Whereas the foot passenger of today feels like a second-class citizen, decanted by an obscure train onto a boat catering primarily to motorists ('Foot passengers please await further announcements'), Arrow passengers were accompanied onto the Canterbury by the conductor of the train, who was on hand to give advice about the onward journey, for which duty he exchanged the cap he'd been wearing on the Arrow for a jauntier, more seagoing one.

And whereas the modern ferry is an indoor affair, apart from a 'deck space' (in effect, a smoking space) about the size of a prison exercise yard, the Canterbury supplied a distinctively maritime experience. As Maxwell writes:

In good weather the Boat Deck offered a real promenade and the awning deck became virtually a single, huge saloon. All along its sides and down the centre were comfortable bays or recesses composed of high-backed armchairs arranged face to face with a table in-between in groups of four, almost like the coupéd [sections] of a Pullman car.

At the end of this extended lounge was 'nothing less than a palm court'. A palm court was the ultimate 1930s' amenity, but they were usually found in grand hotels or ocean liners, not cross-Channel ferries.

The dining-room, reports Mr Maxwell, was on the main deck. It resembled a Parisian brasserie or, as Maxwell writes, was 'predominantly Empire in character', featuring light cream walls and mahogany pillars with 'a delicate golden arrow running vertically up their flutings'. Aside from the public rooms there were eighteen private cabins for use if, for example, you were the king of Spain.

But it couldn't last. The whole operation was anachronistic from the start, what with all those cars and electrical trains swarming around, and the aeroplanes massing overhead. Maxwell knew this. His book is as much a condemnation of the world that killed the *Arrow/Canterbury* as a celebration of the *de luxe* combination. We might as well get it out of the way here: the painful story of the *Golden Arrow* falling to earth.

First came the economic depression and devaluation of sterling, which discouraged foreign travel, Prime Minister Ramsay McDonald refusing the 'modest reduction in unemployment relief' that might have eased the crisis, according to our Mr Maxwell (who was evidently no socialist). In 1932 a couple of the Pullman carriages on the train were replaced by ordinary Southern Railway second-class ones. On the *Canterbury* the Palm Court became the second-class deck saloon. By 1939 the number of Pullmans on the train had dwindled to four.

The *Arrow* was suspended during the war, and the *Canterbury* served in the Dunkirk evacuation, in which patriotic cause she finally reached – indeed exceeded – her passenger-carrying capacity.

The *Golden Arrow* was reinstated with much fanfare – and intertwined Union Jack and Tricolour flags on the buffer beam – in 1946. There were now ten first Pullmans, each in the traditional umber and cream livery. The Labour government of Clement Attlee was happy to flaunt the luxury of the restored *Arrow* as being a return to business as usual, and the *Arrow* was once again teamed up with the *Canterbury*.

But the Palm Court was not restored, and, as Maxwell

notes, a 'rather regrettable' notice appeared advertising 'Restaurant Bar and Tea Lounge'. From October 1946 *Arrow* passengers were usually carried on another vessel, *Invicta*. Folkestone became the home port of the *Canterbury*, the vessel ceding her pre-eminent position 'with her customary grace', although Maxwell records her captain as resenting having to use the *Canterbury* to carry these 'hordes of trippers' to Boulogne. Then came BR and the 'grotesque colour scheme which our nationalised railways have seen fit to adopt for what they all too aptly designate as "ferries"'.

In 1951 Pullman built a rake of new cars (including firsts and seconds) for conveying dignitaries to Paris during the Festival of Britain celebrations. Among the names were *Aquila*, *Carena*, *Cygnus*, *Hercules*, *Orion*, *Pegasus* and *Perseus*. These cars, which are considered the last 'traditional' (if not quite 'vintage') Pullmans, then began to operate on the *Golden Arrow*. The rationality of the '50s did not mix with Pullman sumptuousness. The cars were more pallid and spartan than their predecessors, and the occluded lavatory windows were rectangular rather than oval, making the whole car appear less Palace of Versailles-like. (Pullman lavatory windows had been oval since 1906.) The cars still had the armchairs, the silver service, the wood panelling (albeit without marquetry), the pressed white tablecloths and the table lamps, now 'with French old gold finish'. (According to George Behrend: 'A Pullman car in service without its table lamps is like a Mayor attending an official function without his chain of office.')

In 1953 the first roll-on, roll-off car ferries were operated from the Dover Eastern Docks. The final steam working of the *Arrow* was on 11 June 1961. The engine was named *Appledore*. The next day the train was drawn by an electric locomotive: E5001.

On 15 September 1961 the *Canterbury* was put to the

indignity of a 'bingo cruise' from Folkestone to Boulogne and back. By now, Maxwell conceded: 'The aeroplane and the motor car between them have taken the cream of the passenger trade away forever.' In 1963 BR integrated the Pullman Car Company, which it now owned, with British Transport Hotels Ltd, and this company took over management of the *Arrow*. The last Trianon bar car was removed from the train. 'Attendants' became 'stewards'; what had formerly been 'chairs' were now 'seats'.

On 29 July 1965 the *Canterbury*, this 'product of the era of studied elegance and inviolable proportion … the Augustan age of marine architecture', was towed from Dover to Belgium for scrapping. Let Maxwell have the last word: 'She was spared the journalistic sentimentality and vulgar obsequies of a "Last Voyage" … Last salutes were blown to her from the sirens of her consorts on the Channel service and from the tugs and tenders of the Dover Harbour Board as the final cortege passed out of the harbour.'

By then, the *Arrow* was down to four first-class Pullmans, supplemented by ordinary second-class BR coaches, with a second-class buffet to serve this rabble. In 1967 the cars were painted in the new BR livery of blue and grey, and a generic 'Golden Arrow' was painted over their original names. In 1969 the last Pullman/*Wagon-Lits* car running on the French side was removed, and the name *Flèche d'Or* was dropped.

According to a memoir written by Alec Hasenson for the website *Coupe News*, there was a 'mad scramble' for seats on the last 'down' *Arrow*, which, on 30 September 1972, was seen off from Platform 8 at Victoria with 'cheers and bangs'. He supplies a photograph of the white-coated stewards, most with 1970s' bouffants, toasting the train on its arrival at Dover Marine. But when the last 'up' *Golden Arrow* arrived at Victoria in the early evening, 'no one came to cheer ... The Pullman cars were taken back empty stock to Clapham carriage sidings, then eventually to Brighton for disposal.'

It's a good job Henry Maxwell did not live to see the 'Family Bar' of the *Pride of Burgundy*, with its TV and fruit machines, scampering children, tables loaded with bottles of Chardonnay, pints of lager, foaming cappuccinos in paper cups and bags of crisps. If he had done, and he'd seen *me* in it, I'm sure he would have disapproved of me as well. 'The holiday starts here,' observed the man sitting directly next to me, as he observed the raucous scene. His name was Steven House, and he too was a foot passenger. He now lives in Antwerp, but he'd grown up in Aylesham, Kent, and as a boy he had often waved at the *Golden Arrow* from various Kentish fields. He was returning from visiting his mother, who still lives in Kent. He had travelled at short notice, and this was a cheaper way of doing so than *Eurostar*.

I told him about the *Canterbury*, and said that I thought the *Pride of Burgundy* could do with an oak-panelled smoking-room, or a Parisian-style restaurant. 'There's always the Club Lounge,' said Mr House, who knows a lot about crossing the Channel. The words seemed familiar. I checked my ferry voucher. I had grandiosely requested 'first-class all the way' when booking my tickets, and while there is, strictly speaking, no class system on a cross-Channel ferry, I saw that I had paid a small supplement entitling me to use this 'Club Lounge'. Making my excuses to Mr House, I went in search of it.

Opening the door, I entered a plush, pinkish room ... and a *Golden Arrow* sort of world: unquestionably middle-class people sat at low tables eating prawn mayonnaise sandwiches, or something that turned out to be called 'salmon timbale', while talking quietly, or reading *Great Golf* magazine, copies of which were available on a complimentary basis, along with tea, coffee, soft drinks and snacks. I decided against ordering a sandwich – unwisely, as it would turn out – but took two packets of complimentary peanuts and gave one to Mr House when I returned to the Family Bar.

He was looking through the window. The sun was glimmering on the sea, and I thought of what the Maltese gent had said: 'I'd rather be on the sea than under it.' As we approached the dock, Mr House began trying to locate the site of the old Calais Maritime railway station ...

On arrival at Calais, *Arrow* passengers would have been ushered through Calais Maritime (counterpart to Dover Marine) and onto the *Flèche d'Or*, which would have wound its way through the second Calais station, Calais Ville, in the middle of the town, before proceeding to Paris. Calais Maritime had been an elegant château-like building, which was flattened by bombs in the war, and replaced by a single-storey concrete building. It was demolished in the mid-'90s. 'I think it was over *there*,' said Mr House, as we disembarked from the *Burgundy* at nearly mid-day (1 p.m. French time). I tried to picture the station, which I myself had used as a boy, but I could conjure no image to replace the bleak modern reality, which is a vast hinterland of car parks.

My father says of Calais Maritime, 'It always made me anxious. Every time we got off the ferry there'd be half a dozen trains waiting, and this cacophony of announcements in French. I never knew which one to board, and if you got on the wrong one, you ended up in the wrong country.'

For now, I was faced with the question of how to get to Calais Ville, from where my train was due to depart. I didn't quite trust the connecting bus on this side. I had once waited half an hour for it at the ferry terminal, and I recall a languid Frenchman, a member of the port staff, who was in no hurry to go anywhere, lighting a cigarette and saying, 'Why not take a taxi?' It had arrived eventually, and I had made my connection at Calais Ville with a minute to spare. 'If the bus doesn't come,' said Mr House, 'we can walk it – takes about twenty-five minutes. You just keep the station clock tower in sight.'

But the bus was already waiting outside the ferry terminal. On boarding with Mr House, I realised that two of our fellow foot passengers were Americans, father and son. I asked them why they'd come by this route: 'To see the White Cliffs of Dover,' said dad, 'also Calais, the last part of English territory given up during the Hundred Years War.' In view of this knowledge of English history, evidently better than mine, it seemed likely they'd heard of the Golden Arrow. They hadn't.

'Sounds great, though.'

As a station, Calais Ville is comatose, having been completely eclipsed by Eurostar and the French TGV network, both of whose trains rocket away from nearby Calais Fréthun or Lille, neither of which was ever touched by the Golden Arrow. About five years ago the bar in Calais Ville station was called The Golden Arrow, and there was a painting of a steam locomotive on the window. Now the bar is simply the Buffet de la Gare, and the painting has gone. I said goodbye to Mr House, who was checking out the connections for Antwerp, and I stepped down onto the platform.

French platforms are lower than British ones, and the trains are both higher and wider. This enhances the charisma of the train. In the days of steam the engines also had great presence. Driver and firemen really looked as though they meant business (they wore goggles), and the big Pacifics of the Nord railway that pulled the Flèche d'Or triggered

the familiar response of the British to French locos: they
looked to be inside out. Here is an anonymous account of
travelling on the Flèche in the '30s: 'To British eyes the first
appearance of a French locomotive comes as something of
a shock. It seems to carry a large proportion of its internal
economy spread in the form of parts of various shapes and
sizes, pipes and rods, all over its exterior.' The same account
describes the carriages as 'a symphony of brown cream and
blue'. (Blue because there were some Wagon Lits sleepers at
the rear, which would be taken around the Petite Ceinture –
a railway M25 of Paris, now closed – from Gare du Nord to
Gare de Lyon for onward journeying to the south of France.)

My own train was a symphony in violet and white: a fat,
short slug of an electrical multiple unit with a DayGlo interior. I couldn't find the first-class because there was no first-
class, but I wouldn't have to rough it for too long. I required
this train only to go to Boulogne, half an hour to the south,
where I changed for the Paris-bound service, so boarding
the first proper, loco-hauled train of my journey. It was an
electrical train, a French Intercité, of what SNCF calls the 'classic' (i.e., slower than high-speed) service, and it would go to
Paris over the route of the Flèche d'Or.

This 'classic' being a marginal service, I had a first-class
carriage all to myself, and a big, well-upholstered seat (black,
with orange antimacassar). These seats approximated in my
imagination to the fêted armchairs of the Flèche/Arrow. The
last properly comfortable, bouncy seats in Britain were on
BR Mark I carriages of the late '50s. They were, I believe, the
last to be stuffed with horsehair before fire-retardant foam
was sensibly, but disappointingly, introduced. There was no
buffet car or trolley, however, and I had only the complimentary peanuts from the Club Lounge of the Burgundy to see me
through to Paris.

I had taken so long to cross the Channel that I was now on *Golden Arrow/Flèche d'Or* time. In other words, I was leaving Boulogne at about the same time of day (2.30 p.m.) as the *Flèche/Arrow* would have been passing through. As I tried to decide between finishing my peanuts (I was starving) and not finishing them (they might trigger a thirst, and I had nothing to drink), I recalled reading how it was at Boulogne that the French attendant walked through the luxury train tinkling a bell to announce the service of lunch, for those who had not dined on the *Canterbury*.

I have seen an *Arrow table d'hôte* luncheon menu from the '60s. It cost 12s. 6d., or the French equivalent (about £20 in today's money), and consisted of chilled fruit juices, followed by soup of the day with golden croutons. For main course there was a choice of cold collation, omelettes or, from the grill, Dover sole, lamb chop or minute steak. These came with two sorts of potatoes and a second veg. There was then 'Sweet du Jour'. Drink was extra. The more spoilt *Golden Arrow* passengers complained that the French passport inspection by the gendarmerie, which occurred at around this time, disturbed the luncheon.

From my seat I could observe in detail the countryside of northern France, as I would have been able to on the *Flèche d'Or*, and as you cannot do on the TGV or *Eurostar*, which go too fast, often through cuttings. The countryside has been accommodated to the train rather than the other way around. John Ruskin wrote: 'All travelling becomes dull in exact proportion to its rapidity. Going by railroad I do not consider travelling at all; it is merely "being sent" to a place, and very little different from being a parcel.' My train travelled slightly faster than the 60 m.p.h. of the *Flèche*, but then again it had stopped four times by the time I reached Abbeville. The River Somme now appeared on the left. Two men sculled calmly along, but even today the name of the river creates a knot in the stomach, and I trust its appearance would have given pause to the guzzling of the *Flèche d'Or* passengers, who were finishing their desserts hereabouts. The Battle of the Somme took place 20 miles to the east – as many ruined buildings would have reminded the first travellers on the *Flèche*. They would have seen new ruins after the Second World War as well. They might have felt justified in their enjoyments, since the luxury train they were aboard was meant to banish the spectre of war. But the sight of an ordinary civilian funeral being conducted in a churchyard at Longpré-les-Corps-Saints was enough to cause me a spasm of guilt. (The *Eurostar* route is to the east, running right through the heart of the battlefields, but you'd never know it.)

At the big junction of Amiens – which survived the First World War intact but was partly destroyed in the Second – my carriage became a quarter full, and the guard spoke on the intercom for the first and only time. In French, then in English, he said 'I would like to wish everyone a very good afternoon' – a very classy announcement, I thought. In the late years of the *Flèche* an electric loco was put on at Amiens for the run into Paris. Here also the luncheon tables were cleared, and passengers turned their mind from the important matter of luncheon on the train to the even more important matter of dinner in Paris.

After Creil we ran through the pretty forest of Chantilly, then downhill to Paris, with a TGV alongside us. We seemed to have picked up a lot of speed, which may have been illusory. A place like Paris seems to magnetise a train towards it. As Vladimir Nabokov wrote in his novel *King Queen Knave*: 'The first chapter of a journey is always detailed and slow. Its middle hours are drowsy, and the last ones swift.'

At Louvres we entered the Parisian suburbs. On the *Arrow* I would have left a tip for the waiter and stood up to check my tie was straight in the oval mirror at the end of the carriage. I would then have taken out my *Plan de Paris* and verified the location of my hotel. *The Southern Railway Continental Handbook* recommended the Grand Hotel Suisse, at 5 rue Lafayette, commended as 'best situation in the centre of Paris', in other words, nowhere near Gare du Nord – it's now the Hotel Excelsior and the Tivoli pizzeria – or, at 86 rue Lafayette, Hotel Cavour ('Rooms 10fr. Hot and cold water in every room. English proprietor'), which is now flats and an optician's.

We drew into Gare du Nord at 5.20, fifteen minutes earlier than the *Arrow* if we take the classic timing. But my journey had taken ten hours and ten minutes, as against six hours thirty-five. The Gare du Nord has a melancholic grandeur, especially in the morning. In *Confessions of a Young Man* (1886) George Moore wrote: 'We all know the great grey and melancholy Gare du Nord at half past six in the morning; and the miserable carriages, and the tall, haggard city.' In *Les Mémoires de Maigret* (1951) Georges Simenon wrote: 'In the morning the first night trains, arriving from Belgium and Germany, bring in the first load of crooks, with faces as hard as the light that falls through the window panes.' In the evening it is more welcoming, being lit by glass globes like so many pale orange suns, and these would have been in place – and illuminated – when the *Arrow/Flèche* first arrived at the station, and the steam and smoke would have been swirling around them. I would have collected by coat, umbrella and fedora hat – I have seen two posters for the *Arrow* in which male passengers wear fedoras – and I would have been off, hesitating briefly, perhaps, before the entrance to the Métro, but then striding confidently on to the taxi rank.

TWO

THE
BRIGHTON
BELLE

TWO

THE BRIGHTON BELLE

A PARADOXICAL TRAIN

The *Brighton Belle* also left from Victoria, as does its nearest modern equivalent. Just as the *Arrow* was the star of the eastern side – which was all about serving the Kentish ports – so the *Belle* was the star of the central side, where the emphasis was on moving people, and moving them especially to Brighton. Each train left from the most easterly platform of its side: number 8 for the Arrow; number 17 for the *Belle*, above the gateway for which a yellow and black arch proclaimed the name of the train.

The *Belle* being the ultimate party train, I might – if it hadn't been 10 a.m. – have prepared for my journey with a Bloody Mary in the sparkly bar of the Grosvenor Hotel, which overlooks the circulating area of Victoria (central side). The Grosvenor used to boast that it 'connected by private entrance with Victoria Station', and 'hotel porters meet all trains.' Today you can still access the hotel from the station by a humble back door, but you have to know where to look.

As I took my place in the ticket queue, I was resigned to paying for first-class. Unlike the early *Golden Arrow*, the *Belle* always offered both first- and third-class accommodation. The operator liked to boast that passengers, on boarding, would enquire in wonderment, 'Are we in first or third?' In fact, third on the *Belle* was slightly cramped, since the 2+2 seats were bench-like rather than armchairs. But the sheer Art Deco exuberance of the Belle's third so exceed the modern *standard* class that I would have to go first on the present-day train to get anywhere near it.

... I say 'I', but I was taking my wife to Brighton. This is bad form, I know. You should take someone else's wife to Brighton. She was only vaguely aware of my book's conceit, and when I told her we would be going first-class, she looked at me blankly. Eventually, she said, 'Well, all right, if you're paying.' When I put my Prince of Wales check suit on for the trip, she said, 'Why are you wearing that? It's ridiculously formal for a day at the seaside.' I said, 'Because it's the sort of thing men would have worn on the *Brighton Belle*,' short-form for what had really inspired me: a quote from Antony Ford's book *Pullman Profile No. 4: The Southern Belle and Southern Electric Pullmans*, about how the *Belle* interiors were 'ideally suited for Bertie Wooster and his entourage ... and the racy gents in spats and ladies whose cigarette holders glinted over the bubbly; men who were good judges of port and the 2.30 at Goodwood and ladies who were not afraid to giggle and join in the judging'. My wife was not giggling, but she was judging. 'There's a stain on the lapel,' she said. I didn't bother saying so, but the stain made the suit still more appropriate, given the decadent reputation of both Brighton and the *Belle*.

Between 1933 and 1972 the *Brighton Belle* ran half a dozen times on weekdays, and four times on Sundays, between

London and Brighton. The original weekday timings were as
follows: the Belle departed from Victoria at 11.00, 3.00 and
7.00; it departed from Brighton at 1.25, 5.25, 8.25. Fixed and
memorable departure times like that are called 'clock-face',
and they are designed to make automata out of commuters.
The *Belle* ran non-stop, and the headline was that the journey took an hour. Throughout its history that eleven o'clock
departure from Victoria was a constant. In other words,
one running of the *Belle* coincided with the departure of the
Golden Arrow from the other side of the station. But the *Belle*
was an electrical train, therefore quicker off the mark, and it
would soon overtake the *Arrow* as it wheezed its way up the
1-in-61 to Grosvenor Bridge.

That is one of the virtues of electrical trains. You can get
them away quickly from stations. This is why they're suited
to the intensive commuter traffic that was the main business
of the Southern Railway. Electrical trains are also cheaper
to run. They require only a driver – depressingly styled a
'motorman' – rather than a driver and a fireman, and they are
easier to keep clean, and to reverse out of a terminus. (The
in-house Pullman magazine, *The Golden Way*, conceded that
'The motorman's cab holds no thrills for the guest therein.
The cheery coal-grimed fraternity of the footplate is absent
… Instead, a grave mechanician sits in a little room, looking
through plate glass windows. A couple of electric bulbs glow
dully, telling him all he wants to know and you nothing.')

We arrive now at the first of many paradoxes about the
Belle. It was a glamorous express, yet it was an electrical
multiple unit, a train – as explained – lacking a locomotive,
resembling a series of carriages and therefore looking bereft.
It ran over a relatively short distance, and, for all the racy reputation of the train and of Brighton, it was a product of one
of the great suburb-making movements: the electrification

7. Platform 17 at Victoria, home – as it was difficult
to avoid noticing – of the *Brighton Belle*.

of the Southern Railway. It was an individualistic train arising from a culture of conformity.

In order to compete with predatory buses and trams, that
predecessor of the Southern, the London, Brighton & South
Coast Railway, had begun electrifying before the First World
War. It had used overhead wires, but the Southern resolved
on electrification from below, by means of a conductor rail.
This had worked on the Underground; it was more aesthetic
and, more importantly, cheaper. But the third rail has its
disadvantages. Anyone who logs onto the websites of the
modern-day southern operators in snowy weather will see a
sprinkling of red exclamation marks, denoting services put
out of action by snow and ice on the third rail. And electrical trains, being lighter, can't ram their way through snowdrifts, as steam locomotives could do with a snowplough
on the front. (You can see a locomotive doing just that in
the famous British Transport Film of 1955 *Snowdrift at Bleath
Gill*).

In his book *The Brighton Line* John Eddolls writes: 'The
Southern Railway did more to suburbanise Southern England than any other institution ever had, or probably ever
will. The company worked hand-in-glove with the major
property developers by encouraging families to set up
homes in the south.' In *Semi-Detached London* Alan A. Jackson
speaks of 'a marriage between the Southern and the specu-
lative builder', adding that 'a third of the additional stations
opened in the London area after 1919 were on the Southern
Railway.' Anyone who thinks London is a city for commuter
drudges can put much of the blame on the Southern Railway, which advertised the generality of its electrical services
with the image of a train heading towards a happy-ever-after
sunset and the slogan 'So swiftly home.' The other main cul-
prits would be the Great Eastern Railway, which in the late

nineteenth century offered cheap fares for working men, so triggering a building boom in north-east London, and the London Underground.

Both the Southern and the Underground were encouraged to create homes for 'small-c' conservatives (as suburbanites are usually characterised) by a government policy that was almost socialistic. In the '20s and '30s the railway companies were offered financial incentives to generate economic activity and alleviate unemployment through line-laying, which in turn led to house-building, which in turn led to higher fare revenue. Sometimes their plans for spending this largesse brought them into conflict. In 1926 the Southern Railway opposed the extension of what became the Northern Line to Morden. It was appeased by being allowed to take over the Wimbledon-to-Sutton line, which had originally been an Underground project. In *Underground to Everywhere* Stephen Halliday describes how the legacy of the Southern Railway 'is felt to this day as commuters south of the Thames are far more dependent on main line railways than are their fellows to the north, the incursions of the suburban Underground system being confined to Richmond, Wimbledon and Morden'.

The conflict between the Southern and the Underground might have been worse if the clay of central and north London had spread over more of the south, because that would have enabled the building of more Tubes south of the river. In effect, the Southern Railway was the continuation of the London Underground by other means. The Southern aspired to run its electrical trains almost as intensively as those on the Underground, so that timetables would not be required.

By 1927 the Southern had 300 miles of electrified line, extending 25 miles from south London. The first *main line* in Britain to be electrified was the line to Brighton, and the job was done by the Southern between 1929 and 1933. In persuading people to live near the newly electrified stations, the Southern took a leaf from the Underground's book. Frank Pick, second-in-command on the Underground, promoted the Underground suburbs with posters showing bucolic idylls and slogans such as 'A Place of Delightful Prospects' – which was Golders Green. His counterpart on the Southern was that pioneer of PR John Elliot. He commissioned a watercolourist called (and only a watercolourist could be called this) Ethelbert White to depict similar bucolic scenes above the slogans 'Live in Kent and be content' and 'Live in Surrey, free from worry'. Unlike Pick, Elliot had a sense of humour, and he disclosed that some joker had sent him a letter proposing a slogan beginning 'Live in Bucks ...'

There were also booklets in a series called Southern Homes, with long lists of 'house agents'. The book for the towns growing up as a result of the Brighton-line electrification – Croydon, Purley, Coulsdon, Merstham, Redhill, Horley, Gatwick, Three Bridges, Haywards Heath, Brighton, Hove and Worthing – was called Southern Homes for City Men. The towns other than Brighton were given a harder sell than Brighton itself, which was already full of commuters. As electrification spread, other publications appeared, including Southern Homes in Kent and Southern Homes on the Conqueror's Coast (East Sussex to Hastings). The Southern knew that people aspired to live where they'd been on holiday, and so these books ran in parallel with a series called Hints for Holidays, with spin-offs such as Hike for Health, Southern Rambles and Walking at Weekends. Attendant slogans included 'In Southern Sunshine', 'There is Sunshine in the South' and 'South for Sunshine Holidays'. The accent was on health and longevity, and the Southern constantly quoted 'a doctor' who had conveniently declared, 'So far as expectation of life is concerned, it is better to live in the Country than the town, and the south than the north.' Again Brighton was a special case, acknowledged to be not so innocent and wholesome. The healthy message was more associated with places such as Bexhill, Seaford ('most excellent for anaemia, debility, convalescence; for tuberculosis, chronic bronchitis and catarrh') and Eastbourne ('recommended by doctors') than with Brighton, which was not recommended for anything in particular, health-wise. This was only right, since Brighton was the first of the original spa resorts to abandon the genteel quackery of taking the waters in favour of just having fun. It was more likely to be promoted for 'Party Outings' or 'Evenings by the Sea' – this particular poster showing a high-heeled vamp certainly not dressed for rambling.

A new fleet of electrical multiple units was built to serve the Southern electrification, and many of these would feature a single, luxury Pullman carriage. But a whole train of Pullmans? That would seem excessive for the utilitarian business of commuting. But while the 'clock-face' timing of the *Belle* reflects the pro-commuter, anti-timetable movement, it does not indicate a train for the normal sort of commuter. Here was a train for late-risers. The timings changed over the years, but no *Belle* ever left London or Brighton before 9.30 in the morning.

Brighton did not need its *Belle* for the many Brighton–London commuters. There were other electrical trains for them. It needed the *Belle*, as we will see, because Brighton had its upmarket populace, and also because it had its downmarket populace. I was beginning to explain something about the balancing role of the *Belle* as my wife and I boarded our modern-day equivalent ...

BRIGHTON AND THE *BELLE*

It was a Saturday morning, but since the Belle experience was not a *commuting* experience that did not matter. I had selected the 11.06 to Brighton as being near to that regular 11 a.m. departure. The 11.06 – which awaited us at Platform 10 – was also fitting in that it is one of the fast trains to Brighton, meaning it stops only at Clapham Junction and East Croydon. There are no longer any non-stopping trains to Brighton, just as there are fewer non-stoppers generally.

The train was an Electrostar, like the one that took me to Dover, but whereas that had been a 375, this was a 377, a distinction unlikely to be of any interest to my wife. We boarded alongside five Brighton-bound women wearing pink bubble wigs, and T-shirts with their names on them. Ominously, one of them clutched a bottle of pink Lambrusco. I wondered whether the women – a hen party – would have got past the white-coated attendants guarding the doors of the *Brighton Belle*. It had been suggested to me there was a dress code on Pullmans. Sir Laurence Olivier, who lived in Brighton, was a regular on the *Belle*, and, when he became Baron Olivier of Brighton, he was about as eminent a customer as the train was ever likely to have, but he was a scruffy dresser, and in his book *Pullman* Julian Morel tells how an attendant new to the job in the late '60s blocked Olivier from boarding his regular first-class carriage, and pointed him firmly down the train, saying, 'Third-class is that way, sir.'

We all took our seats, the five women in standard, my wife and I in first. The woman holding the Lambrusco uncorked it. We heard the popping of the cork very clearly, being separated from it only symbolically, by a partial screen of toughened glass. 'This is a right rip-off,' my wife said, surveying our accommodation, and you'd almost think she'd paid the fare herself. I ought to have been warned by what the ticket clerk had said when I asked for a first-class ticket to Brighton: 'Why?' He had warned me there was very little difference between first and standard except the price: £37.90 as against £25.20. Standard seats had green-blue stripes, whereas ours in first had green-blue checks. And we had antimacassars, which as a matter of fact the *Belle* passengers did *not* have ...

The *Belle* was one of the new, early 1930s' breed of Southern Electric Pullmans. Its cars were not what are considered the 'vintage' Pullmans of the early *Arrow*. Such fusty words as 'Renaissance', 'Pergolese' or 'Adam-Style' did not apply. Words like 'Art Deco' and 'Jazz-Modern' were more appropriate. Yes, there was still elaborate marquetry in the wood panelling, but it displayed abstract forms, such as the sunbursts appearing on the cocktail cabinets, radios or other mod-cons fashionable in the suburbs the Southern Railway promoted. Yes, there were still thick-pile carpets, but also linoleum on the car floors; and the marquetry was dyed yellow, violet and orange. The brass fittings of the earlier cars were replaced by oxidised silver. The famous table lamps now had celluloid rather than silk shades, but they had lost none of their totemic importance. (One observer of the *Belle* on the move referred to a 'blur of table lamps'.) The colour schemes of the seat moquettes were positively futuristic: stolid reds, blues and greens were replaced by apparently wayward peaches, fawns, mauves, orangey browns and exotic reds, the continental-looking 'autumnal shades' favoured at the time. Anthony M. Ford quotes an 'Art Deco historian' called Alastair Duncan to the effect: 'Tastes in colour changed more rapidly in the field of textile design than in any other medium ... vivid, sometimes discordant shades of lanvin blue, tango and hot pink were juxtaposed with lime-greens and chrome yellows to generate a psychedelic palette rivalling that of the 1960s.'

We pulled away dead on time. It is depressing to leave from the central side of Victoria these days, since a glass office block sits atop Platforms 9 and upwards. It is said that one's first impression on boarding the *Belle* was one of silence, so solidly built and closely muffled was the train. I, by contrast, contended with shouts from standard of 'Drop more fizz, Tray?' as I attempted to interest my wife in the above-mentioned social-paradox of the *Belle* ...

Brighton was put on the map by the patronage of the Prince Regent, later George IV, but that's not to say it was made respectable thereby. He went there to consort with his mistress, Maria Fitzherbert, to whom it turned out he was secretly married, which might have been to his credit had he not also been married to Caroline of Brunswick. So began the association of Brighton with dirty weekends. Even in those pre-railway days there was a rackety element. In *Rural Rides*, written in the 1820s, William Cobbett described Brighton as

> naturally a place of resort for 'expectants', and a shifty, ugly-looking swarm is, of course, assembled there ... You may always know them by their lank jaws, the stiffeners around their necks, their hidden or no shirts, their stays, their false shoulders, hips and haunches, their half whiskers, and by their skins, colour of veal kidney suet, warmed a little, and then powdered with dirty dust.

These were the sorts of reprobates who used telescopes to watch women emerging from the bathing machines on the beach. An attraction of Brighton was that its bathing machines did not have the canvas awnings that screened bathers at other resorts as they entered the sea.

George IV set the town on a course of frivolity by block-
ing the building of a harbour, on the grounds that it would
muddy the bathing waters. (Mud ought not to have been
George's main concern, given that the sewers of Brighton
discharged directly into the sea.) Newhaven would become
the Sussex port. Seaborne arrivals at Brighton would be confined to the few steamers arriving at the pier. Brighton was
confirmed as a place for people rather than commerce, and I
am reminded of a sentence in a history of the Southern Railway: 'The railway had far less freight than the other companies and served hardly any coalfields.' (There was one: near
Dover.)

The town proceeded to sell out. What had been Bright-
helmstone became the catchier Brighton (probably, it had
always been pronounced that way), and moved on from
being a spa resort. As Alain Corbin writes about Brighton in
The Lure of the Sea: 'for the first time, a shift took place from
therapeutic aims to hedonistic ones, and this was to charac-
terise all the great continental resorts during the Nineteenth
Century.'

The railway from London arrived in 1841, which is an
easy thing to write, and most people do think of London to
Brighton as a well-trammelled groove. Before the railways,
Brighton had been connected to London by particularly fast
stage-coaches, which took five hours. In *Rural Rides* Cobbett
described the town's 'stock jobbers ... [who] skip backward
and forward on the coaches and actually *carry on stock-jobbing*,
in 'Change Alley, though they reside in Brighton'. Brighton is
known as London-on-sea, and it was an early centre of commuting to London, but the connection is not as natural as it
might seem. The railway had to work hard to get to Brighton.

The first engineer consulted on the project, Robert Stephenson, normally preached the 'straight through' doctrine,

but came out against it in the case of Brighton because the chalk escarpments of the North and South Downs and the intervening sandstone ridges and clay valleys of the Weald were in the way. But Stephenson was brushed aside. 'Straight through' was adopted, and an engineer called John Rastrick, a friend of Stephenson's, was brought in to build unprecedentedly long tunnels at Merstham (through the North Downs), Balcombe (The Weald) and Clayton (South Downs). A viaduct would also carry the line over the Ouse Valley in the Weald.

Within a year of the opening of Brighton station in 1841 the residential population of the town had increased from 7,000 to 47,000, and it has been estimated that the number of trippers visiting the town every year increased thirty-fold to 3 million. Cue the departure of Queen Victoria, who now preferred to take her holidays on the Isle of Wight, finding the expanded populace of Brighton 'very indiscreet and troublesome'. The wealthier patrons hung on, but shifted their season, and their social round – conducted in the magnificent houses of the Royal Crescent – from summer to autumn, so as to avoid the excursionists. Here was the start of what John K. Walton in his book The English Seaside Resort called the 'complicated informal system of internal social zoning' that operated in the town, a function of its willingness to take all-comers.

The London, Brighton & South Coast Railway was a snobbish outfit, and did not want to be known solely as a carrier of third-class excursionists. It wanted to keep its prosperous clientele, whether they were commuting or not. This meant luxury trains.

In 1881 the LBSCR brought in what was unofficially called the Pullman Limited Express between London and Brighton. This was the first all-Pullman train in the UK. It operated only on weekdays, but the following year a Sunday service called the *Pullman Drawing Room Car Train* began running, known to its opponents as 'the Sabbath Breaker'. (Brighton was something of a pioneer at Sabbath-breaking.) In 1898 these services were re-launched as an all-week service officially called the *Pullman Limited Express*.

In 1908 this became the *Southern Belle*, billed as 'the most luxurious train in the world'. A return to London was 12 shillings – about half a week's wages for an unskilled labourer. The LBSCR held a party at the Hotel Metropole in Brighton to celebrate, the earl of Bessborough, chairman of the railway, presiding. According to a report in the *Daily Telegraph* of 2 November 1908, he said the new train 'showed the railway were doing their best to encourage first-class traffic to Brighton, and they hoped this would not be the only train of its kind'. The mayor of Brighton responded by saying he 'hoped the new train would bring to Brighton the class of passengers the place wanted'.

Between 1929 and 1933 the Brighton line was electrified. It would have been possible to continue with the steam-hauled *Southern Belle* over the line, but you couldn't creditably have a steam train as your flagship on a line you'd gone to all the trouble of electrifying. So the new *Southern Belle* would take the form of the other expresses being introduced on the Brighton line: it would be a five-car electrical multiple unit. But this EMU – or these three, because there would be three five-car *Belle* units – would be a Pullman. Two of the five-car units would be in operation at any one time, the third kept in reserve. Each unit featured two first-class carriages. These were in the form of kitchen cars, and were given names suggesting the sort of young lady that a young (or not so young) man might want to take to Brighton: Audrey, Doris, Gwen, Hazel, Mona and Vera.

In 1931 the Southern Railway had begun running a *Bournemouth Belle*, which left the newly electric *Southern Belle* sounding generic. So it was renamed the *Brighton Belle*, to the delight of Brighton Council. On 29 June 1934 the mayor of Brighton, Miss M. Hardy, christened the train. Of all the *Belles* of the Southern, the Brighton train was *the Belle*, and no train has ever been so closely associated with a single town.

The *Belle* suited Brighton in that it offered slightly decadent luxury, but with a demotic touch. The third-class fare (and supplement) was within the reach of the ordinary sort of passenger who thought he or she deserved a treat. In their book *The Great Days of the Express Trains* David St John Thomas and Patrick Whitehouse describe the *Belle* as 'the only luxury service in Britain which the working man, if he could afford to travel at all, could for a small supplement use for a day out at the seaside'.

When visiting the preserved Bluebell Railway in Sussex, I met a man called Martin, a volunteer on the line. He told me he'd travelled on the *Brighton Belle* in 1971, needing to unwind after a harrowing interview for a place to read engineering at Sussex University. 'They'd made me an offer of three Cs at "A" level. I knew it was a tall order.' He paid 2s. 6d. for the third-class Pullman supplement, 'about the price of a pint'. Once on board, he splurged. 'I ordered a bottle of Double Diamond, plaice, chips, peas and tartare sauce.' It was the tartare sauce that made the meal special. Martin told me that he believed there was 'a certain amount of pressure' on the *Belle* passenger to order something from the menu, and that the question was not so much, 'Would sir require lunch?' as 'What would sir require for lunch?' I asked whether a glass of tap water would have been complimentary. 'Mmm ... they might give you a funny look. They might expect a tip for that.'

FOO GO

Our Electrostar was gaining speed as we approached Wandsworth.

The inexorability of the old express run to Brighton was demonstrated by a film made in 1953 that was often used often to fill the 'interludes' that occurred in the days of black-and-white TV. *London to Brighton in Four Minutes* was a speeded up film of the *Belle*'s journey from London to Brighton. The train is seen to travel at the speed of sound. It was more exciting than *The Potter's Wheel*, let's put it like that. The BBC repeated the exercise in 1983 and 2013, but for this third film the current operator of the line, Southern Trains, had to lay on a special service in the absence of any Brighton non-stoppers. Paul Clifton, Transport Correspondent for BBC South, travelled on this 'special' and compared the trip to the earlier two for the BBC News website. Mr Clifton noted the less ethnically diverse railway staff of the past, and the fewer women. He also noted: 'In the 1950s film passengers are soberly dressed. By the 1980s Brighton style has become more relaxed, but still most men wear suits and ties.' In 2013, 'as for fashion, well, anything goes. The Brighton passengers', Mr Clifton concludes damningly, 'are fatter and slower on their feet sixty years on.'

Being mentally on the *Belle* put me in a snobbish frame of mind, and when, at 11.12, we called in at Clapham Junction, I couldn't help but think of it as a place the *Belle* wouldn't have touched with a bargepole. Thereafter, it all looked so common: Wandsworth Common ... Streatham Common. If I had been on the eleven o'clock Saturday *Belle*, I would by now have been studying the menu. And I would have been torn. Full meals were served at all times. It was a little too early for lunch, but was it too early for a quarter-bottle of something?

Since I was not actually on the *Belle*, I had to go looking for the 'at-seat service of snacks, sandwiches and hot and cold drinks' that would be 'available for all or part of the journey'; or maybe not. Certainly the at-seat service had come nowhere near my seat. I asked my wife if she wanted anything. 'Mineral water,' she said automatically, from the depths of a novel.

My search for the trolley took me past the hen party. The women wore T- shirts with their names on, and it would have suited my ghostly purposes if six of them had been called Audrey, Doris, Gwen, Hazel, Mona and Vera, but I only noticed Tracy and Sue. Most of those *Belle* names seem quaint today, although I do know an Audrey who's about my age. It is said that baby girls stopped being christened Mona because of Mona Lott, a depressed laundrywoman in the radio comedy *It's That Man Again* (1939–49) whose catchphrase was 'It's being so cheerful as keeps me going.'

I found the at-seat service in the next carriage along. A forthright, competent East European woman was in charge of it. Yes, there were quarter-bottles of white and red, but I decided it *was* too early. Food-wise, I could see only biscuits, crisps and snacks on the trolley. 'Do you sell sandwiches?' I asked. 'Yes,' she said, 'in fact, I have sold them all.'

'What were they?' I asked, 'just out of interest?'

'Egg and rocket, BLT, cheese and tomato and lettuce.'

I asked about hot food.

'We have cheese toasties, pizza snacks and sausage roll – on Monday to Friday.'

'They're all hot, are they?' I asked, the question purely academic since this was a Saturday.

'They are hot in the mornings.'

Well, she didn't have a kitchen, unlike the *Brighton Belle*, but the selection of hoot food did have something in common with the *Belle* fare, as described in a menu of 1966. Among the highlights were:

Deep fried fillet of fish tartare with French Fried
   Potatoes 8s. 6d.
Pan fried egg and grilled bacon: single 4s., double 8s.
Welsh rarebit 2s. 9d
Buck rarebit 4s.
Toasted bacon sandwich with pickles 4s.
Double-decker egg and bacon sandwich 5s. 6d.

In short, heart-attack-on-a-plate, and Southern Trains
were carrying on the tradition with their cheese toasties
and pizza. It must be admitted that the catering on the *Belle*
declined over the years. A three-course *Table d'Hôte* (written in
French until 1937) gave way to *A la Carte*, and then something
more snack-like. One *Belle* regular told me of his dismay at
discovering that the 'mashed potato' was Cadbury's Smash.

The trolley-keeper waited patiently.

'Perhaps I'll have something to eat on the way back,' I
said.

'The last train back with a trolley leaves at 17.49,' she
warned me ... and she was eyeing my Prince of Wales check
suit. 'Are you from first-class?'

I proudly replied in the affirmative.

'Then you are entitled to a free coffee.'

I graciously agreed to accept one, and as it was being
poured, I thought about train dining.

On the earliest trains passengers could not dine, since
they were trapped in their corridor-less compartments.
Meals were taken in haste at refreshment stops. These were
at York on the East Coast route to Scotland, at Normanton
on the Midland route, at Preston on the West Coast. On the
Great Western the stop was at Swindon, where the passing
trains were obliged by a fateful deal, struck in 1842 between
the railway and the proprietor of the refreshment rooms, to

stop for ten minutes. The railway unchained itself from the dreaded Swindon Refreshment Rooms when it bought out the caterer in 1895.

Refreshment rooms in general had a terrible reputation, partly because of Charles Dickens. On 25 April 1866 the great – but rather touchy – author was travelling from Liverpool to Euston with two companions, including William Henry Wills, writer and sometime secretary to Dickens. At Rugby the carriage in which the three were sitting was discovered to be on fire. (This was barely a year after Dickens had nearly died in the Staplehurst smash.) They were turfed off the train, and Dickens and Wills went to the refreshment room, where a woman stood at the counter. What happened next is told in *The Express Train and Other Railway Studies*, by Jack Simmons:

> [Dickens] and Wills had each asked for a cup of coffee, which was supplied to them. While Wills was feeling in his pocket for some small change with which to pay, Mr Dickens reached across the counter for the sugar and milk, when both articles were suddenly snatched away from him and placed beneath the counter, while his ears were greeted with the remark, made in shrill and shrewish tones, 'You shan't have any milk and sugar till you two fellows have paid for your coffee.' The young page boy of the refreshment rooms was looking on, and he burst into laughter at seeing the two fellows confounded in this way.

And so the short story called *The Boy at Mugby* – one of three with a railway theme written by Dickens for the Christmas number of his magazine *All the Year Round* – begins, 'I am the boy at what is called the refreshment room at Mugby Junction, and what's proudest boast is, that it never yet refreshed a mortal being.'

Three years later, in his novel *He Knew He Was Right*, Anthony Trollope described the railway sandwich as 'the real disgrace of England'. In his day sandwiches would curdle under a glass dome in a hot refreshment room. Later, they would do the same on the buffet counters of hot trains. It wasn't so much the railway sandwich that was a disgrace as the sandwich-prepared-long-in-advance.

The first dining car with kitchen – it was a Pullman – was run on the Great Northern in 1879, between King's Cross and Leeds. There were balconies at either end. Passengers boarded by one of these. The other balcony was a sort of backyard where a scullery boy would peel potatoes, scattering peel on the tracks as the train raced along. There was a central gangway, red plush armchairs and tables with white cloths on either side. But there was no through corridor to connect the dining car with the rest of the train. Once in the car, you stayed in it.

On most trains, compartments were the norm, and passengers had to be released from these to access a dining car. This required corridors alongside the compartments and gangways between the corridors. The first side-corridors came in during the 1870s. The first train fully gangwayed along its length was introduced by the Great Western in 1892, but, as one wit noted: 'The paths of glory lead but to the luggage van.' They also led to the lavatory, but they did not lead to any dining car. By 1893 there were dining cars for all classes on the East Coast, West Coast and Midland services from London to Scotland, but only one of these, a 2 p.m. Euston-to-Scotland service, was gangwayed throughout, so that passengers could return to their seats afterwards. As the *Oxford Companion to British Railway History* says, 'The interior decor [of a dining car] is generally of a higher standard than other carriages.' So why would any passenger *want* to leave after a meal, instead of lingering on with a cigarette and coffee? I remember Robert Robinson hosting a radio discussion about the morality of spending the entirety of a journey in the restaurant car (effectively first-class accommodation) while travelling on a second-class ticket.

The rule with most 'de-classed' diners was that first-class ticket-holders would be tipped off first about the service of a meal. They got priority, and I used to feel vaguely ashamed when, in the days of dining cars on the East Coast, I was beckoned from my seat by the announcement, 'Will all passengers in *standard* class wishing to take their seats for dinner please come forward to the restaurant car now.' When I arrived, all the diners from first would be well into their first courses. They would eye me beadily as I rolled up my jacket and put it on the rack.

Dining cars might be de-classed, or divided into first and third seating, or there might be separate carriages for each class. A third-class Midland Railway dining carriage from the late nineteenth century is displayed at the National Rail Museum in York. Examining its monogrammed silver plate cutlery, bone china and crystal glasses, visitors exclaim, 'And you got all this in third-class!'

During the 1930s many restaurant cars were converted to buffet cars, which did not have a full kitchen and which provided snacks, including 'grilled tea cakes' or, for the delectation of post-war passengers on the East Coast Main Line, a 'plain tea'. In the buffet car the essence of the appeal of the dining car was retained. You did not have to take the food away, in the manner once complained of by Victoria Wood: 'I'm not a fan of the modern railway system. I strongly object to paying twenty-seven pounds fifty to walk the length of the train with a sausage in a plastic box.' You sat down in the buffet; it provided a seat away from your own seat, and the accompanying sense of expansiveness.

Dining cars seemed luxurious partly because of contingencies imposed by the train. Breakfast was doled out by a poised waiter (braced against the shaking of the carriage), who picked the bacon and sausages from a silver salver with tweezers. You could point to the particular rasher of bacon you wanted; and the fried egg was lifted towards you on a triangle of fried bread. This seemed very refined, but the fact is there wasn't space in the galley to lay out the breakfasts on plates.

Where once there had been many hundreds of trains with restaurant cars, by the end of BR days the number was down to about 250. These had survived the rise of snacking in preference to formal dining, the steep decline in rail use and the rise of the at-seat trolley. Today dining cars are deemed uneconomical. The carriages are needed for normal seating on trains that are once again crowded. The lure of first-class is increased by the way coffee, snacks and – at the right time of day – wine are brought to your seat at no extra cost. At the time of writing, dining cars survive only on the trains of First Great Western, as we will be seeing in the next chapter.

On the Brighton train I had to carry the coffee back to my seat in a paper bag. All 'takeaway' coffees must be served like this on British trains, but not on Eurostar, which is majority-owned by the French. The bag reduces the risk of spillage and scalding. You'd think there was no such danger on the Belle, but the cars were poorly suspended and rough-riding. The steam-hauled Southern Belle had been smoother. The trouble was something to do with the wrong sort of bogies. These were replaced in 1955, but the problem persisted. Attendants would know not to pour coffee at certain points on the route, and a napkin was always placed between cup and saucer. *Belle* menus included the disclaimer: 'Our staff take every care and precaution in the service of refreshments, and the company cannot be held responsible for accidents or spillage etc., which may occur on account of excessive movement of the train.'

BEYOND CROYDON

I returned to my seat as we were approaching Croydon. I was thinking about kippers. A pair of grilled ones constituted the healthier options on the *Belle* menus. But in 1969 Laurence Olivier found no sign of the 'marvellous, juicy and succulent' kippers that he ordered every time he boarded. According to Julian Morel in his book *Pullman*, 'An over-zealous official had streamlined the menu for "economic" reasons.' The particular problem with the kippers was that 'certain famous passengers' (i.e., Lord Olivier) would order them late on during the 11 p.m. 'down' service that had been introduced in 1962, often ordering after Haywards Heath. Consequently, the end-of-shift cleaning of the kitchen was thrown late. Lord Olivier got up a petition, and the kippers were restored. On 24 March 1970 a man called Collie Knox wrote a letter to the *Daily Telegraph* outlining the story and concluding, 'Not even when nightly strangling Desdemona at the National Theatre has Sir Laurence acted to more noble purpose.'

Collie Knox was a journalist and broadcaster, and his letter was addressed from the Garrick Club. This was a sort of annexe of the *Brighton Belle*, which was known as 'the Equity express'. Max Miller, Terence Rattigan, Peter Jones, Jimmy Edwards and Dame Flora Robson were regulars on the train – also Dora Bryan, whom I actually saw approaching the *Belle* at Victoria in about 1971. My sister ran across the concourse and got her autograph.

Alan Melville, broadcaster and playwright, lived in Brighton and travelled on the *Belle* several times a week. In his autobiography, *Merely Melville*, he wrote about the train: 'The most lethal of the Belle's journeys is the 11 p.m. from Victoria ... and you have to be very careful indeed if, after a long day's grind, you don't want to be trapped with a lot of gay chat about how fabulous the business was tonight, or how unreceptive the audience was all through Act One but how they brightened up after the interval.' Before boarding, Melville would buy the *Evening News* rather than the *Standard* because the *News* was bigger and he could hide behind it on the train. 'Not that this attempt at camouflage always works; Dora Bryan has an endearing habit of turning down the top of one's *Evening News* and saying, "Oh it's you, dear."'

Celebrities were often seen on the *Belle*. It became, according to the *Daily Telegraph*, 'an autograph album on wheels'. In September 1938 King Boris of Bulgaria, described in *Life in Brighton*, by Clifford Musgrave, as 'one of the most engaging of the lesser monarchs of Europe', travelled on the *Belle*. King Boris had two principal interests – butterflies and railways – and he combined them by taking the *Belle* (travelling some of the way in the driver's cab) to inspect the collections of Lepidoptera in the Booth Museum of Natural History in Brighton. According to Musgrave:

A luncheon was given for the king, together with the Mayor of Brighton and the Chairman of the Museum Committee, in the Central Saloon of the Royal Pavilion, which was undergoing restoration. A plumber who was working in the building accidentally blundered into the room, clutching a bag of clanking tools. Two members of the king's retinue pulled automatic pistols and flung themselves in front of their master. The king thought it

was all very funny: 'That is the sort of thing that could
only happen in England!'

It was big of him to find it funny, given that he had survived two assassination attempts by anarchists up to that
point. When he died, in 1943, it was suspected that King
Boris had been poisoned on Hitler's orders for refusing to
become more involved in the war.

A latter-day *Belle* might be serving its kippers to Julie
Burchill, Zoe Ball, Simon Callow, Peter Andre, Julian Clary
– all Brighton residents. About twenty years ago I was waiting to use the WC on an ordinary Brighton train, when the
door opened and Elvis Costello stepped out to the sound of
the lavatory flushing. I watched him as he retreated to a first-
class seat, a much bigger man than you would have thought
from his early, nerdish persona. But I could see no celebrities
on the 11.06.

We called at East Croydon (11.23), another place the *Belle*
used to cut dead. Well, Croydon was more ignorable then,
a humble market town when the *Belle* was born rather than
the mini-Manhattan of today. Before we departed, the guard
announced, 'This train will be calling at Brighton only', and
so from now on we would be more *Belle*-like.

After South Croydon, at Stoat's Nest, I watched the older,
and slower, line to Brighton wandering away to the left. A
moment later, we would cross over it. The slow line goes
through Redhill, the scene of rivalry between the London,
Brighton & South Coast Railway and the South Eastern.
The latter would design its operations so as to obstruct the
former's trains there. (Redhill station, a generally problem-
atic spot, was known as Reigate station in those days, after
the bigger town near by.) The LBSCR built a line avoiding
Redhill; it was opened in 1900.

Being on that newer, faster line, we penetrated the North Downs through Quarry Hill Tunnel, whereas the slow train goes through Merstham Old Tunnel. The *Belle* was always on the fast line. After crossing over the M25, we rejoined the slow lines at Earlswood. Most of the slow trains running over the slow line to Brighton go from London Bridge.

We sped through Gatwick Airport station, 26 miles from London. The airport lay to the right, parked Easy Jet planes alarmingly proximate. On the tile map at Victoria, Gatwick is denoted by two benign symbols: a green 'V' meaning 'golf links' and a red horseshoe shape meaning 'racecourse', and the railway station at Gatwick was called Gatwick Racecourse until 1935. In their book *The Brighton Belle: The Story of a Famous and Much-Loved Train* Stephen Grant and Simon Jeffs write, 'The Belle never called at Gatwick, even for special working.' Gatwick was designated Britain's second airport in 1952; it got a new station in 1958. The present station is being rebuilt at a cost of £50 million. Since 2008 Gatwick has trumped Brighton, in that some of the trains from Victoria dubbed 'Gatwick Express' run on to Brighton, as a sort of afterthought.

After Three Bridges, which serves Crawley new town, we were in the Weald, which is manicured like a giant golf course, but sufficiently rolling to require the Balcombe Tunnel and the graceful Ouse Valley Viaduct, with its Italianate pavilions at each end. After Haywards Heath the South Downs came into view ahead of the train – proper hills these, even to a northerner's eye. We sped through Wivelsfield, Burgess Hill, Hassocks (the footstools on the *Belle* were called hassocks), then into the South Downs Tunnel – Clayton Tunnel – whereupon we broached what I, on my trips to Brighton, think of as the Vale of Death.

THE VALE OF DEATH

The north end of Clayton Tunnel looks like a medieval castle, but on top of the tunnel mouth, in between the mock turrets, sits a perfunctory single-storey house. The house was built at the same time as the tunnel, but its purpose is unclear. Most likely, it accommodated some functionary whose job related to the tunnel.

The Victorians were moles. They built 90 per cent of Britain's railway tunnels, but they were also scared of them. Tunnels were often painted white so as to mitigate claustrophobia. The Clayton Tunnel was painted white. It was also illuminated by gas jets, and it is thought the house was built to accommodate the man who maintained the lighting. But illumination did not remove the real danger of railway tunnels, which lay not in suffocation or tunnel collapse, as Victorian travellers feared, but in the invisibility of the trains to signalmen.

On Sunday 25 August 1861 three trains left Brighton for London spaced at five-minute intervals, the minimum permitted at the time. The first two were excursions, the third an ordinary timetabled train. One train was not supposed to follow another into a tunnel until it was established that the first had cleared the tunnel. But the signal at the south end of the Clayton Tunnel was broken, so the first excursion did not change it to 'danger' when it entered the tunnel. The signalman in the box at the southern end, a man called Killick – who was working a twenty-four-hour shift in order to earn a day off on the Monday – tried to stop the second excursion by waving his red flag. He failed to do so. He then used his telegraph connection to ask the man in the north signal box, whose name was Brown, 'Is the tunnel clear?' Brown signalled back 'Tunnel clear', because he'd just seen the first excursion emerge. Killick took the reply to refer to the second excursion, which had in fact stopped in the tunnel and was now reversing, the driver intending to ask Killick what he'd meant by the red flag. The ordinary, time-tabled train then entered the tunnel and smashed into the second excursion with such force that the chimney of that third engine hit the tunnel roof, twenty-four feet above the ground, an impact that must have resonated horribly in the house above. Twenty-one people died and 171 were injured in what was the worst railway accident up to that point. It was said by the pious to be a punishment for the railway's willingness to run excursions on the Sabbath ... and (the Sabbatarians might have added) for allowing a signalman to become exhausted through working a twenty-four-hour Sunday shift.

The Clayton smash was probably in Charles Dickens's mind when he wrote his ghost story *The Signalman*, one of the three railway sketches of 1866. It concerns a terrible accident in a tunnel, and a signalman haunted by the telegraph bell that rings when the other unseen signalman, at the other end of the tunnel, warns of an approaching train. The epony-mous character – a sallow, neurotic functionary – inhabits a signal box sunk in a dank cutting, where he is fixated on the adjacent tunnel mouth and a glimmering red signal light. The narrator observes: 'So little sunlight ever found its way to this spot, that it had an earthy, deadly smell; and so much cold wind rushed through it, that it struck chill to me, as if I had left the natural world.' The signalman is tormented by a precognitive vision of a railway accident, and in an essay called 'Blood on the Tracks: Sensation Drama, the Railway and the Dark Face of Modernity' Nicholas Daly sets the story in the context of Victorian railway accidents. Daly discovers in the popular perception of them something

qualitatively different ... they occur in 'machine time' not
human time. Human agency cannot usually move rapidly
enough to intervene, and there are few rescues. In fact,
such incidents are often too quick for the eye, and
perception takes place after the event: if you see it, you are
still alive.

It is this dimension that Dickens captures. The signalman
sees the accident happen *before it takes place*.

Our Electrostar traversed the South Downs, before entering the less ominous Patcham Tunnel. We emerged at the
Brighton suburb of Preston Park. On the afternoon of 27
June 1881 a bloodied man staggered out of a London Bridge-
to-Brighton train at Preston Park. He was a dandified, thin,
chinless, suspicious-looking man who announced himself
as Percy Lefroy. He said he'd been attacked in his compartment when the train had been running through Merstham
Tunnel by an assailant who had subsequently alighted. In
fact, Lefroy, who was really called Mapleton, was found to
have attacked and robbed another man – a Mr Gold – when
the train had been running through another tunnel: Balcombe Tunnel. Mapleton had then pushed Gold's body out
of the train and into the tunnel. A murder *would* occur in
Merstham Tunnel, but not until 1905, when the mutilated
body of a Mary Money was found there. Her killer was never
apprehended.

Both Gold and Money were trapped with their killers, as
was the victim of the very first railway murder, a City clerk
called Thomas Briggs, attacked in a first-class compartment
of the North London Railway at Hackney on 9 July 1864. His
killer was almost certainly the man hanged for the crime,
Franz Muller. The Briggs murder led to the introduction
of the communication cord, but not until 1868, too late for

Gold and Money. Some companies also drilled apertures – peep-holes – between compartments. These were known as 'Muller Lights', and today there is a yoghurt with the same name. In the 1870s side-corridors began to appear on compartment coaches, as we have seen. But corridor-less compartments were still in use for short runs, especially on the slam-door trains of the Southern Region – including some Brighton trains – until the late 1980s.

Walter de La Mare wrote: 'It is a fascinating experience, railway travelling … One is cast into a passing intimacy with a fellow stranger, and then it is gone.' In his introduction to a collection of railway crime stores, *Crime on the Lines*, Bryan Morgan wrote, 'There were times during my reading when it seemed that half the crime short stories published before the first world war began, "The stranger in the astrakhan coat leaned towards me across the first-class compartment."' Compartments marked 'Ladies-Only' – still to be found in the mid-1970s – were meant to keep the astrakhan-coated men at bay.

The Victorian sensationalist novels of Mary Elizabeth Braddon typically featured a middle-class woman sitting alone in a railway compartment. She is minding her own business when, in spite of the fact that the train is going at 60 m.p.h., a top-hatted stranger clambers into the compartment from the window, having been – for some reason he may or may not deign to explain – travelling on the roof of the carriage. Sealed-compartment murder occurs in various railway crime short stores by Canon Victor Lorenzo Whitechurch, and in *The Mysterious Death on the Underground Railway* by Baroness Orczy. Alfred Hitchcock was alive to the dangerous intimacy of compartments, as shown in his film versions of *The Thirty-Nine Steps* (much better, and more railway-oriented, than the novel) and *Strangers on a Train*.

The fiction exaggerated the dangers. I have written a series of crime novels set on Britain's railways in the early twentieth century: nine books, with an average of two murders per book, whereas in fact there were only seven murders on Britain's railways between 1827 and 1929.

This talk of closeted death may also seem a long way from the festive, open carriages of the Brighton Belle ... but not quite.

Between the 1890s and 1963 the aforementioned Preston Park was the location of the Brighton Pullman works (the half-derelict shell of the building survived until 2008). The works were a little way north of some others sidings and workshops called Lover's Walk. Today Network Rail occupies part of this latter site, with something called the 'ECR infrastructure and maintenance depot'. The Belle used to be stabled at Lover's Walk between runs. At 5 p.m. on Friday 14 October 1960 the door of one of the third-class lavatories was found locked while the train was being cleaned and prepared after the 3 p.m. 'down' run from Victoria, and prior to the 5.25 'up'. A Pullman attendant opened the door with a master key, to find the blood-soaked body of a twenty-two-year-old woman. There was also a medical dissecting razor, and with this she had slit her throat. The dead woman was about to begin medical studies at Guy's Hospital in London. Meanwhile she'd been working as a psychiatric nurse, and it was suggested at the inquest that this work had disturbed her. Some accounts have claimed the woman had been jilted – with no more evidence than the loose association of suicide and 'Lover's Walk', which, in any event, ought to have been renamed long before 1960 ...

In 1831, before it was a railway depot, the name denoted a small wood and picnic spot. In that year the torso of a woman called Celia Bashford was found in a trunk buried

in the woods. She had been strangled in a house on Donkey Row, Brighton, by her husband, John Holloway, who
had then chopped off her limbs, assisted by his other wife,
Ann Kendall (Holloway being a bigamist). The limbs were
dropped into an outside toilet in Margaret Street, Brighton.
Celia Bashford was very short and had a misshapen head.
It seems Holloway had never loved her, but merely impreg-
nated and then reluctantly married her. (Four years earlier,
she'd given birth to a still-born child.)

The killing of Celia Bashford has been called the first
'trunk murder'. A series of subsequent ones took place a
hundred years later, and one is somehow not surprised that
two of these occurred in Brighton. The first in the series
occurred in May 1927, and a man called John Robinson was
executed for it. He had picked up a prostitute called Minnie
Alice Bonati at Victoria station; he killed her in Rochester
Row, put her body in a trunk and took it to left luggage at
King's Cross (so the whole thing is railway-haunted). The
trunk began to smell ...

The second London one came to light later in the same
year, when the suspicious wife of a Patrick Mahon discovered a Waterloo station cloakroom ticket in one of his pockets. Given the events of the previous May, you'd have thought
she would have left it where she found it. But she took it to
Waterloo and was handed a Gladstone bag full of bloodstained female clothing. Mahon, it transpired, had killed
and dismembered his mistress at their Sussex love nest.

On 17 June 1934 – the year after the inauguration of the
Belle – an unclaimed trunk in Brighton station left luggage
office began to smell. A female torso was found inside. The
matching legs were found at King's Cross after a general left
luggage alert had been put out. The victim was about twenty-
five and said to have had 'pretty feet'. Neither her identity

nor that of the murderer was ever discovered, although a Brighton abortionist called Massiah was suspected.

The investigation of this first Brighton trunk murder unearthed a second one. A search of premises near Brighton station discovered the remains of a Violette Kaye in a trunk in a house at 52 Kemp Street, an address recently vacated by one Toni Mancini. On 10 May 1934 Kaye had had a violent quarrel with Mancini at the Skylark Café on Brighton seafront, and she was never seen alive again. Mancini was tried and acquitted, but in 1976, shortly before his death, he confessed to a *News of the World* journalist.

In 1946 incriminating luggage was also found at Bournemouth West Station. It included a metal-tipped whip and a bloodstained scarf; it had been deposited by Neville Heath, the sadistic RAF officer who killed two women in that year.

The common denominator is not so much trunks as left luggage offices, towards which killers who might otherwise have gone undiscovered seem to have been fatally drawn. But this was a railway era, and the killers did not have cars in which to transport the bodies to some lonely spot. The left luggage office would not be so attractive today. If the attendant missed the tell-tale smell and ooze of blood, the X-ray machine (universal since 9/11) would probably discover the contents. And the CCTV camera would identify the luggage-leaver.

I once walked into the blandly named Travel Centre on the east side of Brighton station, and asked one of the men advising passengers there, 'Which building used to be the left luggage office?' He turned to me with a mournful expression: 'I'm afraid this did.' He knew what I was getting at, and the Travel Centre still has all the dimensions of a left luggage office.

The trunk murders earned Brighton the informal title

'Queen of Slaughtering Places', a modification of its claim
to be 'Queen of the Watering Places'. Brighton resented the
slur, but in 1938 came further slurring, with the publication
of Graham Greene's novel of Brighton low life, *Brighton Rock*.
One biographer of Greene suggested *he* was the Brighton
Trunk Murderer. Specious, of course, but Green did spend
a lot of time in Brighton, and a trunk murder does occur in
his novel *England Made Me* (1934). The body is found at Paddington, in similar circumstances to the Brighton discovery,
which Greene appeared to have prefigured, having made
notes about his fictional Paddington crime as early as 1932.
(He had dreamed it, he said.)

Incidentally, a plausible explanation of the unsolved
Brighton trunk murder is given in Brighton resident Peter
Guttridge's teeming, cross-generational crime novel of a
couple of years ago, *City of Dreadful Night*. Guttridge himself lives in Brighton, as do so many of the writers who have
painted the place on felonious colours. The late Keith Waterhouse – for many years a Brighton resident – said the town
'looked as though it was helping the police with their enquir-
ies'. Waterhouse often used the *Belle*, which has not escaped
being tarred with the same brush. Antony M. Ford quotes
a certain Edward Woollard as follows: 'Since the 1930s,
people have made love on the *Belle*, jumped to their deaths
from it, while theatre stars learned their lines, and crimes
have been plotted on it.' Chapter and verse are not given.
The *Belle* does not feature in the principal Brighton horror,
Brighton Rock, and *Brighton Belle*, a recent murder mystery by
Sara Sheridan, is so-called because of the heroine's name,
Mirabelle Bevan. But I think the *Belle* does figure in Patrick
Hamilton's murder novel of 1941, *Hangover Square*. The traveller is the alcoholic George Harvey Bone, who is obsessed
with a manipulative female called Netta. Bone is certainly

in a third-class Pullman car, probably on the *Belle*, although that is not stated. (Most fast services to Brighton had at least a single Pullman car in those days.)

Bone intends to book a hotel room in Brighton, where Netta has promised to join him after he had visited her in London. Ecstatic at the news, he had begun drinking beer and gin in London, and continued drinking on the train, which is now travelling through Haywards Heath 'in the sunny, sticky, streaming afternoon'.

> He was in a Pullman car. He sat on the right facing Brighton, and there was no-one else at his table. There were only a few other people in the car. Lunch was over, but the lunch-spotted white cloths were still visible on the tables. He was drinking beer and he all at once became gloomy and saw that he had probably made a fool of himself again, after all.

He cannot believe that Netta will really come to Brighton, and as the thought settles upon him, the train stops. A blue-bottle buzzes in the carriage. 'A bored fellow-passenger rattled a newspaper in turning it ... And you could hear the clinking of crockery and the conversation of the attendants in the kitchen behind.'

I called the media office for Sussex police.

'Does Brighton have a high murder rate?'

'Crime across Sussex is falling,' said the spokesman, not quite answering the question.

I rephrased it: 'Is there anything alarming about the murder rate in Brighton?'

'That's a matter of opinion. I would say certainly not.'

'Did it ever have a high rate?'

'I've no idea.'

Let me stress that Brighton is booming as a commuter town, and often listed high among the most desirable places to live in Britain.

THE DEATH (AND RE-BIRTH) OF THE *BELLE*

As our train approached Brighton, I approached the loo. 'We think it's out of order,' said one of the hens who, against all precedent, had become quieter rather than louder throughout the trip. I walked along to another loo – one of those with an electronic door. I don't like these. I worry the door won't lock; then I worry it won't re-open. A sign said, 'Press button when flashing', which was somehow like a joke on a bawdy seaside postcard. And there was another comedy sign: 'WARNING: Magnets fitted to toilet lid and seat.' Everything was plastic, of course. There was just enough soap in the dispenser to make me worried there wouldn't be enough water to wash it off with.

I have read accounts of the *Belle* WCs. They were at the ends of the cars, approached along a short mahogany passageway. The occluded window was a four-coloured oval with inset ventilation dial. Walls were polychrome panels coloured eau-de-Nil, with black beading. The sinks were black porcelain, with vanity unit above and chromium-plated brush and comb racks. There was a basket for soiled towels, and a fixed ashtray. The floor was marble mosaic inlaid with mother-of-pearl.

As the Electrostar pulled into Brighton, I was dabbing water on the stain on my jacket, and only making it worse. I gave up, collected my wife, and we stepped down. I looked at the gilded clock that hangs from the elegant blue vault of Brighton station. We had arrived dead on time, at 11.57. The journey had taken fifty-one minutes, nine minutes faster than the *Belle*, even with the two stops. We approached the barrier, where the attendant looked to be in his sixties. I asked him if he remembered the *Belle*. He did. 'The best-dressed passengers walking through the ticket gate had always come off the *Belle*.' And he was eyeing the stain on my jacket.

But in its last years the *Belle* itself was not so well dressed. In 1968 it was repainted in the grim new BR livery of blue and grey. The interiors were also refurbished. The second-class seats were upholstered in what Grant and Jeffs call the 'common or garden' blue and green of all second-class at the time, while the first-class seats were also regularised with the BR fleet, so becoming black and grey. (This was called Inter-City 70 Moquette – the colour, in effect, of my childhood.) The carpets became uniformly mustard, but the marquetry was untouched. This redecoration may seem perverse, a case of tall poppy syndrome. But by the late '60s the *Belle* resembled a museum on wheels. In effect, customers were paying a supplement to go back in time, and the supplement ('the Pullman racket') was resented.

The *Belle* was expensive to run, and in the recession of 1972 BR was keen to economise. So the *Belle* died in the same year as the *Golden Arrow*. The last run was on Sunday 30 April 1972, a final fit of Sabbath-breaking on the Brighton line. A sign was put up over the entrance to Platform 13 (which had become the *Belle* platform in 1971): 'Farewell to the *Brighton Belle* on her last day of public service.' A special commemorative tea tray was issued to mark the occasion – an inappropriately domestic object for the racy *Belle*, you would have thought. The long inscription was only perfunctorily apologetic about the decline of the *Belle*. Instead, the un-sentimentality that had seen off steam engines was now applied to the most famous electrical train. 'It's goodbye to Hazel, Doris, Audrey, Vera, Gwen and Mona. And their frilly lampshades and old world charm ... We will miss them. But one can't survive on nostalgia ...'

The line-side was crowded on the last day. There were a number of special services, including an evening cheese-and-wine special from Brighton to Victoria. The still more alco-holic 'Champagne Special' then left Victoria at 22.30. The TV news cameras were present, and the film is on *YouTube*. Jimmy Edwards slavers over a beauty queen on the crowded Brighton platform (although he was in fact gay). On the train he doesn't so much sip as *quaff* champagne in company with Moira Lister, Dame Flora Robson the DJ Alan Freeman and other famous people of the time that I can't recognise. The train was seen off by a brass band, and long-haired people dancing in vaguely 1930s' clobber, so that they looked like members of the Bonzo Dog Doo-Dah Band, who combined the jazz age and the pop age in a way that the *Belle* no longer could. The train was greeted at Brighton by another brass band, and more dancing.

Brighton station suits festivity, even though one enters it through a Vale of Death, as I have mentioned. In 1841 the *Brighton Gazette* said, 'The Brighton terminus is a beautiful structure [that] will not suffer from comparison with any railway in existence.' The white chalk cutting rearing up on the western side is a foretaste of cliffs and the sea. The wooden platform on the east side is a foretaste of the pier. I own a book that contains a photograph of the concourse from 1900. A thin workman's ladder ascends towards the pretty clock, and it's like an allegory to do with aspiration and time. Such nearby locations as Terminus Road, Railway Street and (and the name of the pub opposite) The Railway Bell are testament to the power of the railway, which sucked the town up towards itself via Queen's Road. *Belle* passen-gers would probably have taken a taxi from the station, but in *Hangover Square* George takes a tram along Queen's Road, discovering the town packed with girls from the 'Lucky Tip'

8. The *Belle* at Victoria sometime after 1962, when the
Pullman coat of arms seen here – bigger and even more
florid than the old one – was applied to the cab fronts.

cigarette factory in London. 'They looked boldly, nastily, and yet perhaps not uninvitingly at him as he passed on his way to the sea.'

In 2013 my wife and I stood on the station forecourt amid a great lighting of fags and (with eyes on the Railway Bell) 'Shall we have a pint first?' Nobody batted an eyelid as two police cars went screaming past.

Fourteen of the fifteen *Belle* cars survive. One of the third-class cars was partially destroyed by fire at Carnforth in 1990, then finished off by vandals when it was moved to the East Lancs Railway. Like retired footballers, several of the cars went into the licensed trade, becoming restaurant annexes to public houses. One car, *Hazel*, became part of the Black Bull Public House at Moulton, North Yorkshire. (The publican had proposed to his wife on the *Belle*.) Venice Simplon Orient Express now owns some of the cars, and operates them in its 'British Pullman' railway cruises.

A charity called the 5BEL Trust has acquired six of the cars. At the time of writing, they are completing the restoration of the cars at their base in Barrow Hill, near Chesterfield, and altering the 'go-bits' underneath, so they can run at 75 m.p.h. This is a requirement for main-line running, and the 5BEL Trust aims to do nothing less than restore the *Belle* as a regular, albeit Sunday-only (Sabbath-breaking!) service between Victoria and Brighton. Apparently much of the certification – known as the 'grandfather rights' – of the *Belle* remains in place so that, for example, passengers in 2015 will be allowed to sit in armchairs un-bolted to the carriage floor, just as they did on the original. Neil Marshall, who speaks for the Trust, says that, with the new bogies, the rough ride will finally be cured. 'It will be possible to drink a cup of tea!' If anything is spilled on the resuscitated *Belle*, which ought to be running from 2015, I trust it will be champagne.

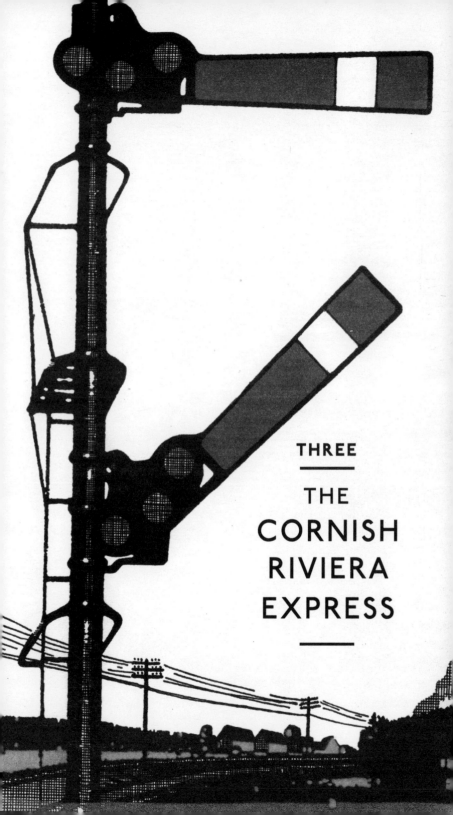

THREE

THE
CORNISH
RIVIERA
EXPRESS

3

THE CORNISH
RIVIERA EXPRESS

THE MOST ROMANTIC TRAIN OF THE MOST
ROMANTIC RAILWAY

The *Cornish Riviera Express* began running in 1904 and still exists, after a fashion. It was the flagship service of the Great Western Railway (GWR): the most romantic train of the most romantic railway. It was not a Pullman. The haughty Great Western did not need to borrow style from the Pullman company. That the train ran from Paddington to Penzance, in Cornwall, is fitting. A company called the Great Western *ought* to be famous for going west, rather than to Birmingham and Birkenhead (to which its tentacles also extended), which are more north than west.

The train began its journey with a great leap to Plymouth, travelling the first 225 miles of its 305-mile journey without stopping. It was the longest journey without stops that it was possible to make on British railways at the time. At present, the longest hop is 283 miles, the Newcastle-to-London stretch of the 5.40 a.m. from Edinburgh, a train that has inherited the mantle *Flying Scotsman* and is the subject of the next chapter. The present, depleted *Riviera* still goes to Penzance, but makes its first stop at Reading. Trains stop more often these days, as explained.

Part of the romance of the GWR lies in the fact that it was almost the personal train set of one man: its civil engineer, Isambard Kingdom Brunel. He surveyed the line from London to Bristol, and as far as Falmouth in Cornwall. He frequently designed the stations, and had a hand in designing the engines, all the while chain-smoking cigars and pursuing his two grand visions: first, the notion of the railway as the start of a further thrust west, aboard his giant Atlantic-crossing steamships; second, the 7-foot-track gauge – the broad gauge – which he rightly believed would offer greater stability and speed. He either hoped it would crush the standard gauge (4 foot 8½ inches), to which the majority of railways were committed, or he just didn't care about the other railways.

There is a pub opposite Bristol Temple Meads station called *The Reckless Engineer*, and that was Brunel. It is speculated that he became this Alpha Male – determined to be 'the first engineer' – as a reaction against the character of his father, Marc Brunel, a refugee from Revolutionary France, who was an equally brilliant engineer, but easy-going, and prone to being exploited by his employers. When, in 1825–43, Marc Brunel was digging the world's first under-river tunnel, to link the two sides of the London docks, the Thames would keep breaking in, flooding the tunnel. On one occasion when this happened, Marc Brunel said, 'We have been honoured with a visitation of Father Thames', which was particularly forbearing, given what the Thames was full of. Contrast Isambard, who – in a question designed to expose the inadequate signalling of the early Great Western – was asked what he would do if, when rattling along the track at 50 m.p.h. (because he would often drive GWR engines himself), he met a train coming head-on towards him. He replied, 'In such a case I would have put on all the steam I could command with a view to driving off the opposite engine with the superior velocity of my own.'

Brunel's railway continued in his image: headstrong, a combination of *gravitas* and silliness. To take the *gravitas* first, the GWR distributed the coal from the mines of south Wales. It brought 'perishables' by fast goods trains from the south-west to London. For much of its existence, the GWR was known to have the fastest engines in Britain. It ran, as noted, the longest non-stop journey, and for this probe into the *terra incognita* of Cornwall, time itself had to be amended. In 1840 Truro was twenty minutes behind London. So the GWR imposed 'railway time', establishing the precedent for another three-letter acronym: GMT. At Swindon the company established the largest railway works in Britain, and a railway colony run – eventually – on enlightened and paternalistic lines. It was the GWR that, from 1906, pioneered modern signalling by its adoption of Automatic Train Control, by which a train that passed a danger signal would be automatically stopped.

And yet there was a whimsical, antiquarian streak. In his diverting book *Britain from the Rails*, Benedict le Vay finds it in a horse trough at Reading marked 'To Be Used By Great Western Horses Only', as though horses ought to be able to read, and it was their fault if they could not. John Betjeman found it in the way that celery and radish were always served with cheese in the dining cars. Early engine drivers on the GWR were perversely kitted out in white corduroy suits, to prove their cleanliness in a dirty environment. The company persisted with the antiquated spelling of a ubiquitous notice, 'Tickets will be Shewn', and – a more expensive anachronism – maintained the broad gauge until 1892, when it was obviously a lost cause.

GWR signals were on the 'lower quadrant' principle: a down-pointing signal arm meant 'line clear'. The other companies used an up-pointing signal arm for that, because a down-pointing one might result from the effect of gravity on a broken signal. But the Great Western solved this entirely self-inflicted problem by incorporating a counterweight, whereby the signal arm would be sent upward – meaning 'danger' – if the cable broke. The Great Western was also the most salubrious railway, famous for its many, intensively worked, country branch lines and its charmingly naive slogan (from 1923) 'Go Great Western', spelt out in trackside flower beds. It had a charming colour scheme for the rolling stock: Brunswick green for the locos, with a smart copper band around the chimney tops; chocolate and cream for the carriages.

It has generated numerous misty-eyed recollections. 'Adlestrop' – the title, and setting, of Edward Thomas's poem encapsulating the slumberous beauty of rural England before the First World War – was a GWR station. R. P. Lister's poem 'Nostalgia' is a catalogue of railway memories by a much-travelled man: 'Awhile my tastes were fickle: but the seeds/ Sown there have proved the stubbornest by far:/ Upon my heart is graved G.W.R.' ('There' refers to Bristol Temple Meads, where he changed trains as a boy.) The last edition of the *Great Western Railway Magazine* appeared in 1947, when the company was absorbed into BR. It concluded with a poem by N. Ross Murray:

Alas! The curtain falls, the lights are low:
Pride of Brunel, now it is time to go;
But when old days are dim, when we have gone,
May all thy grand traditions live on.

Many of them did. The company's identity was almost indestructible among those who thought that GWR really denoted 'God's Wonderful Railway'. The less reverent had called it the 'Great Way Round', since trains to the West Country had originally all gone via Bristol.

It was the only railway to keep its name after the grouping of 1923. Even after nationalisation, when the territory was nominally BR Western Region, you would, according to John Betjeman, 'still find officials who, out of their own pockets, buy the round pill-box hats of the GW and wear the company's badge of twin shields bearing the arms of the cities of London and Bristol'. The old name re-emerged in slightly modified form after privatisation, in that the franchise is run by First Great Western, whose management is haunted by the old company whether they like it or not. It seems that at first they did not, because about ten years ago they dropped the train names associated with the old company – including that of the Cornish Riviera Express – before reviving them a couple of years later. Today Paddington bristles with the GWR logo of the 1930s, in which the three letters appear in a circle. (It is known as the 'shirtbutton logo'.) The Didcot Railway Centre, a sprawling museum-cum-shrine to the GWR, stands slap bang in the middle of First Great Western territory. Many of those Great Western branch lines that Beeching tried to murder have been revived as GWR-themed steam railways, and the Cornish Rivera Express refuses to die ...

The express began running in July 1904. At first, it was un-named, but in August the GWR organised a competition in conjunction with the *Railway Magazine*: 'Three guineas for the name of a train'. The magazine, being pretty confident of the gender of the eventual winner, promised that 'His name will become known, and will be handed down to future generations of railway officers and railwayacs, as the originator of the title ...' A 'railwayac' was a railway maniac, a perfectly respectable thing to be in Edwardian times.

There were 1,286 entries, and the prize was divided between ... well I'm sure I need hardly mention the names of those two immortals: Mr F. Hynam of Hampstead and Mr J. R. Shelley of Hackney, who suggested *The Riviera Limited*, which is *not* what the train came to be called. It is irritating to have to unpick this complication, but let us try to do so. 'Riviera Limited' was a shrewd suggestion in the sense of being sycophantic towards the GWR, which, a few months beforehand, had published a book called *The Cornish Riviera*, the start of the company's campaign to depict Cornwall as a glamorous and exotic destination. ('If he [the traveller to Penzance] walks in the Morrab Gardens, where a good band lays amongst a wealth of sub-tropical vegetation which Nice or Monte Carlo might envy, he may without any great stretch of imagination find himself in Algiers.') Part of the genius of calling Cornwall the Riviera was that the other Riviera was principally a winter resort for the British at the time. So Cornwall was made to seem attractive in winter as well as summer.

But even the Great Western Railway had to face the fact that, until such time as Cornwall was established as the Riviera, the clarifying prefix 'Cornish' would have to be added. Hence a revision of the Hynam and Shelley name. It became the *Cornish Riviera Limited*. The train was also known to staff as 'the Limited' or 'The 10.30 Limited', after what became its usual departure time, and a book of that name would be published by the GWR in 1924. The train was formally rechristened the *Cornish Riviera Express* in 1958, when it began to be pulled by diesels, but it had been informally known by that name since the start, and that's what I'm calling it, even though the train is indicated on the current pocket timetables as 'CR', which, a footnote explains, stands for 'The Cornish Riviera'.

The drama of the *Riviera* lay in the fact that Cornwall was like a foreign country to Edwardians. The Great Western had only reached Cornwall in the mid-1870s (by the acquisition of smaller railways), and Paris was a more familiar destination for the well-to-do traveller. The GWR targeted this market with its posited Cornwall–Riviera equivalence and, from 1908, the peremptory command, 'See your own country first.' Many people were responsive to the idea: the *Cornish Riviera* booklet sold – it wasn't free – a quarter of a million copies, at 3d. each.

The middle classes began travelling to the West Country for holidays, but not the working classes. Paid, week-long holidays were not the norm for working people until the 1950s. The GWR promoted resorts in Somerset, Devon and Wales as well as Cornwall, but Cornwall was the plum, and by the time of the First World War the company was able to publish a picture of a wistful nymphette in a floaty dress standing on a rock and looking out to sea with the words 'The Cornish Riviera' and the suffix, 'On the sunny shores of the Atlantic.' There was no need to state the name of the railway company, so strong had the association become. It is fitting that, whereas the Southern Railway's holiday brochures of the 1920s and 1930s would be called *Holiday Hints*, the Great Western's series, initiated in 1906, were called *Holiday Haunts*, because the accent was on 'a dash of adventure': antiquarian lore, stone circles, granite crosses, ghosts, smugglers, white witches, the evil eye, a perpetuation of the myth-making seen in the works of authors such as Sabine Baring-Gould and Arthur Quiller-Couch.

A stream of books was issued by the company, under the direction of the publicity officer, Felix Pole. While the *Holiday Haunts* titles were little more than lists of places to stay near the railway line, ranging from the company's own opulent Treganna Hotel, near St Ives, to attractions commended for being 'homely' and 'moderate' (a farm in Gloucestershire offers 'attendance, bath and piano'), there were also more high-minded publications, in which the name of the railway is hardly mentioned. In 1925 the ghost story writer, and provost of Eton, M. R. James, wrote a book called *Abbeys*, about the abbeys on the Great Western territory. There was no advertising matter except a folding map, with the note, 'Readers desirous of further information write to Superintendent of the Line, Paddington W2. GWR.' Two years before, the equally scholarly *Cathedrals* had appeared, written by G. E. Beer. It had been proofread by various deans and had a foreword by the Archbishop of Canterbury. The Great Western Railway also produced more jigsaws than any other railway company: more than eighty, as opposed to the three produced by the London & North Eastern. They included *Exeter Cathedral, Swansea Docks, Cornish Riviera Express, Ann Hathaway's Cottage, The Vikings Landing at St Ives, Sir Francis Drake at Plymouth*, and *Cornwall – Preparing for a Catch*.

From the mid-1920s there began to be books about the Great Western's own engines and train services. A similar curve was traced by the other railways' publicity machines. As competition from road transport increased, so the accent came to be on the virtue of train travel per se rather than on the places to be seen by train. Today almost all railway publicity concerns the cheapness of fares and the comfort of the journey, rather than the attractiveness of the places served, but recently First Great Western has reverted to the old idea of Cornwall-as-enigma, with a posters showing a lonely-looking man on a beach, and the slogan 'Sometimes, I just want nothing.'

PADDINGTON

The journey to those mysterious, yet definitely sunnier, places begins at Paddington station. In the second chapter of *Howard's End* (1910) E. M. Forster writes, 'In Paddington all Cornwall is latent and the remoter West', which is perhaps not so much a metaphysical insight as a testament to the power of the GWR publicity machine. It is worth taking a look around Paddington before we board what remains of the *Riviera Express*, because the station itself is all too likely to be the high point of any journey starting from there.

Paddington was a collaboration between Brunel and his architect friend Matthew Digby Wyatt. They, like the builders of many Victorian stations, were inspired by Paxton's Crystal Palace, which used an iron rib-cage to support glass. Each rib is prettily perforated with holes that are star-shaped, reminiscent of those cut-outs of snowflake patterns made by primary school children. The train shed at Paddington had an overall span of 238 feet, the widest in Britain until St Pancras, which was 2 feet wider. It has no side-walls, and no frontage except for the Great Western Royal Hotel, which is a very effective icing on the cake. In *The Railway Station: A Social History*, Jeffrey Richards and John M. Mackenzie describe it as

perhaps the earliest major building in Britain to show a marked French Renaissance influence ... It is interesting

9. Platform 1 at Paddington. The *Cornish Riviera Express*
always left from there; the *Night Riviera* still does.

to observe how frequently the French style prevails not just in the building of hotels but in the whole 'architecture of pleasure' in Britain. It is as if somehow the puritanical, work-obsessed British associated the idea of pleasure with the saucy, sinful continent.

Brunel wanted the station to be 'an enormous conservatory in a cutting'. Why in a cutting? That seems uncharacteristically modest. It has been suggested that, having an inkling that the underground Metropolitan Railway was about to come to Paddington, he wanted to be close to its level. He also wanted to provide a flat grade for departing trains. As for conservatories, he ended up with a train shed made of three side by side, with soaring glass and iron roofs, and iron arabesques decorating the glass screens at the ends. A fourth arch would be added in 1916, because Paddington was deemed too small by then, as it still is.

These west–east arches would seem long and worm-like were they not twice intersected by north–south transepts. These correspond to, and are stared into by, vaguely Elizabethan arched bow windows and balconies placed high on the south wall of the station. The stationmaster used to occupy the office behind one of those arched windows, and it's a good job he no longer does so, because his dignity would be undermined by the Ladbrokes and McDonalds that have been accommodated below. Today the stationmaster is located in Tournament House, an Art Deco block on the north-eastern corner of the station. It overlooks the ramp that used to correspond to the 'departure' side of the station. Another ramp, overlooked by another Art Deco block on the south-eastern corner, used to correspond to the arrival side. Now that most trains are reversible, stations no longer have arrival and departure sides, but the terminological distinction was still used at Paddington until the 1980s. Users of Paddington will know the departure ramp as the place where smokers are allowed to stand. The other ramp is, at the time of writing, closed off because Crossrail is coming to Paddington, and it will be fitted in along that south side, with no disruption to Brunel's train shed.

Along the top of the block overlooking the smokers' ramp is another testament to the obstinate persistence of the old company, in the words 'GWR Paddington'. I have seen images – or perhaps dreamed – of those words blazing forth in the London night sky, and there are uplighters beneath them, concealed in concrete conch shells. The uplighters no longer work, but the interior of Paddington has an almost Christmassy glow at night, explained by the way the station lights illuminate the corrugated iron screens running half-way up the glass arches like venetian blinds. By day these look grubby and nondescript, but under electric light they become a warm, rusty red.

I particularly like Paddington on Friday nights, because of the band.

In the late 1990s, when I was writing a column about transport in London, I received a letter from a man who signed himself, 'Reverend Gareth Edwards, The Vicar of Bayswater, and 1st Tuba BB Flat, Paddington Band', which, he explained when I met him, was a contraction of 'Great Western Railway Paddington Military Band'. The vicar wanted to publicise the shifting of the band from a prominent spot on the circulating area to an ignominious location between Burger King and the ticket gates of Platforms 8 and 9. The band played – and plays – every Friday night, 'between 1930 and 2100'. In sympathy with the trains, it observes the twenty-four-hour clock. The band members had once all been railway workers, but that has long since ceased to be the case. It used to play next to a placard proudly announcing 'GWR Paddington Band'. After nationalisation, the 'G' was grudgingly – and only partially – crossed out. The band is well known for playing 'Plymouth Hoe', which is geographically fitting. Tearful farewells at Paddington have been soundtracked by the band playing another of its specialities, 'A Bunch of Roses'.

Having interviewed the Revd Edwards, I interviewed some of those standing and listening to the band. A man called Ron explained that his Friday night routine was to drive in from Stevenage, drop his wife at bingo in Edgware, then come to Paddington to hear the band. He said you often saw Bill Oddie doing the same (not the bingo part, but listening to the band); also 'that tall man from Blue Peter'. He must have meant Simon Groom, who is a railway enthusiast, and recently produced and directed a Channel 4 documentary called *The Flying Scotsman: A Rail Romance*. Ron told me, in awed tones, that the trumpeter with the band had once played with Sid Millward and His Nitwits, a musical comedy act of the '40s and '50s. There was also Cathy, who taught nursing at Ealing and, as a girl, wanted to be 'the person who plays the records at Waterloo'. (Martial music used to be played at Waterloo to speed up circulation in the circulating area; nobody seems to know when it stopped.)

I happened to be in Paddington one Friday in late 2013. It was about seven o'clock, and I collared a station official, and asked if the band would be playing. 'Yes,' he said, 'but they're all pretty angry.' I asked why. 'Because they've been moved to a part of the station they don't like.'

'But that happened years ago!'

It seemed that the band had been demoted again. Having been moved *towards* Platforms 8 and 9, they have now been moved *on to* those platforms, and must compete with the noise of trains arriving and then departing. As I walked in that direction, I saw the band in place, and they struck up with 'Plymouth Hoe' just as the tannoy blared, 'This is a security announcement!' Whatever emendation of signage was going on during BR days, the band has now somersaulted smartly back in time. The banners on the music stands say simply Great Western Railway Paddington Band. Who can blame them for evoking the days when they were in their rightful place: on the main concourse?

We have veered into nocturnal Paddington, but it is also attractive by day, when a sufficient amount of light filters through the glass arches. It might be that Paddington is the most upmarket terminus. The early Victorian village of Paddington was described by John Betjeman as 'stucco Grecian and leafy'. The station itself was leafy, in that the eastern, or town, end was the stationmaster's garden, and a child who picked a flower there in the early years was fined for stealing the company's property. This area became a park for horse-drawn vehicles and steam lorries. In the early 1930s it became a sparse circulating area, still known as 'The Lawn'. In the '90s it was rebuilt, becoming a bright atrium, and a 'retail revolution' was implemented. Now it is host to T. M. Lewin, Accessorize, Caffe Ritazza, Yo! Sushi, Smith's, Cards Galore, Boots, Monsoon, M&S Food, EE Mobile and Sainsbury's, among others. This shopping centre is still called The Lawn on numerous signs pointing towards it, some with the suffix 'cash machines'. 'Lawn ... cash machines': it would be interesting to know what foreigners with limited English make of that.

I used to be against station retailing. I thought the shops clashed with the trains. In his novel The Information (1995), Martin Amis wrote: 'The railway station had changed since he had last had call to use it. In the meantime its soot-coated, rentboy-haunted vault of tarry girders and toilet glass had become a flowing atrium of boutiques and croissant stalls and limitless cappuccino.' The train sneaks in 'apologetically', upstaged by the garish shops. But the railways have always rented out retail space. W. H. Smith established his bookselling business in railway stations (starting at Euston in 1848) before branching out into the surrounding streets, and in the mid-1860s Felix Spiers and Christopher Pond went from running railway buffets at Victoria and Ludgate Hill stations to creating, in the West End, the first chain of mass-market restaurants. Surely a Sainsbury's that is drawing people towards a railway station is more use than a Sainsbury's drawing motorists to an out-of-town shopping centre. Shops have taken over many of the old ante-rooms of stations, and who wouldn't rather have a Sainsbury's than a First-Class Ladies Waiting Room?

The Lawn used to be a bleak space, a misty, deserted yard. Today it is full of light, and bustle and money, which suits the station. Paddington was always moneyed, in the sense that the GWR was keen to promote long-distance, first-class travel above all, and did little to encourage commuting west of London. It served Oxford University, and the public schools of Eton, Radley, Marlborough, Shrewsbury and Malvern; and the porters at Paddington were known to get the best tips.

In the early 1930s Clement Freud took the train from Paddington to Dartington Hall, for which the stop was Totnes. He and his classmates would travel down unaccompanied by adults, and, as he recalled in his autobiography, *Freud Ego*, 'The pervs waited for us in the lavatories, which they did not lock, and one went in to find amiable men telling you not to be afraid. "Have some of you friends got big ones ... like this?" one of them asked me.' In *Uncle Fred in the Springtime* (1939) P. G. Wodehouse wrote, 'The two-forty-five express

– Paddington to Market Blandings, first stop Oxford – stood at its platform with that air of well-bred reserve which is characteristic of Paddington trains.'

The anonymous writer of a book about the route of the *Riviera Express* called *Through the Window: The Great Western Railway from Paddington to Penzance* (1924) introduces a more demotic aspect of the station scene: 'The characteristic patois of Devon and Somerset mingles with the dialect of West Cornwall, which has at times a quaint, musical note and brings into play local words that only a Cornishman would understand.' Paddington has usually been about Londoners going west rather than westerners coming east, but the story is told of one Victorian yokel who came up to London by train, and was so overwhelmed by the scale of Paddington that he concluded London was 'all under glass'.

Paddington has the most mellifluous name of any London station. 'Names are very important', Michael Bond, the creator of Paddington Bear, once told me. He said that he always knew he wanted to call a character Paddington, and before the bear was born, in 1958, he'd been limbering up by writing stories about 'an eccentric uncle called Parkington'.

When the stories became successful, a stuffed Paddington was placed in a Perspex case on the Lawn. The case would occasionally be smashed by drunks and the bear carried off. 'The police at Paddington Green became very good at finding him.' More distressing to Mr Bond were those times when Paddington would slump within his display case, as though he himself had been on the booze. 'I would phone BR about it,' said Mr Bond, 'but I could never get through to the right person.' One day in the 1980s he carried his own toolkit on to the station, jemmied open the back of the case, set Paddington upright and re-sealed the case. 'Nobody batted an eyelid.' None of these problems can arise now, because Paddington is sculpted in bronze on the Lawn. Incidentally, Mr Bond – who was born in Newbury, and used to stand on Reading station as a boy to watch the *Cornish Riviera Express* go past – could not explain how Paddington Bear had got from his well-known point of origin, Darkest Peru, to Paddington station. I wonder whether the feature film about Paddington Bear – forthcoming at the time of writing – will resolve this back story. He perhaps came up from Plymouth on one of the Ocean Liner Specials, effectively the last of the tidal trains, in that they ran at variable times – this because they were meeting ocean liners arriving at Millbay Docks, which received ships of the P&O, Union, Royal Mail, Castle and Orient Lines. Some of those must have sailed from South America, if not Darkest Peru specifically.

ON PLATFORM I

The above-mentioned book of 1924, *Through the Window* (from now on *TTW*), begins, 'No need to enquire which platform for the Cornish Riviera Express – Number One every time!' So I waited for the modern-day 'CR' on Platform 1. This would turn out to be a mistake, but one is irresistibly drawn to number 1 at Paddington. Here are the iconic (as people did not say in 1924) three-faceted clock, the statue of Brunel and the GWR's war memorial. The sleeper to Cornwall, the *Night Riviera* leaves from Platform 1, usually coming in early, waiting in a thoughtful sort of way for its 23.45 departure time, and allowing people not intending to travel to walk along its length and peer into the cosy sleeping compartments.

Most of the 'usual offices' of the station have been located along the wall adjoining Platform 1. Gentlemen's and ladies' lavatories and waiting-rooms, book stalls and dining-rooms have shuffled up and down it, all indicated by signs that used to project from the wall like signal arms. You can hire a towel and have a shower in the Gents on Platform 1, and the last time I did so the towel was clean and warm, and the shower was hot. On the down side, there were mushrooms growing in the footwell. Today, besides the Ladbrokes and McDonalds, there is a Costa Coffee and a West Cornwall Pasty Company. The McDonald's might be considered the heir of what the *Railway Magazine* called 'the first ever "Quick Lunch and Snack Bar" on a station', which came to Platform 1 in 1935, boasting its 'twenty-seven bar stools'. It, like the West Cornwall Pasty Company, served Cornish pasties, approved of by the *Railway Magazine* because they 'bespoke the destinations of the trains'. The presence of all these retail outlets explains the absence of barriers from Platform 1.

For its first few years, before it became a 10.30 fixture, the *Cornish Riviera Express* left Platform 1 at 10.10, and today's version leaves at 10.06. I arrived at ten to ten, to find no passengers and no train. I decided to kill time by entering the room off Platform 1 that was formerly the Royal Waiting Room (the GWR regularly carried Queen Victoria to and from Windsor) and is now the FGW First-Class Lounge. A red carpet, slightly ruched and stained, protruded from the entrance. I entered by flashing my first-class ticket at the receptionist. My understanding is that the *Cornish Riviera Express* was first-class-only in its first couple of years, and I wanted to do the trip as stylishly as possible. A notice in the waiting-room assured me that First Great Western were attempting to facilitate this: 'We are making it our aim to make your visit here today the best it can be.' A TV was showing twenty-four-hour rolling news with the sound turned down, but subtitles meant you couldn't escape various foreign traumas. There was bad smog in Singapore that it was very important we knew all about. A dozen people sat in the lounge, most with complimentary coffees going cold as they either watched this TV or looked at their electronic devices. In other words, not one of them was mentally on Platform 1 at Paddington, and nor was I, because I was wandering through some Golden Age GWR engine sheds ...

The GWR had acquired a reputation for speed in 1840 with the Firefly locomotive of Brunel's engine builder, Daniel Gooch, and its sister machines, which all had incendiary names, including the fate-tempting Fireball. That reputation then fell away, Gooch's locomotives seeming increasingly antiquated, and the broad gauge not delivering the speed boost that Brunel had promised. In 1902 George Jackson Churchward became Locomotive Superintendent of the GWR. One of his engines, City of Truro, was reported as averaging a record 100 m.p.h. on a run from Plymouth to Bristol. His engines classed Saints and Stars were fast and elegant, made missile-like by tapering boilers. In his book *Great Western Railway: A History* Andrew Roden writes: 'Stars and Saints were – and by a very wide margin – the finest express passenger locomotives in Britain, as well as quite possibly all of Europe.' In 1922 Charles Benjamin Collett took over from Churchward, and he introduced the Castles, a bigger and more powerful version of the Stars, and the bigger still Kings. A three-word litany encapsulating the romance of steam runs 'Stars, Castles, Kings', and this was the highpoint for the GWR, which would be eclipsed in the late '30s by the streamlined engines and trains of the London & North Eastern Railway. (The patrician GWR regarded streamlining of steam locos as a gimmick.) I settled, so to speak, on a Star. I would have an Edwardian journey, my previous two having been inter-war affairs. And so, when I stepped back out on to Platform 1, the year was, say, 1910.

The platform is now wooden, and I am inhaling the sharp tang of the Welsh coal that powered the GWR. Over on the arrival side, a tank engine is backing some recently emptied coaches out of the station, its bark reverberating under the roof glass. As it fades from sight, and from earshot, its steam lingers in the station, and I watch it slowly dissolve under the footbridge. Now the station is full of the clattering of milk churns being rearranged at the 'country' end of Platform 1. Some goods spill over from the goods station – fuming away a quarter of a mile west of Paddington – and enter the passenger station, having been brought in on passenger trains: milk especially, but behind the coal tang there is also the fusty smell of fruit and flowers.

Behind me on Platform 1 stands the new Empire Fruit stall, overseen by a severe-looking woman in horn-rimmed glasses, under a banner ordering, 'Eat Empire Fruit'. Some of it – not the bananas, obviously – has come up from Cornwall that very morning. The platform is now crowded, both with passengers and porters. The porters congregate in groups around their barrows laden with suitcases, trunks, parcels wrapped in string, golf bags and gun bags. (A common offer in the Holiday Haunts directories is 'Rabbit shooting'.) The majority are at the 'town' end, where the brake van will pull in. They are surrounded by some of the less trusting passengers, who want to keep an eye on their luggage for as long as possible. Some of the porters are working with pots of paste, labelling the luggage to go into the van. The GWR labels are vivid orange and yellow, showing a train emerging from a giant sunset or sunrise.

In the open air beyond the 'country' end of the station a hot, early summer day is developing, and the light filtering in makes some of the ladies' white dresses slightly transparent, I note with interest, as I walk past them, touching my

THE "GOLDEN ARROW LIMITED"

WORLD FAMOUS DE LUXE PULLMAN SERVICE DAILY BETWEEN LONDON [VICTORIA] AND PARIS [NORD]

Copies of the illustration above, in colour, price 1/- and Jig Saw puzzles 5/- each post free from S.R. Advertising Dept, Waterloo Station, London, S.E.1. and through Messrs W.H. Smith's bookstalls & shops.

PARIS 6½ HOURS

SOUTHERN RAILWAY
KEY TO THE CONTINENT

SOUTHERN RAILWAY ADVERTISING   Ad 1088   PHOTOCHROM C^o L^TD. LONDON & TUNBRIDGE WELLS

1. Poster of 1929 to promote the new *Golden Arrow* service. It takes longer than six-and-a-half hours today to travel over the *Arrow*'s rail-sea-rail route.

2. The poster dates from 1936, but it is one of many produced by the Southern Railway from the mid '20s onwards, showing a small child next to a big engine. The clever publicity of the Southern was under the aegis of John Elliot, 'Britain's first PR man'.

3. This LNER poster from 1932 satirises the Southern's series of posters showing children looking up at the footplate men. It was not popular.

THE
BRIGHTON BELLE
ALL-PULLMAN TRAIN

DAILY THROUGHOUT THE YEAR

WEEKDAYS

LONDON (VICTORIA)	dep	11	0 am	3	0 pm	7	0 pm
BRIGHTON . .	arr	12	noon	4	0 pm	8	0 pm
BRIGHTON . .	dep	1	25 pm	5	25 pm	8	25 pm
LONDON (VICTORIA)	arr	2	25 pm	6	25 pm	9	25 pm

SUNDAYS

LONDON (VICTORIA)	dep	11	0 am	7	0 pm
BRIGHTON . .	arr	12	noon	8	0 pm
BRIGHTON . .	dep	5	25 pm	8	25 pm
LONDON (VICTORIA)	arr	6	25 pm	9	25 pm

FOR FURTHER INFORMATION PLEASE ENQUIRE AT STATIONS AND TRAVEL AGENTS

SOUTHERN

AD 7544

4. The *Brighton Belle* depicted in 1958; a 'train for late-risers' (note timings).

5. The *Brighton Belle* emerging from the Clayton Tunnel. In 1861, long
before the Belle was born, there was a bad smash in the tunnel, which
probably inspired Charles Dickens's ghost story, 'The Signalman'.

6. Great Western poster of 1939 showing a King's class locomotive. According to GWR publicity of the time, 'Somewhere in the breast of every normal homo sapien there stretches a chord which vibrates only to the sight of a fine locomotive.' This, the company hoped, held true 'even now, with airplanes and motors to bid against it.'

7. Poster of 1928 advertising the new, non-stop service of the *Flying Scotsman*. The arrow points to the little corridor in the tender that permitted a crew changeover on the move.

8. The *Night Scotsman* sleeper ran on the East Coast
Main Line from the 1920s to the '80s. There are no longer
any sleepers on the East Coast Main Line.

brown bowler hat. Unfortunately, it is the porters who are eyeing me, rather than the ladies. They're annoyed at my independence from them, betokened by the fact that I am fit enough to be carrying my own portmanteau. The first-class return to Penzance nestling in my pocket book cost nearly £3, twice their weekly wage before tips. Beyond the end of the station, I see that our train is approaching. With all the surliness of a scene-shifter, a pannier tank engine is dragging the giant Dreadnought coaches (named after a strain of battleship currently under construction) of the *Cornish Riviera Express* along Platform 1. Two middle-aged 'railwayacs' (one of them a vicar) are rushing up to the 'country end', to witness Act II of the drama: to see which green engine is going to back down on to the carriages. But of course, I know it's going to be one of the new and still rare Stars ...

THE HST

I was snapped out of my reverie by an announcement: 'Platform 8 for the *Cornish Riviera Express*, the 10.06 First Great Western Service for Penzance.' I was torn between delight at the use of '*Cornish Riviera Express*' and indignation that it should be leaving from Platform 8. I bustled over there, joining a crowd flowing towards the train, most of whom, not having been told to wait on Platform 1 by a ninety-year-old book, had been standing about on the circulating area.

There were a couple of backpackers, but the school holidays had not yet begun, and this was not a holiday crowd. Most were 'executives' – obviously bound not for Penzance but for the more businesslike stops on the way. Then there were some older leisure travellers, likely candidates for connections to Newquay or Torquay.

The train was what a BR loyalist might call a 125, but

which the modern-day operators who are stuck with this ageing stock call 'HST's, standing for High-Speed Trains, that being more generic and less evocative of the nationalised railway than '125', which was the fast and futuristic brand name of the trains, advertising their top speeds. HSTs are like the dogged family Volvo that the children hope will break, so that a more stylish – or at least new – car can be bought. Yes, the HSTs are old – introduced in 1976 – but this attests to their durability, for which they are admired by engineers. They are reliable and strong ('crashworthy').

HSTs are diesels. The overhead wires at Paddington cater to the whims of the electrical Heathrow Express, allowing it to pull in at a variety of platforms. By 2017 the lines from Paddington to Bristol, Cardiff, Swansea and Newbury will all be electrified, which isn't much to celebrate – not when you think that the 5,500 mile Trans-Siberian Railway was fully electrified a couple of years ago. The trains running over those electrified lines will be the new Intercity Expresses. But nowhere west of Bristol will be electrified. The HSTs are 'fixed formation'. The trains can't be uncoupled, or not without difficulty. They don't exactly have locomotives. Their aerodynamic-looking front ends (so exciting in 1976) are called power cars.

The colour scheme of the First Great Western HSTs is mainly purple-blue with bluey-pink doors, and a transfer showing white, pale blue and fluorescent pink running straight, then becoming wavy, like an oscilloscope connected to a person who was apparently dead but then revived. I once asked a senior First Group man *why*. 'It's the First livery,' he blandly replied. 'You see it on First Capital Connect, and TransPennine Express.' This was not in itself a justification, nor is the need for a degree of colour contrast to help the visually impaired, which accounts for the fluorescent yellow strip on the handles of the pink doors.

There is nothing wrong with blue as a train or engine colour. The Blue Pullman, the direct predecessor of the 125s, was blue: 'Nanking Blue'. Mallard was blue – garter blue. The *Flying Scotsman* loco was briefly blue under BR. Thomas the Tank Engine was blue. But the classic colour for engines was green: 'all the forest tints', as one railway poet had it. The famous steam locomotives of the Great Western were green before and after the grouping of 1923. To mention some other pre-grouping railways ... the engines of the North Eastern, the London & South Western, the Great Northern and the Great Central were mainly green. 'There is a reason for it,' writes G. G. Chapman, in his pedagogic work *All about Our British Railways*,

> a reason that shows our early railway engineers as folk with a thought for their men. It is that green, as you probably know, is the most restful colour for the eyes. The eyes of the driver must always be running along the boiler of his engine. From the 'spectacles' of the cab the boiler is the first thing seen – hence the engines were painted green.

The driver of a modern train sits as the very front, so is spared whatever colour scheme his bosses have imposed on the train.

As for the interior of the First Great Western HST carriages, which are BR Mark 3s tarted up ... blue, pink and grey predominate in standard. The tops of the seats have hand-holds to grab on to while walking along the gangways, and these protrude absurdly like Mickey Mouse's ears, except that they're a pinky red. FGW is generally dedicated to colours you can't describe. The plusher seats in first are a sort of blue-brown-beige, resembling the *Mastermind* chair.

They're comfortable enough, but the armrests are solid plastic. I once met a man who had worked on designing interiors for prisons and hospitals. He told me that elusive, pastel shades were favoured. Any strong colour was a 'statement' that might be considered provocative. When it came to trains, or any public interior, he suspected that designers just shrugged and went for the meekest option: 'Let's go hospital', as he put it.

The guard welcomed us aboard the 'Ten-oh-six First Great Western train for Penzance'. The words 'Cornish', 'Riviera' and 'Express' did not feature. He listed the stops: Reading, Exeter, Newton Abbot, Plymouth, Liskeard, Bodmin, Par, St Austell, Truro, Redruth, Hayle, St Erth, Penzance. (Seventeen GWR stations between Plymouth and Penzance have been closed, perhaps penalised for having the best names, since they included Defiance Platform, Doublebois, Respryn, Burngullow.)

As the boarding scrimmage intensified, I thought more about porters. On the eve of the First World War 625,000 people worked on the railways. About a fifth of those were designated 'porters', but they might also be selling tickets, oiling lamps, feeding horses, cleaning wagons, assisting with shunting. In 1948, when the workforce was a quarter of a million, BR rechristened the hard core of porters – the bag carriers – Railmen. Their numbers were thinned out in the '60s by the decline of railways and rising wages elsewhere. They were all gone by the end of the '80s, replaced by luggage trolleys that you pushed yourself.

Privatisation brought a small revival of portering. A dozen, smartly uniformed, appeared at King's Cross. I remember seeing one of them riding down the escalator towards the Tube. He was accompanied by three middle-aged women, and their three big suitcases. He was chatting animatedly to the women, probably in hopes of a good tip. As they descended, I thought: 'That guy's going to have to get his act together with those bags, or there'll be a pile-up.' When they reached the bottom, the first suitcase toppled over and two of the women fell onto it; then the porter and the third woman fell on top of the first two. When the Heathrow Express came to Paddington in 1998, eight porters came with it. They wore red uniforms, and badges proclaiming 'Porter £5', which seemed a bit steep, but apparently they would be willing to assist with bags to any destination within half an hour of Paddington. They were what used to be called 'outside porters'. A press release boasted, 'The smartest rail porters ever, and the politest people in the UK'. But they didn't last long, and if you travel on the Heathrow Express today, you carry your own bags.

I settled into my seat, glad I wasn't in standard class. On First Great Western HSTs, standard carriages are as tightly packed with high-backed seats, as in economy class on an aeroplane, and this is indeed called 'airline seating'. Trains ought not to be cravenly mimicking planes. Some operators provide sick bags, and ask you to 'take a minute to familiarise yourself with the safety features of this carriage' (as if anybody ever would). A friend of mine was on a First Great Western Train approaching Bristol when the guard announced, 'We are now commencing our approach to Bristol Temple Meads.' As on a plane, you can't see over the seat backs unless you stand up. The effect is of people sitting invisibly in holes, only activated as human presences when their phones ring, and they pipe up.

THE BILLIARD TABLE

As we pulled away, I settled into my mental compartment. The Dreadnought coaches of the early *Riviera* were built by Mr Churchward, and they had compartments and corridors. They were roomy, taking advantage of the clearances allowed by the broad gauge, even though the broad-gauge tracks themselves had gone. On the Dreadnought I would have gone for the optimum spot: corner seat, facing. On the HST I tried to block out the phone conversation of the man behind. It wasn't hard, since he spoke softly in Arabic.

In the old days the departing passenger would see on the right what looked like a factory with the words 'Paddington Goods Stn.' in dirty white lettering. The goods station closed in the early '70s; a bland tower block called Sheldon Square stands on the site. We passed Royal Oak Underground station, which is not underground, and stands in the middle of wilderness of railway lines with the Westway rearing up behind. With its pretty, valanced canopy, Royal Oak looks like what it is: a station built in countryside, then overwhelmed by the city. It is on the Hammersmith & City line, a spin-off from the Metropolitan Railway. The GWR was happy to let the Underground soak up the growing demand for commuter services in west London, which is not as magnanimous as it sounds, since the GWR had a stake in the Metropolitan.

We approached Old Oak Common train depot, also on the right. The blue trains of First Great Western stood in orderly rows, because they are stored and maintained there just as the trains of the GWR were. The only structure readily apparent is a grey hangar. In BR days Old Oak Common was the place where HSTs were maintained, and the small fleet of trains that were the forerunners of the HST: the Blue Pullman. In 1960 car and plane use between Scotland and

London was rising fast, and the Pullman company, recently acquired by BR, was pitched into the fight. It was a bit like reaching for a beautiful, bejewelled sword to combat an opponent with a machine gun. The Blue Pullmans antici- pated the HSTs in that they were built for speed, had sloping fronts and were fixed-formation, meaning they were gener- ally kept coupled together as single units. The interiors were plush with red or powder-blue seating, and Japanese motifs. In 1960 British Transport Films made a documentary pro- moting the new trains. Businessmen were shown doing all the things you couldn't do in a car, like reading the *Financial Times* while eating lobster. There are many close-ups of the vast gins and tonics being served by the white-coated attend- ants. The Blue Pullmans were stylish but unreliable. By the early '70s their white-coated attendants and supplementary charges seemed as quaint as those on the other Pullman ser- vices expiring at the time. They were mothballed in 1973.

Old Oak Common is about to become famous as a railway hub, junction of Crossrail and High Speed 2. At least, that is the plan at the time of writing. There is a mayoral scheme to create a mini-Manhattan (another one) on the site. In other words, something not nearly as interesting to look at from a passing train as the Old Oak Common of GWR days, with its green locos, its loco shed, coaling station, ash shelter, coppersmith's shop, refuse destructor, all coming and going under a shifting cloud of smoke and steam.

To the right, I kept seeing small clusters of workmen in bright orange. They were plotting the arrival of Crossrail, which will come from Reading and go underground just before Royal Oak station. Soon they will be many more men, a moving sea of orange.

'High-vis' clothing originated on the railways. Some time in the early 1930s a young American called Robert C. Switzer suffered a head injury while working in a Californian rail-yard, and he was required to convalesce in a darkened room. Switzer, who was trained in chemistry, began experimenting with fluorescent materials in his gloomy confinement, which led on to his invention of a fluorescent paint that he called DayGlo. He covered his wife's wedding dress in the stuff, and so the first high-visibility clothing was made.

It is likely that high-visibility clothing had its first industrial application on the railways of Britain. In July 1964, the *Railway Magazine* reported that fifteen platelayers working on the Pollokshields to Eglinton Street line in the Scottish Region of BR had been issued with 'a new kind of luminous safety jacket which shines in half-light conditions'. In the absence of a photograph, the magazine strained to explain this bizarre phenomenon to its readers. The jackets, 'made from a fluorescent orange plastic material', were 'similar in appearance to old fashioned ships' lifejackets'. The writer speculated that these 'human fire-fly jackets may be adopted throughout British Railways.'

High visibility clothing received its decisive boost with the Health and Safety at Work Act of 1974. Employers are required to remove hazards if possible or guard against them if not, and there's no cheaper way of guarding against hazards than to dole out high-visibility vests, which can be bought for about £1 each wholesale.

Once adopted, the vests can't be relinquished, because that would smack of irresponsibility. If you speak to sellers of high-visibility clothing, they will tell you, in a bored tone, as though the point were hardly worth making, that sales go up every year. Children on school trips wear them. My postman wears a high-visibility vest, as do police on the beat – and theirs are stab-proof, so they are garments designed both to attract and repel. Who could ever speak out against high-visibility clothing? You won't catch me doing it. True, Edwardian track gangers, like all Edwardian men, wore dark suits and ties that gave them a dusky, cowboyish elegance; but they didn't stand out. In *The Country Railway* David St John Thomas writes that track gangers 'had the highest accident rate among all railwaymen, and on scarcely a mile of track in Britain has a ganger not been run down by an unexpected train, its approach often drowned by a gale'.

We were accelerating rapidly. The early stage of the main line from Paddington was known as 'Brunel's billiard table' because it was flat, the line following the valley of the Thames. In effect, our HST was being driven by the ghost of the diminutive young man – because Brunel was always a young man – whose remains lie in Kensal Green cemetery somewhere not very far to the right of our speeding train. Among the interred, TTW name-checks 'Thackeray, Leigh Hunt and other famous people' – no mention of Brunel, the man who built the railway that forms the subject of the book. Perhaps the author did not want to admit Brunel's mortality, but the book consistently ignores Brunel, as we will see. Perhaps, in 1924, the broad gauge was still unforgiven; or maybe Brunel was regarded as too embarrassingly primitive for the first-class passengers of the *Riviera Express*, with his dusty boots, comical stove-pipe hat and incessant cheroot. Brunel died at the age of fifty-three, on 15 September 1859. Steven Brindle's book *Paddington Station: Its History and Architecture* includes a haunting photograph of his office at 18 Duke Street, taken a few days later. The office is beautifully wide and rangy. Everything is in the 'broad gauge'. Framed photographs are propped on the wide mantelpiece. No time to hang them up, you see. It is sparsely furnished. A globe, a calendar, a clock are the salient objects.

We thundered through Southall. A man sitting near me

was saying, in a clipped voice, 'I was speaking to the Admiral.' TTW speaks of the 'dash of naval uniform' generally to be seen at Paddington – men coming from or going to Plymouth. So I hoped this man was in the Navy. He looked the part: trim, with short grey hair. He was not in uniform, but I had been told that forces personnel prefer not to go uniformed on trains, and certainly not in large numbers. It is a security risk.

We thundered through Hayes & Harlington station, junction – via a 4-mile tunnel – for Heathrow. Hayes & Harlington is served by Heathrow Connect, the *slow* shuttle to Heathrow, whose every train to Paddington is fated to be overtaken by the Heathrow Express.

Of Hayes & Harlington TTW notes: 'the enormous buildings in which HMV gramophones are made stand close to the station.' In 1931 the site was taken over and expanded by EMI. Soon afterwards, a man called Alan Blumlein climbed on to the roof of the factory, which incorporated a research laboratory. He began recording and filming the trains leaving Hayes station. The idea was to capture the sound of their puffing going away into the distance ('barking', the railway-acs call it). The resulting film and soundtrack, 'Trains from Hayes Station', is not publicly available as far as I know. If it was made in the late morning, then the *Cornish Riviera Express* would have been captured. All Beatles records were marked 'Manufactured in Hayes'. Today the complex stands empty and half derelict, but it is about to redeveloped.

Between West Drayton and Iver the M25 is carried over the line by a bridge that seems negligible from a hundred-mile-an-hour train. TTW was more concerned with the crossing over the River Colne, 'which marks the frontier between Middlesex and Buckinghamshire. We are well clear of London now.' That is still more or less still true, thanks to the Green Belt.

We went through Slough, too fast to make out the station signs. Reading TTW, you can see the beginning of the process that would lead, in 1937, to John Betjeman's poem beginning 'Come, friendly bombs, and fall on Slough!': 'Slough is an old country town which has been modernised a good deal in recent years. On either side of the line is the Slough trading estate, occupying the site of the motor transport "dump" which was established during the latter part of the War.' Later, real rather than rhetorical bombs fell on Slough, and Betjeman regretted writing the poem. He tried to emphasise that it was the new 'trading estates' he objected to rather than the town in particular, but Slough apparently doesn't care, because the clearest indication of the town to passing trains is a giant sign reading 'Slough Trading Estate'.

Before Maidenhead, 24 miles from London, a quick thrum indicated that we had passed over Maidenhead Railway Bridge, which was built by Brunel, and kept low so there should be no hump in the billiard table. It was typically audacious. Its low brick arches were the widest ever built at the time, and the directors of the GWR did not trust them. They thought they were too low, and would collapse, so Brunel built wooden supports in the Thames beneath. But the wooden supports were not needed, as he knew perfectly well, and as he was proved when they were washed away.

J. M. W. Turner stuck his head out of the window while going over the bridge, and found the experience exhilarating. In 1844 he painted *Rain, Steam and Speed – the Great Western Railway*, showing a loco of the Firefly class speeding over the bridge. The painting is in the National Gallery, and I was nearly ejected from there when I pointed out to my sons the tiny hare fleeing from the engine in the bottom right-hand corner. The security guard thought I was going to touch the painting. The symbolism of the hare is ambiguous. It might represent the threat to nature from the trains; or it might be a testament to the speed of the engine. It was feared that the overhead wires for the coming electrification of the Great Western main line – and for Crossrail – will spoil the elegance of the bridge but I am assured that Network Rail have liaised closely with English Heritage to design the most delicate and unobtrusive 'overhead'. Maidenhead was lucky with its bridges. Pevsner called the adjacent road bridge, which has thirteen spans, 'this beautiful piece of 1772'. From our fast train it appeared momentarily to the right: almost subliminal, like a single frame in a period film.

We raced through a high cutting: Sonning Cutting, by name. On Christmas Eve 1844 a train crashed into a landslip here; eight people 'of the poorer class' died when third-class carriages at the front of the train were crushed by goods wagons behind. The inquest found 'great neglect' on the part of the company, so there is no mention of it in TTW, only a sketch of an engine puffing peacefully through the cutting.

We were closing in on Reading. The big landmarks on the station approach were always the Huntley & Palmer biscuit factory and Reading Gaol. Only the latter survives, currently as a Young Offenders' Institution but about to close. The prison is modelled on the Eastern State Penitentiary in Philadelphia, where Charles Tyson Yerkes, who built much of the London Underground, had been imprisoned for fraud. The prisoners used to know Reading Gaol as 'the biscuit factory' after the adjacent premises of Huntley & Palmer, which in the 1930s were served by 7½ miles of railway siding, and which were flattened between the mid-'70s and the mid-'90s. Huntley & Palmer liked to boast that it had supplied the biscuits to Captain Scott for his Antarctic expedition. Unfortunately, of course, he ran out towards the end. Until the late 1960s, the firm also supplied small tins of biscuits ('Huntley & Palmer's Railway Assortment') to first-class diners on trains that would be running past their factory. The biscuits came with a promotional leaflet, telling passengers exactly where to look out for the factory.

We stopped at Reading, which the *Cornish Riviera Express* did not. Reading is a big interchange. Five routes come together there, and a reorganisation of the station is attempting to cease what had been a bottleneck. It will also be the western terminus of Crossrail. A suntanned, late middle-aged couple boarded our carriage. They evidently knew another, younger couple already in the carriage. The question came from the younger couple: 'Oh hello, where've you two been?' to which the female half of the older couple answered: 'Mexico – just landed at Heathrow.'

'What was it like?'

'Really, really hot.'

I felt embarrassed on behalf of the Cornish Riviera, whose main meteorological advantage over the rest of Britain was that it was slightly milder in winter.

WHITE HORSES

After Reading we diverged left. Trains to the West Country used to bear right, heading for Bristol and the 'Great Way Round'. A couple a day still go that way. The 'new' route, opened in 1906, cuts the corner to Taunton. It's known as the Berks & Hants cut-off, but it's nowhere near Hants.

An affable 'customer host' came up and presented me with the Travelling Chef menu. Yes, the Travelling Chef – an actual person – was on board, and, as a first-class passenger, I could have the food brought to my seat rather than having to walk up and order it from the counter of the Express Café. I looked at the menu. I was quite tempted by *The Great Westerner*: 'Choice of fried, scrambled or poached egg with sweetcure smoked Wiltshire back bacon, Cumberland sausages, button mushrooms, tomato and Heinz baked beans with a choice of buttered white or malted bloomer toast.' The man across the aisle from me was having a toasted bacon sandwich, brought without asking. It was his 'usual', and it smelt good. The trouble was the time. I had already had breakfast, and I put it to the customer host that it was a bit early for lunch.

'It's not a lunch menu, sir,' he said. 'It's an all-day menu.' Actually, it was more like a half-morning menu, since I'd only just heard about it, and the Travelling Chef would be ceasing operations at Exeter, where we were scheduled to arrive at mid-day. In other words, the Travelling Chef would be shutting up shop at *lunchtime*. But to give First Great Western credit, they do operate the last remaining dining cars or British trains. They are available on lunchtime (the correct time for lunch) and evening services between Paddington and Plymouth, although not on the *Riviera Express*. They are open to standard- or first-class passengers, but only first-class ticket-holders can book a seat in advance. The menu features a lot of fish, as was traditional on the railways. (Fish is quick to prepare, and the railways carried a lot of it.) I accepted a complimentary coffee from the customer host, as we began flashing through verdant Berkshire, Wiltshire and Somerset. 'Talk about heat,' the Mexico returnees were saying. 'I mean, it was really hot.'

Pewsey – where the rolling Marlborough Downs give way to Wiltshire – came and went. Then came the bleaker, denuded Salisbury Plain, haunted by prehistoric ghosts: long barrows, few trees, no people to be seen ... and sky momentarily darkening. This is not the cosy sort of landscape that railway modellers make out of *papier mâché*.

The strangely elongated Westbury white horse came into view to the left, It is the oldest of several white horses in Wiltshire, but it is not known how old. It might be a commemoration of King Alfred, who was born near Uffington in Oxfordshire, where there is another, definitely older, white horse, which gives its name to a locality with a railway resonance to some of us: the Vale of White Horse. The Vale's pretty stations on the GWR main line between Didcot and Swindon were closed by Beeching in the '60s, but they survive in 1/76 scale at the Pendon Museum in Long Wittenham, Oxfordshire ...

The museum was founded by Roye England, who died in 1995, and who was the finest railway modeller the world has ever known. A model of Roye himself appears on the layout, the figure resembling a tiny Charles Hawtrey, or a superannuated boy scout. It was made by a woman, one of the team of crack modellers schooled by Roye, and when he saw the figure, he peevishly observed: 'But the socks are wrong, aren't they? They're knee-length, and I only ever wear ankle-length.' There spoke a man of such extreme fastidiousness that he once spent six years making a model of a country pub in the Vale, far longer than it took to build the seventy-six times larger original. But England had duplicated every quirk of brickwork and thatch. He would spend days modelling a single flower. Hollyhocks were made using a cat's whisker, or the spine of a bird's feather.

Roye England was born in Perth, Australia, in 1906. The focus of his young life was *The Wonder Book of Railways*. One day, 'when everyone was out', he built a Meccano model of the Forth Rail Bridge in the family sitting-room. It was sixteen

feet long. In 1925 he sailed for the Mother Country, dock-
ing at Plymouth and travelling to Paddington in the chocolate and cream embrace of the Great Western, whose trains
he found 'more beautiful than I had ever dared picture'. On
arriving in London, he began 'really seeing the sights': Victoria station, Waterloo station, Euston station. He went to stay
with a curate friend in the Vale, and fell in love with the landscape and the railway. He began photographing and measur-
ing, plotting the miniaturisation of this 'pageant that went
by in the high noon of steam'. As he tramped the Vale – or
traversed it on his Triumph motor bike – he wore, aside from
the ankle socks, hiking boots, shorts, raincoat and beret. He
had a limited diet: boiled eggs, black bananas and *Crunchie*
bars. Railway modelling, he believed, was 'something for
which I had been set apart. It was no mere hobby; it was a
vocation.' He conceded that he was better at the line-side
scenes than the actual trains. 'Card,' he wrote, 'that is my
medium.' By scratching away at the right sort of cardboard,
he could create the texture of weathered brick or stone, and
it became imperative that he get on with doing so as the old
Vale changed. 'One by one the chalk roads were being tarred
over. Here and there a length of wire replaced a falling hedge
... Concrete had come in as well.'

But this mission conflicted with another possible vocation: for the priesthood. Roye England was a devout Christian, who took Communion every day. He eventually tried to
reconcile the two by forming the Guild of St Aidan, whose
members would practise railway modelling in a somehow
Christian way while corresponding in Esperanto ('a beautiful language, logical, efficient, easy to learn'). The Guild
was inaugurated with a specially written collect, read by
Roye to the small congregation of a church at Coalpit Heath,
Gloucestershire, on 31 August 1939, St Aidan's Day. The next

day Hitler invaded Poland. Roye could immediately see the terrible implication: supplies of decent cardboard would be jeopardised. He took the train to Bristol, where he bought a vast amount of good cardboard for £10.

During the war he couldn't get much modelling done. As a conscientious objector, he was put to agricultural labouring. There were many vicissitudes over the next forty years. He employed a female secretary for the Guild correspondence, but 'Without the least warning, she became amorous. I had to terminate her services.' He built what would become the museum in Long Wittenham, but was swindled out of ownership of some neighbouring land. He acquired a 38-foot-high old Great Western semaphore signal (the Up Main Distant from Culham) and erected it outside the museum. But he had to take it down again when planning permission was refused. As his private income dwindled, he attempted to fund the museum and its slowly expanding layout by running a youth hostel in Long Wittenham. The Silverwing Cycling Club were loyal clients, but the venture didn't pay. He also worked for a stint at the Morris factory in Oxford, even though he hated cars just as much as Charles Dickens had hated trains. And just as Dickens's enmity was confirmed when he was involved in a near-fatal train crash, so Roye England was badly injured when, cycling back from church in 1986, he was knocked off his bike by a car. He never fully recovered, but the Pendon Museum accumulated followers and co-modellers, determined to go forward with Roye into the past. It is now established as a charitable foundation, and is open on Saturday and Sunday afternoons, and some Wednesdays. The highlight of any visit is when the lights are dimmed and an illuminated night train comes through the Vale.

The career of Roye England is a reminder that religion

and railways go together. The connections have often been plotted: the stations are cathedrals, and for a long time the smaller ones tended to close down, like churches. The time-table is the Bible, and the steam was incense. A dispropor-tionate number of the early 'railwayacs' were clergymen, partly because they had time.

Among the number of devout railwaymen is Cecil J. Allen, who declined a chance to travel behind Mallard on its record-breaking run in 1938, because it was scheduled for a Sunday. The man who built Mallard, Sir Nigel Gresley, came from four generations of rectors. Bishop Eric Treacy was 'the railway bishop', and he died at Appleby station while photographing the last steam locomotive built for BR, Evening Star. Treacy's see was that of Wakefield, but the railway–church connec-tion was particularly strong in the territory of God's Own Railway. Aside from Roye England, there was William Tem-ple, Christian socialist and Archbishop of Canterbury in the Second World War, who apparently knew Bradshaw off by heart. He was born in Exeter. Canon Victor Lorenzo White-church, author of railway detective stories, was chaplain to the bishop of Oxford. The Revd Wilbert Awdry, creator of Thomas the Tank Engine, grew up in a house called Jour-ney's End, near the west end of Box Hill Tunnel, on the Great Western main line. Only the GWR was confident, and camp, enough to put a model of a bishop's mitre on the front of an engine and call the train – in letters suggesting the involve-ment of a medieval monk – the Cathedrals Express because it connected (not very quickly) the cathedral cities of London, Oxford, Worcester and Hereford.

One morning in the late '70s, David Maidment, a lifelong Methodist, and employee of British Rail Western Region, was waiting for a train to Paddington at Maidenhead. He was on his way to work. Normally, he commuted from Beaconsfield, but he had gone to Maidenhead because 'it had a railway model shop that sold *Crownline* paints for detailing models'. He was reading the theological novel *Mr God, This is Anna*, and he had come to a passage where the precocious six-year-old Anna stresses the importance of not being 'afraid of life'. In terms of his own life, the message seemed to be that Mr Maidment should stop worrying about dogma and 'get on with life working to the humanitarian and compassionate demands of the person of Jesus as recorded in the Gospels'. He was confirmed in this thought by an epiphany that occurred on the platform. Whereas Mr Maidment had been expecting a humble diesel multiple unit, the train that pulled in for him was loco-hauled, pulled by a Class 50 diesel engine named, like the carriages of our Edwardian *Riviera*, Dreadnought. (Dread nothing, you see.) David Maidment OBE would go on to found the Railway Children charity, which has raised millions to help street children around the world, who tend to congregate around big railway termini.

'Iguanas just wandering around in the jungle,' the Mexico people were saying. 'Well, why not? It's their jungle.' The naval man was saying, 'I'm in Switzerland next Tuesday', which rather suggested he wasn't a naval man after all.

We went fast through Westbury. The Edwardian *Riviera* would have done the same, but this is the first of the places where it would have slipped a coach. That is, a coach would have been uncoupled while the train was in motion. It is self-evident, I hope, that the first coach to be slipped would be the one at the back. There was no gangway connection between one slip coach and another, or between any slip coach and the rest of the train. That way, a person who just happened to be walking the length of the train would not find themselves slipped. Slip coaches would be composite, a little world of their own, or a train within a train, with first and other classes, a lavatory and a control unit, where a special slip guard, who was something between a guard and a driver, presided. The slip coach was connected to the rest of the train by a special hinged coupling retained by a wedge. At the right moment, the slip guard pulled a lever to withdraw this wedge. He then applied the brakes of the slipped coach. He also had at his command a bull horn, to warn anyone who might have strayed on to the tracks, because a slipped coach would move silently on the inherited momentum of the train.

The slipped coach would usually be collected by a shunting engine, like a bone thrown to a dog, and taken to the right platform or carried forward along a branch line. The driver of the actual train had to remember not to make an emergency or unscheduled stop immediately after the slipping, because in that case the slipped carriage would smash into the carriage from which it had just been slipped. Slip coaches have been a gift to thriller writers (who usually haven't made much of it). See *The Slip Coach Mystery*, by Canon Whitechurch (1898), or then again *The Mystery of the Slip Coach*, by Sapper (1933). Bradshaw did not go out of its way to finesse the matter. There was the word 'slip', followed by a not very reassuring footnote: 'The carriage is detached. The train does not stop.'

According to Cecil Allen, slipping is 'confined entirely to the British Isles', and 'far and away ahead of all other lines' for slipping was the GWR ... 'on which no less than 67 slips are detached daily'. (Next came the Great Eastern, with twenty-six slips.) The challenge, for anyone being slipped for the first time, would be to remain blasé about it. In *The*

Railway Journeys of My Childhood (1963), Brigadier John Faviell describes being slipped from a GWR train before the First World War. Faviell was a schoolboy at the time, heading, on the Worcester express, from Paddington to his school at Cheltenham:

> I knew we were to be slipped at Kingham; so to other passengers' disgust and discomfort, I insisted on struggling to the window as we approached the station. The brakes of our carriage were put on very hard; and the rest of the train accelerated briskly. Then after this initial breaking our carriage continued slowly and gently into Kingham station while the express rocketed away in the distance. The carriage was collected by a tank engine which then crossed the main grain of the Cotswolds, sweating and puffing ... Stow-on-the-Wold, Bourton-on-the-Water, Notgrove, Andoversford, Charlton Kings, Cheltenham.

Slipping wasn't done in reverse. No train ever collected a carriage while on the move, although I bet Brunel could have thought of a way. Slipping faded after the war, and the last carriage was slipped on the Western Region of BR, at Bicester North on 10 September 1960.

We passed through Frome – low hills, copses, broken barns, lonely horses, all under a sunny but slightly milky sky. Between Castle Cary and Taunton is Somerton Tunnel, and we now went through it. This took only forty-five seconds, but a murder occurred on the *Cornish Riviera Express* while it was in this tunnel. A fictional murder, I mean – in *The Cornish Riviera Mystery* (1939), by John Rowland. We will be returning to this work. We came to Taunton, where the *Express* would have slipped another coach. From Taunton the West

Somerset Railway extends 20 miles to Minehead along a branch that Dr Beeching thought he'd closed. It is the longest preserved railway in Britain. Beeching seemed to have it in for Somerset, and today none of its main attractions – Wells, Glastonbury, Burnham-on-Sea – is on the railway.

The train guard came up to inspect my ticket. I asked him why he didn't refer to 'the *Cornish Riviera Express*' in his announcements, and he produced what he called his 'working diagram, my worksheet if you like. There's no mention here of the Cornish Riviera. To be quite honest with you, ninety-nine per cent of people want the train to run on time, and they don't give a monkey's what it's called.' Also, he had been told to cut back on announcements: 'People have a low attention span ... less is more.' I learned from a typically well-informed column by that railway sage Christian Wolmar that reminders about 'personal belongings' and 'take a moment to familiarise yourself with the safety features' are required by Transec, the government's transport security committee, and can't be dispensed with. So it is the lighter stuff that must go. In Transec's climate of fear, it would seem frivolous to suggest something along the lines of 'A warm welcome to the *Cornish Riviera Express*.'

We were now climbing Wellington Bank, coming *down* which Churchward's engine City of Truro may have touched 102 m.p.h. on 9 May 1904 while pulling the *Ocean Mails Special* from Plymouth to Paddington, in which case it would have been the first steam locomotive to reach 100 m.p.h. It was unofficially timed at that speed by a *Railway Magazine* journalist. The GWR did not claim the record, for fear of seeming reckless. The feat was brushed further under the carpet in 1906, when a Plymouth–Waterloo boat train of the LSWR crashed at Salisbury, probably because the driver was trying to match the faster timings between the West Country and

London that had become available to the GWR by the opening of the Berks & Hants cut-off. Twenty-eight people were
killed. In 1922 the company admitted the alleged speed, but
an experimental electrical railcar had reached 126 m.p.h.
near Berlin in 1903.

THE SEA WALL

We entered Devon or, as TTW calls it, 'Glorious Devon'
through the Whiteball Tunnel, and at 12.08 we stopped at
Exeter St David's, where we exchanged executives (including
the man who was probably not a naval officer) for passengers who were either older or younger, and not so prosper-
ous-looking. Exeter St David's is a pretty station: airily blue
and white, the balustrades of the staircases shaped like locomotive connecting rods.

The London & South Western Railway tried to compete
with the GWR in the West Country, and the LSWR trains
from Waterloo used Exeter *Central*, which still serves Waterloo trains. But LSWR trains also called at St David's on their
way to the company's West Country strongholds. The layout at Exeter St David's was such that LSWR trains heading
west and away from London pulled out of the station in the
same direction as those of the GWR heading east and *towards*
London. As a volunteer at the GWR Museum at the Didcot
Railway Centre took great satisfaction in explaining to me:
'If the engines of the LSWR and the GWR were facing the
same way, you knew they were going in opposite directions.'

Did the LSWR have an equivalent to the *Cornish Riviera
Express* on its route west? Yes. It was called the *Atlantic Coast
Express* – ACE for short – and it lasted between 1926 and 1964.
The ACE ran from Waterloo, and constantly subdivided
as it approached north Cornwall. It was the brainchild of

that pioneer of PR John Elliot, of the Southern Railway. He sought a name by running a competition in the *Southern Railway* Magazine.

In *An Illustrated History of the Atlantic Coast Express*, John Scott-Morgan recounts how the competition was won by Frederick Rowland, who worked for the Southern at Waterloo. His prize was 3 guineas. 'The runners up, from Nine Elms and Richmond, were each consoled with a paperweight in the form of a model King Arthur 4–6–0.' Frederick Rowland was a guard based at Waterloo, but he was originally from Devon, and he may have regarded his success in naming a Devon-bound train as an affirmation of his Devonian identity. A year later he moved back there, becoming based at a little station called Torrington. On Friday 9 September 1932 he slipped on to the track at the next station along the line, Marland, while supervising the shunting of a goods train. A wagon ran over his legs and, as he lay dying, he heroically called up to the driver, 'It was no fault of yours, Jack!' The name *Atlantic Coast Express* lives on, designating some First Great Western services to Newquay, and it is the name used by First Group for its X9 bus route from Exeter to Bude. 'These,' says John Scott-Morgan, form 'a fitting memorial to Frederick Rowland.'

Incidentally, the LSWR trains running west of Exeter went to Plymouth via Okehampton and Tavistock; there were also branches to Bude and Padstow. These lines were nicknamed 'the withered arm', and would be lopped off by Beeching, so trains from Waterloo now go no further west than Exeter St David's.

On our HST, a crew change occurred at Exeter, and the new people all had strong West Country accents. ('All right, honey?' 'You look really well, chick.') On the *Riviera Express* the restaurant car would come into play after Exeter, and there was no shortage of these. Andrew Roden writes of whole trains of restaurant cars being taken west from London in the inter-war summers to be attached to the 'up' services. After Exeter the steward from the luncheon car would walk the length of the train, opening compartment doors and perhaps tinkling a bell to announce the service of lunch. In *The Cornish Riviera Mystery* (1939) the two principals are asked by the waiter on reaching the luncheon car, 'Usual lunch, gentlemen?'

'What is the usual lunch?'

'Tomato soup, sole and fried potatoes, apple tart and cream.'

'I think that will do, don't you?'

In 1928 the Great Western boasted that lunch on the *Riviera* cost 3s., while pointing out that the lunch on the Canadian Pacific Railway cost 7s. 11d., as if it was a toss-up for most punters whether to travel on the one railway or the other. In his memoir *Gone with Regret* (1961) George Behrend writes of the same *Riviera*, 'Do not ask why the luncheon fish was invariably a nice piece of turbot. It always was ...' He speaks of white napery and 'silverine cutlery, all emblazoned with the company crest'. In 2013 I took out my prawn sandwiches, crisps and fruit smoothie, bought from Marks and Spencer's at Paddington.

Pulling away from Exeter, we embarked on the most scenic part of the route: the sea wall (two words probably more familiar to the public than when I made my trip; see below). The sea wall proper is at Dawlish, but the term is also used to describe the whole stretch from Exeter to Newton Abbot. TTW recommended that passengers sit on the left, so I moved to that side, waking a late middle-aged man in the process. We began running south along the edge of the Exe estuary, so close that we seemed to be on top of the mild blue

10. The *Cornish Riviera Express* running along the Dawlish sea wall in September 1928. It is said the passengers hoped for delays on this stretch so they could savour the view.

water. Then came Dawlish Warren, and we began to skirt the actual sea. Brunel's fast, flat line is deemed too close to the water. A diversion inland was pencilled in for 1939, but the war intervened. The *Railway Magazine* seemed relieved: 'A journey from Exeter to Teignmouth at high tide during a severe gale can still provide an impressive spectacle of raging waters and windblown rain clouds that it is still worth coming miles to see.' It reported that the GWR had set up a machine on the low red cliffs above Dawlish to monitor the speed of the wind eroding the dunes protecting the sea wall. I wonder if it's still there, a few rusted shards of metal, most of it blown away.

At Dawlish the train is almost on the beach. Instead of signals by the side of the track, there are the masts of boats. This is the Number One photo opportunity on the railways of Britain. The cover of TTW itself shows a King class locomotive on this stretch. The late middle-aged man was grinning. 'I grew up in the Midlands, and we used to come here for our holidays in the Fifties. I would be sitting there,' and he indicated the sea wall just as we went into the first of the five quick tunnels in the cliff that follow, 'and so I'd be facing the trains, while my parents would be sitting on the beach facing the sea. Some of the trains would be delayed there, and it was the one delay that people used to love. But if the sea was rough, and the windows were open, you could get soaked.'

The sea was very rough in early February 2014, and an 80-metre stretch of the sea wall, corresponding perfectly to the photo-opportunity stretch, was destroyed. Reading about this, I learned that the wind machine on the cliff has been superseded by sensors on Network Rail buoys floating offshore, which had predicted trouble, and which must be among the few remnants of our railways' involvement with the sea. The storm left the track hanging in a void, like a hammock. The hanging track was bowed, like my Hornby double-O track when, aged nine or so, I would try to make a bridge by using two books placed a foot apart. The whole of the country west of Dawlish was cut off from the railway network. Journalists discovered the plans for the inland diversion, and demanded to know why it hadn't been built, or why the 'withered arm' had been cut off, denying the West Country an alternative route. At the time of writing the sea wall has been fixed, and if there are plans to replace it, they are proceeding very quietly behind the scenes.

After our progress through the five cliff tunnels of the Dawlish Warren, beautifully described by Benedict Le Vay as being like 'a needle heading through gathered cloth', we came to Teignmouth, described in TTW as 'a highly picturesque seaside resort as well as a seaport in a small way of business'. (The latter claim no longer stands.) We continued by the water, skirting the River Teign, in complete harmony with the small sailing boats, and then we came to Newton Abbot, where we stopped, and our HST emptied out considerably. Those alighting were mainly retirees. Nothing against Newton Abbot, but I assumed they would be changing for the branch ('The Riviera Line') to the railway-made resort, and retirement town, of Torquay.

We passed through Totnes, from where the preserved South Devon Railway goes through the Dart Valley to Buckfastleigh. The SDR station is visible to the right from the main line. It is beautifully kept, and painted in the intriguingly unambitious Great Western station colours of 'light stone and dark stone', two shades of greyish brown. We rolled through undulating country, in cuttings for much of the time, but we would periodically surface to see sun-dappled small fields. At five past one we came to Plymouth, where, writes the author of TTW, 'we actually stop!', whereas our HST had already stopped four times.

For most of the life of the *Cornish Riviera Express* this, the main station at Plymouth, was called Plymouth North Road. It was rebuilt, and opened as plain Plymouth in 1962. It is a long, grey tin-roofed shack. An equally grey seagull was flying lazily through it. No Castle or King locomotive ever stood next to the famously nondescript Intercity House which abuts the station, but we must cut Plymouth some slack, the town having been so badly bombed in the war. An article on the railways of Plymouth in *British Railways Illustrated*, from September 1995, begins despairingly: 'the subject is far too vast to deal with in a single article.' There were a multiplicity of stations in Plymouth, mainly because both the LSWR and the GWR went there. Also it was a naval base, a civilian port and a shipbuilding centre, so branches were needed for the docks, and it should be remembered that what is now Plymouth was three towns until 1914, the largest two being Plymouth itself and Devonport. Even today there are six stations in Plymouth.

We went through Devonport, Dockyard and Keyham, after which a picturesque branch skirting the Tamar and heading to Gunnislake diverges. This is a Community Rail line, one of half a dozen under the auspices of the Devon and Cornwall Rail Partnership.

The Community Rail movement was founded in the early 1990s by Professor Paul Salveson, that namer of trains mentioned in the Introduction. A Community Railway line is formed of contracts between the train operator, the local authority and other stakeholders. It's not meant to be a way of getting lay people to do the train operator's job, since the operator is supposed to match funding that comes from outside. Under the auspices of Community Rail, stations

might be publicised, repainted, their gardens tended and
litter picked. Shops or other businesses might be opened
along the line, and what were once called excursions might
be mounted, often in the form of 'ale trails'. Community Rail
saved the branch lines of Cornwall, and traffic on those lines
has doubled in the past ten years. Apart from the Tamar line,
there is the Liskeard–Looe, the Par–Newquay ('The Atlantic Coast Line'), Truro–Falmouth ('The Maritime Line'), and
Penzance–St Ives. The partnership also covers one line in
Devon: the Tarka Line, from Exeter to Barnstaple.

Professor Salveson once spoke to me of stations on a
rural branch being happily interdependent, 'like pearls on
a string', and of the importance as a community hub of the
station itself, in tandem with the nearby railway inn. The
country station has been romanticised in films such as *Oh
Mr Porter*, *The Titfield Thunderbolt* and *The Railway Children*. It
was a place not just to catch a train but also to collect or des-
patch a parcel or a basket of racing pigeons, to check the
time, send a telegram, meet an incoming guest or see one
off. As David St John Thomas writes in his book *The Country
Railway*, 'In most areas for at least two full generations all
important comings and goings were by train ... The pair of
rails disappearing over the horizon stood for progress, disaster, the major changes in life: the route to Covent Garden
and Ypres.'

The country station was more like a farm than a factory.
Horses and cattle were frequently penned near by; the stationmaster tended his garden; there'd be nesting boxes
and perhaps a horseshoe (for luck) on the signal box. It is
a romantic vision that cannot be entirely dispelled by the
introduction of hard fact. Yes, the railway was a focus for
a community. But it also brought cheaper commodities,
the possibility of shopping further afield or by mail order;

and so the coming of the railway meant death to some local businesses.

The smaller Cornish stations on the route of *Riviera*, including those now closed, might have amused the first-class passenger. They had an ambivalent status: country stations on a main line. The *Riviera* ambled through so slowly that the lad porters wouldn't have bothered to tell passengers to stand back. But the stationmaster probably would have put his gold braided cap on and watched it go by – like the opposite of a funeral. The traveller would have seen the local territory summed up in that station, from the nature of produce in the goods yard, the names painted on the private-owner wagons being shunted in the background, the flora of the stationmaster's garden. At those small stations where the *Riviera* did stop, there'd have been an interesting assortment of vehicles waiting in the station yard, reflecting a cross-section of the populace: a chauffeur in a Bentley; respectable carriages, donkey carts, perhaps a charabanc for some club or association, or, scanning the third-class carriages, a young man who'd arrived at the station on a bike while pushing another alongside, to be ridden by the friend he was meeting. In 1906, there might have been a young man who'd done the same with two horses.

OVER THE BRIDGE

We rolled through St Budeaux Ferry Road, another of those halts immediately after Plymouth station that seem designed to increased anticipation of the coming thrill: the crossing of the Tamar on Brunel's Royal Albert Bridge. The railway – just one line – is carried on brick piers over the river. The train then passes through a wrought-iron cradle that is lenticular (eye-shaped); then comes the diminuendo of the piers on the other side. The iron tubes forming the tops of the cradles, or the tops of the 'eyes', serve two purposes. The trusses holding up the track-bed hang from them. They also brace the bridge, stop it collapsing in on itself. Its economical structure makes the bridge seem elegant and airily poised, soaring a hundred feet above the small sailing boats moored below, which seems like overkill, but the great height was insisted on by the Navy, to accommodate the taller masts of the time.

As we rumbled over the bridge at the maximum speed allowed (15 m.p.h.), the water was sparkling, and the day had become unequivocally sunny. We seemed to be doing nothing less than slowly flying on a train. The executive who was the only other remaining occupant of the carriage was shouting into his mobile phone: 'But I do need to see your plan for this twelve month process.' The stone arches are inscribed with the words 'IK Brunel Engineer, 1859', and the curvature of the bridge allows you to read them from the train. When Brunel designed this bridge, he was a dying man. He was drawn over it recumbent in a wagon soon after its official opening, and he 'saw that it was good', so to speak. The bridge merits a name-check for Brunel – the only one – in TTW: 'one of the finest achievements of I. K. Brunel, who constructed the Great Western Railway'.

To the right of the Royal Albert Bridge is the Tamar Road Bridge, opened in 1961. But the actual roadway looks suspiciously new. Whereas the railway bridge has remained single-track, in 2001 the road bridge became the first suspension bridge to be widened. It went from three to five lanes, and there, in essence, is the story of post-war transport to Cornwall. Many more people visit Cornwall than in the inter-war heyday of the *Riviera Express*, but while the trains are jam-packed in summer, 90 per cent of visitors come by car. And they stay for a shorter time. As recently as 1993, 74 per cent of visitors to Cornwall were on their main holiday. Today the figure is 30 per cent.

The tourist industry in Cornwall was founded by those campaigns of the GWR. They were well timed in that the 'heavy' industry of Cornwall was dying even as the *Riviera Express* began operations. It is unlikely that the copper caps of Churchward's engines were made from Cornish copper; tin-mining was also fading in the early twentieth century. China clay-mining continued, although most of that was transported by sea. The main job of the railway was to bring in trippers and take out agricultural produce, particularly milk, potatoes, broccoli and flowers ...

... Of which there were many (rhododendrons and aga-panthus especially) growing along with palms on the pass-ing platforms: Saltash, St Germans, Menheniot, Liskeard. The Cornish flora make up for the cold colour of the stone-rendered houses. You can't make bricks with china clay. The line-side was also made decorative by the presence, after Liskeard, of old-fashioned semaphore signals, permitted to survive because of the slowness of the trains.

After creating his billiard table, and building a very low bridge, a line on the very edge of the sea, then a very high bridge, the First Engineer found a new amusement in Cornwall. Viaducts! There are twenty-six traversing gorges between Plymouth and St Austell, and they dictate a slow speed. Perhaps this is why the operator doesn't have the nerve to call the *Cornish Riviera* the *Cornish Rivera Express*. I am reminded of a continental service Evelyn Waugh once trav-elled on: 'My train was a *rapide*, and God it was slow.'

We stopped at Bodmin, or rather a station 5 miles out-side. In 1859 Bodmin spurned the railway, thereby forfeit-ing its position as the county town of Cornwall to a town

that embraced it: Truro. The station at Bodmin was originally called Bodmin Road. Today it is Bodmin Parkway, but
the names mean the same thing: *it is not in Bodmin*. In 1958
John Betjeman wrote to a friend called Peggy Thomas, who
lived in Trebetherick: 'Perhaps we could all set up at Bodmin
Road station by arrangement with the Great Western – you
in the refreshment room because of drink, Lynam in the signal box because of administrative ability, me in the booking
office because I'm literary, Edward to do the lamps and odd
jobs because he's so clever with his hands ... We won't have
a station master as we'll be one glorious Soviet.' Betjeman
liked Bodmin Road/Parkway, which dreams its life away in a
wooded valley made by the River Fowey.

We passed Lostwithiel station, the town hidden somewhere to the left. The name means 'Lost within the hill',
but it was detectable in winter to passengers on the *Cornish Riviera Express* by the smoke rising from its chimneys.
We stopped at Par, and those silver surfers who had not
got off at Newton Abbot for Torquay now alighted here for
the connecting train to Newquay. But Par is also china clay
country, even today. The last surviving china clay company
is a French-owned outfit called Imerys. It sends clay trains –
white-dusted and fit to be mistaken for a ghost train in some
rackety farce – to the small port of Fowey, using a branch line
that used to carry people as well, but which is now freight
only. Some of the clay also heads east along the Cornish
main line. And so here is a modern-day correspondence with
an industrial scene as described in TTW, which speaks of 'a
district devoted to clay mining', great 'cone-shaped dumps
of clay', and all the streams running white.

After St Austell – a biggish, blanched-looking town – we
approached Truro, where we, like the *Cornish Riviera Express*,
were booked to stop. We viewed Truro from the two viaducts

preceding the station, the tallest structures in the town after the spire of the cathedral. I am made slightly nervous by these Cornish viaducts. I read that one of the few with two tracks running over it was deemed, immediately post-war, not capable of taking the weight of two freight trains. So the two tracks were singled. It now happened that our HST came to a stop on the second of the two Truro viaducts and remained at a standstill for twenty minutes. We were certainly occupying the only line on the viaduct. Was this the vulnerable one? I began looking to the right, away from the town, where the view is less vertiginous.

In December 1909 the *Railway Magazine* profiled Truro under the heading 'Truro as a Railway Centre'. The article paints a picture of an industrialised town: carpets, paper and iron. Truro was also important in 1910 as the head of the railway branch to the port of Falmouth. The branch survives (Community Rail) and is booming, as indicated by the large number waiting to board our HST. The branch is much used by students at Falmouth University, There is ship-repairing and superyacht-building at Falmouth. As for Truro, it is an 'administrative centre'.

In Cornwall's industrial days china clay gave way beyond Truro to mineral mining, and Cornwall's mines were an Aladdin's cave of minerals – iron, copper, lead, arsenic. I saw a couple of crumbling wheelhouses and chimneys, whereas TTW writes of the approach to Redruth: 'the surrounding countryside is heavily scored with tin and copper mines.' That could have meant they were still working or had already closed.

We stopped at St Erth, as did the *Cornish Riviera Express*. A mantra of the time was 'St George for England, St Pancras for Scotland, St Erth for St Ives'. Palm trees on the platform reminded the author of TTW that he was finally on the

Cornish Riviera, as they did me. As our HST pulled away, a pleasant young man, 'a customer host', came along with a bin-liner collecting rubbish. 'This is the *Cornish Riviera Express*,' I said, 'You know that, obviously?' He cleverly side-stepped the question by giving a half-nod and saying, 'I was just thinking – this is a really scenic route.'

'How long have you been on the railway?' I asked.

'Six months. I worked at *Waitrose* before.'

'Do you want to be a driver?'

'Hopefully, yes. My dad's a driver – he works units out of Exeter. But I've got to keep my nose clean in this job first.'

Looking at the kid, I assessed his chances. He seemed bright and competent, but he'd have to wait a while. You can become a train driver at twenty-one, but that's rare. Maturity is what's required, and many train drivers have come from another profession, often the services, where the right sort of vigilance and orderliness is inculcated. The job was always high-status. In steam days the drivers outranked even quite senior railway clerks. Back then, the challenge was to be taken on as an engine cleaner, because that was the start of the route to driving, via the grades of 'passed cleaner' (meaning you could fire an engine under close supervision), then fireman. The fireman did all the hard work, which is why he ended up the dirtier of the two. But the driver took all the credit, and he would stand on the footplate, narcissistically straightening his neckerchief and wiping clean his not very dirty hands while he received the adulation of the 'railwayacs'. The driver had earned his privileges because he himself had spent twenty-five years firing engines. Today it is even harder to be a train driver. I know a man who drives for First Great Western. He was an engineer with BT when he answered a local newspaper advertisement. He was one of seven thousand applicants for eight places – testament, he believes, to the continuing romantic appeal of railways. A hundred applicants were interviewed. He was selected for training, which took a year with an exam every week. He then did 250 hours of in-cab learning.

'You might be driving the *Cornish Riviera* one day,' I said to the young man.

'I might be driving *you* on it.'

Yes, I thought, if we're both very lucky.

Rising to our left from the milky sea was St Michael's Mount, much compared to Mont St Michel in Brittany by the GWR. A couple of minutes later we arrived at Penzance. We were scheduled to do so at 15.11, but we had been made slightly late on the Truro viaduct. When the *Cornish Riviera Express* had settled down to its 10.30 departure time, it reached Penzance at 5.30. So it took seven hours, whereas ours took a little over six with more stops.

There is a Sunday-ish feeling about modern Penzance, a sense of many of its people having been suddenly called away. TTW speaks of 'the picturesque shipping of its harbour'. Today that harbour, as seen from an arriving train, usually holds nothing but sea. The area between the engine shed of Penzance station and the sea was once all railway territory, with a goods shed and a goods yard. It's now of course a car park. The passenger arriving on the *Cornish Riviera Express* might have been just in time to see the departure of the mail train for Paddington, which might also carry flowers brought over on the ferry from the Scilly Isles, which still docks near the station. If he was a railwayac, he might want to wait and watch this loading, asking the friend meeting him if the driver with his pony and trap wouldn't mind waiting a few more minutes in the station yard. His companion, if not a railwayac, might ask, 'Haven't you had enough of trains for one day?'

On a balmy summer's evening the Morrab Gardens of Penzance remain far more vivid and exotically scented than most public gardens in Britain. The heart of the town retains many fine Georgian and Regency buildings, but there are too many charity shops on the high street. In 1963 John Betjeman wrote: 'The older houses in the narrow centre round the market hall have been pulled down and third-rate commercial "contemporary", of which the Pearl Assurance building is a nasty example, are turning it into Slough.' That building is now a Wetherspoon's (i.e., cheap) pub, where I spent some of my evening. I spoke to the young barman, who said that tourism was 'by far the main thing' in the town, and the tourists often had plenty of money, 'but they were too old', and he would rather they were younger. Then they might spend more, and the place would be livelier. In other words, Penzance remains exasperatingly genteel, as it was in 1879, when Gilbert and Sullivan decided it was about the least likely seaside place in which pirates would be found. The barman told me that a marina might be created in the harbour, and that could be the tonic the town needs. Either way, he said he 'wouldn't live anywhere else,' and looking at my notebook, he commanded, *'Write that down.'*

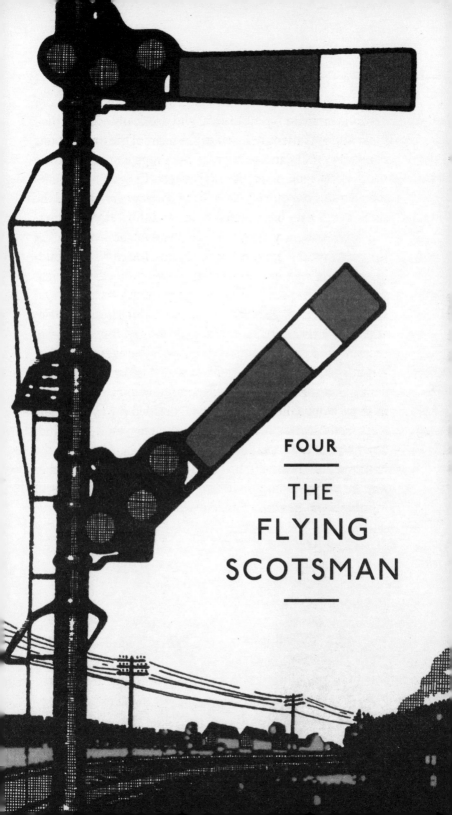

FOUR

THE
FLYING
SCOTSMAN

THE FLYING SCOTSMAN

ECML

It is disorientating to think that in the 1830s the rivalry of East and West Coast main lines did not exist. Trains from York to London went into Euston rather than King's Cross. Why? Because King's Cross didn't exist. They went there via Rugby, Leicester, Sheffield and Normanton, a few miles south and east of Leeds. No town must be more haunted by railway ghosts than Normanton, which for twenty years from the mid-1830s was a big railway player, the stepping-stone between the north-east and the early route to London. If this were one of those heart-breaking 'Where are they now?' articles, I would be writing that Normanton 'recalls the old days with affection but it has made a new life for itself as a dormitory of Leeds. On the whole, it is glad it no longer has all the noise, pollution and stress of being the main railway junction in Britain.'

In 1850 the new Great Northern Railway opened a terminus at Maiden Lane, just north of London. From there, and later from King's Cross (which opened in 1852), they operated what would become the southern stretch of the East Coast Main Line (ECML). At Shaftholme Junction, just beyond Doncaster, the new North Eastern Railway, based in York, operated the continuation of the line to Berwick, from where the North British Railway operated up to Edinburgh. From 1860 these three companies ran trains collaboratively using shared carriages – called joint stock – and with engines changed on the way like a baton being passed.

We might ask, 'What does the East Coast Main Line (ECML) have to do with the east coast?' The sea comes into view only beyond Durham, and then only intermittently, but sometimes gorgeously, and the prestige expresses were marshalled so the compartment windows, rather than corridor windows, were on that side.

The ECML is more coastal than the West Coast Main Line, from which the sea is visible *very* fleetingly, as the trains pass Morecambe Bay. The WCML is like one of those landladies who boast of sea views when in fact you can only see the sea if you stand on the toilet seat and crane your neck. In the early days the ECML was more seawards than it is today. Beyond Peterborough, the line kinked east, running via Spalding, Boston and Lincoln before rejoining what we know as the modern route at Newark. In 1852 the modestly named 'towns line', running from Peterborough to Retford via Grantham and Newark, came into play, and the east coast took another step towards modernity (and away from the sea). Beyond Shaftholme Junction the first incarnation of the line went to York via Knottingley and Church Fenton, but from 1871 the line to York began to go via Selby, thereby inching slightly *nearer* to the coast in this instance. (A hundred years later it withdrew from Selby, as we will be seeing.) In 1872 the Team Valley line opened, bringing Durham on to the route, whereas previously the line had bulged seaward, approaching Newcastle via Leamside and Penshaw.

The ECML, originating at King's Cross and terminating at Edinburgh Waverley, competed with the WCML. That originated at Euston, ran up to Glasgow, but also terminated in Edinburgh – at Princes Street station. The operators of the WCML were the London & North Western Railway and the Caledonian Railway, and they ran their own joint stock carriages. A lesser competitor to both these was the Midland Railway, which went up the middle of the country, running – impractically but picturesquely – over the moorland between Settle and Carlisle. The Midland never offered the quickest way to Scotland, but many chose it for the scenery, and holiday journeys were timed to display the most spectacular parts in daylight.

But the Midland didn't have 'the world's most famous train'.

THE TWO SCOTSMEN

The name *Flying Scotsman*, which had once belonged to a stage-coach, was applied informally to the 10 a.m. services that began to run on the ECML from London to Edinburgh, and vice versa, in 1862. Bradshaw called it the 'Special Scotch Express'. The 392-mile journey took ten and a half hours, including a half-hour stop for lunch or – as it was called – 'dinner' at York. In the 1880s the stops were at Grantham, York, Newcastle, Berwick and Edinburgh Waverley. The stops of its West Coast counterpart, the *Day Scotch Express*, were at Willesden, Rugby, Crewe, Preston, Carlisle, with a couple of further, varying, Scottish stops before Edinburgh Princes Street: a distance of 400 miles.

The *Flying Scotsman* had been first-class only, but in 1887

third-class passengers were admitted. This provoked the
West Coast operators, and in the summer of 1888 the two
consortia raced each other on the route to Edinburgh, with
competing trains running recklessly fast at the same time,
and news reporters also racing – in Hansom cabs along
Princes Street – to compare the arrival times of the services
at the two Edinburgh stations. In August the consortia came
to an agreement, as a result of which the timings were fixed.
The allowance for the East Coast route was eight and a half
hours. There was a further outbreak of racing in 1895, during which the East Coast train achieved six hours nineteen
minutes. Afterwards, a minimum of eight hours was agreed
for the two routes, and this endured until 1932, by which
time it was considered ridiculously sedate, and it was said
that dead fish (on trains from Aberdeen docks) were travelling to London faster than passengers from the north.

In the grouping of 1923 the East Coast consortia were
subsumed into the London & North Eastern Railway, while
the West Coast companies came under the London, Midland
& Scottish Railway. The Chief Mechanical Engineer of the
LNER was Nigel Gresley, and he introduced the American
Pacific style of locomotive to the company. The Pacifics were
long, lean-looking engines with even bigger boilers than the
Atlantic class of engines that had preceded them (the Pacific
Ocean being bigger than the Atlantic). In 1923 the third of a
series of ten Gresley Pacifics – all given the classification A1
– was built and christened the *Flying Scotsman*, thus triggering ninety years of confusion. In 1923 the name given to the
engine was still only applied informally to the train. But in
1924 the *Flying Scotsman* train was formally called the *Flying
Scotsman* as well. So the train was named after the engine that
was named after the train.

New carriages were introduced in 1924, together with roof

boards reading *Flying Scotsman*. In 1928 the *Flying Scotsman* became a non-stop service from London to Edinburgh, with not only the roof boards but also a headboard for whatever loco was hauling the train. This would not make the train any quicker, since the LNER was still bound by the agreement of 1896, but it would attract good publicity, which the service needed. In 1926 a southbound *Scotsman* had been derailed by striking miners. Nobody was killed, but the *Scotsman* seemed besieged. Passenger numbers were falling, train travel generally decreasing in the poor economic climate. Wealthy travellers were increasingly often choosing to fly between London and Scotland, and electrical trains were getting into their stride on the Continent, so the long-distance running of a steam train would have seemed an antiquated feat to some.

It was dramatic, nonetheless. No two men could drive and fire an engine for eight hours, so a crew changeover was required. The 'fresh' crew would travel 'on the cushions', as footplate men referred to travel in the carriages of a train, until the changeover point was reached, just north of York. They would then walk towards the footplate by means of a narrow corridor built into the side of a new series of tenders. It was an Alice in Wonderland-like arrangement, the corridor being so small. Gresley had calculated the minimum width by lining his dining-room chairs against his dining-room wall, explaining to his small daughter, who was looking on amused, 'If I can get through this, my biggest engineman can.'

The first non-stop run was on 1 May 1928. The *Flying Scotsman* locomotive pulled the *Flying Scotsman* train. A couple of days beforehand, the London Midland & Scottish childishly tried to upstage the *Scotsman* by dividing its equivalent of the *Scotsman*, the *Royal Scot*, into two, thus making two relatively light trains that could make it to Scotland without stopping, albeit with barely a scrap of coal left in the tender at the end of the trip, and I assume four – rather than the usual two – men on the footplate. So the LMS had done the first non-stop run, but theirs was a one-off.

The *Flying Scotsman* brand peaked in the late 1920s. The non-stop train was equipped with a cocktail bar and a barber's shop, and four men braved the cut-throat razor on the first run. (I think 'braved' is the right word, even though Gresley was famous for the smooth running of his carriages.) There was also a ladies' retiring-room doubling as a *salon de coiffure*, so that ladies could get their hair done too. The new first-class restaurant cars have been described as being in 'Louis XIV style with low-backed loose armchairs blending with painted wall panels in stone picked out with blue mouldings'. But it was the business of non-stopping that was made the chief selling point by the LNER's dynamic advertising manager, W. M. Teasdale. A poster advertised the 'Without Stop' service. It showed the engine, a big arrowhead indicating the small corridor by which the tender was approached. Another, rather spectral image showed the *Flying Scotsman* cocktail being mixed by hands silhouetted in an expressionist style. Bob Gwynne, a curator of the National Rail Museum, says the cocktail – involving whisky, vermouth, bitters and sugar – could have 'felled a horse'. The *Flying Scotsman* (train and engine) was depicted on one of the three jigsaws produced by the LNER. The engine was modelled for a paperweight 'finished in oxidised silver' with details of the non-stop run on the plinth; a cardboard template was manufactured so that children could make a cut-out of the engine.

In 1928 the LNER offered 'all possible assistance' to the makers of a feature film called *The Flying Scotsman*. Train and

11. The *Flying Scotsman's* cocktail bar served the
Flying Scotsman cocktail, which could have felled
a horse. The advert is from the early 1930s.

engine were made available on a succession of Sundays over
the Hertford Loop, the suburban line running parallel to the
East Coast Main Line immediately north of King's Cross. It
seems inconceivable that the company would have done this
if they'd known in advance what the film was about ...

The Flying Scotsman (released in 1929) is an impressively
wild and nasty film. It tells the story of a *Flying Scotsman* footplate crew. First there is driver Bob (played by Moore Marri-
ott, who also starred in the much more good-natured railway
film *Oh Mr Porter*), a humourless martinet, violently inclined.
Then there is Crow, an alcoholic who drinks on the job, snarls
at little old ladies when they come up to the engine at King's
Cross to thank him for the run, and is even more violently
inclined than his colleague. (If you put the names together,
you get Bob Crow, the late leader of the train drivers' union,
the RMT.) On the eve of his retirement Bob goes to the superintendent at 'top shed' (base for the crack engines and drivers
working out of King's Cross) and reports Crow for persistent
drunkenness on the job. Crow is sacked, and vows revenge.
He will somehow sabotage Bob's final run on the *Scotsman*. He
boards the train as a passenger, making straight for the dining car, and alcohol. Bob's winsome daughter Joan – played
by Pauline Johnson – has got wind of his plot, and she too
boards the train as a passenger. After sitting in a third-class
compartment for a while, giving us the chance to see that it
is surprisingly spartan, with much bare wood, she locates
Crow in the restaurant car. There – strangely undisturbed
by any waiter – she keeps an eye on Crow but, even though
her father's life is at stake, she falls asleep, a testament to the
lulling power of clickety-clack rhythm of a train running over
jointed track. (Tracks are now continuously welded. But there
should be an app that plays the old noise, for use on trains by
those wanting to drown out mobile phone talkers.)

As Joan sleeps, Crow has made his way to the footplate of the racing train, not by means of the tender corridor, which he seems to have forgotten about, but by crawling over the coal in the tender. On the footplate he sees Bob having an argument with his new young fireman, Jim, who Bob has just figured out has been carrying on with Joan. Meanwhile Joan has advanced towards the footplate by walking along the footboard of the carriages in high heels with the train going at 50 m.p.h. (Johnson did this herself, without a stunt double.) On the footplate Bob smashes Jim over the head with Jim's own shovel, thus knocking him off the train. Then Crow hurls a two-foot-wide lump of coal at Bob's head, knocking him out. Joan has seen all this. Crow makes his way back into the carriages, this time using the corridor. He then (and this was the scene that particularly infuriated Sir Nigel Gresley) uncouples the engine from the train, using only a penknife. Joan averts disaster by stopping the engine, then switching some points so that the train does not crash into the back of it. By now Joan can speak, since the third reel has sound, and whereas she is supposed to be a cockney sparrow of the kind likely to marry a fireman, she actually sounds like a member of the royal family. She declares that her father did not push Jim off the train (even though he did) and denounces Crow for trying to kill her father. Gresley insisted that a caption be shown at the start of the film reading: 'For the purposes of the film dramatic licence has been taken in regard to the safety equipment used on the Flying Scotsman.' The peculiar thing is that Freeman Wills Crofts had been a technical adviser on the film, and he was both an engineer and a novelist of the railways, whose own fictions are accurate to the point of pedantry.

In 1932 the trip was speeded up to seven and a quarter hours, and the typographer Eric Gill designed a new Gill

Sans typeface for the LNER, which was used on the *Flying Scotsman* headboard. As part of his fee, Gill requested a trip on the footplate. He wrote in a letter to a friend:

> Here we were on an engine ... attached to one of the most famous of all travelling hotels ... with its Cocktail Bar and beauty parlours, its dining saloons, decorated in more or less credible imitation of the salons of 18th Century France, its waiters and guards and attendants of all sorts, its ventilation and heating apparatus as efficient as those of the Strand Palace Hotel, and we are carrying on as if we were pulling a string of coal trucks.

His theme was the philosophical disconnect between the footplate and the train. The train was just a load to be pulled by 'this extremely heavy sort of cart horse'. He notes that the rhythm of the rail joints, 'iddy UMty ... iddyUMty' as heard in the carriages becomes, on the footplate, 'a continuous idddyiddyiddy', which reminds me of one of my own footplate experiences. When I stepped down, I saw that my mobile phone – set to the highest volume of ring-tone – had rung three times, and that engine had only been doing 25 m.p.h.

In 1934 the *Flying Scotsman* became the first steam locomotive to run at a recorded 100 m.p.h. But from 1935 the loco and train were overshadowed by Gresley's introduction of streamlined engines and carriages. Streamlining was the apogee of the machine-age aesthetic, and the speed obsession created by industrial competition between nations. A welter of famous streamlined engines and trains were introduced on the north–south routes, and their names had a relentlessly monarchical theme that is enough to turn anyone republican. On the East Coast, from September 1935, there was the de-luxe *Silver Jubilee*, which ran in silver-grey livery between King's Cross and Newcastle. A supplement was charged. Also on the East Coast there was the *Coronation*, a streamliner for Scotland, and on the West Coast there was the *Coronation Scot*, pulled by engines of the Coronation class in maroon with gold go-faster stripes. All these engines were streamlined.

The East Coast streamliners were classified – for reasons that need not concern us – as A4s, and the most famous of these was the Mallard, which on 3 July 1938 set the world speed record for steam: 126 m.p.h. The A4s would sometimes haul the *Flying Scotsman* train, but it's doubtful whether they ever eclipsed the fame of the Flying Scotsman locomotive, which we might dispose of, so to speak, at this point.

The locomotive was retired from active service in 1963, and so began its fraught afterlife as an icon of steam. It was scheduled to be scrapped by BR. An organisation called Save Our Scotsman tried, and failed, to raise the scrap value of the engine. Then Alan Pegler acquired the engine. He had fallen in love with the *Scotsman* when it had been displayed at the British Empire Exhibition of 1924. After spending a fortune refurbishing the engine, Pegler used to run enthusiasts' tours in Britain. Between 1969 and 1971 the engine toured the US and Canada. Some states seized the engine as a fire hazard. The tour resulted in Pegler's bankruptcy, with creditors circling around the engine in San Francisco. It later came into the hands Dr Tony Marchington, whose ownership of the engine also resulted in his bankruptcy. The engine is today in the National Rail Museum, which has spent over £2 million making it ready to run again, amid arguments – impenetrable to all but the cognoscenti – over what technical specification, and what livery, would be the most authentic to revert to. The *Flying Scotsman* features in one of the Revd Awdry's *Thomas the Tank Engine* stories, and when the animated TV series of the stories came to be made, the production company couldn't afford to create a model of the loco, so just showed its tender sticking out of an engine shed.

I once made the mistake of suggesting by email to a highly erudite rail enthusiast that here was a locomotive that should perhaps have been put out of its – and a lot of other people's – misery a long time ago. He replied, 'A ghastly combination of post-modernists, theoretical Marxists (via a modern museum training) and free market haters of public institutions would agree with you.' He went on to lament the way the engine had been 'handed around like a fallen woman. At one point, as part of Driver Experience courses, you could drive her for fifty quid. Classy! She ran for twenty years with the wrong boiler. Finally, the National Rail Museum have taken on the task of restoring this masterpiece, and a lot of thanks they get for it.' He invited me to consult the *Guinness Book of Records* for a list of her achievements. 'First officially recorded "ton" [100 mph] by a steam loco ... longest non-stop run, and plenty more. The engine is totally unique and beautiful. You do not have to be an anorak to see this.'

But to go back to the train ...

Newer and still more luxurious stock was introduced in 1938, including a 'buffet lounge'. The train was one of the few named expresses to retain its name throughout the war, albeit with no headboard and the engine – sometimes pulling twenty-three coaches in those fraught days – painted black. In 1948 the last non-stop run was made, and a new set of carriages was introduced. The Gresley exteriors of polished teak gave way to the experimental BR colours of carmine and cream, or 'blood and custard', and this set boasted a buffet with a twenty-two-foot bar. (There were still restaurant cars on the train, but note the waxing of buffets as the taste for formal dining declined.)

The first diesel pulled the *Flying Scotsman* in 1958. In 1962 the train began to be hauled by the diesel-electric Deltic locos, which looked to be full of machismo, had a good name (like 'Daleks'), and took the journey time down to five hours twenty minutes. But these engines that generated their own electricity were only required because the government would not pay to electrify the East Coast route, whereas the West Coast line was being electrified (London to Glasgow) from 1959 to 1974. And the Deltics were not popular with those trainspotters who'd grown up on steam: the slogan 'Sod the Deltics' began to be daubed on tunnel mouths along the line.

By 1982 the train was an HST (still a make-do diesel, in other words, albeit one capable of 125 m.p.h. and more, were it not for speed restrictions). But in the summer of that year the *Scotsman* came adrift of its 10 a.m. moorings, and that departure time from both King's Cross and Edinburgh was given to a train called the *Aberdonian*, which fizzled out in 1994.

The belated electrification of the East Coast line from London to Edinburgh was completed by 1990, and electrical Intercity 225 trains, with Class 91 power cars can run over that stretch with carriages classified as Mark 4. Any East Coast main-line service extending beyond Edinburgh must use the diesel HSTs.

On privatisation, the route was operated by Great North Eastern Railway, the only privatised train operator to have excited rail enthusiasts. It was owned by a shipping firm, Sea Containers, which had been founded by an American graduate of Yale and former Naval Officer called Jim Sherwood, a railway romantic who also founded Venice Simplon Orient Express to run luxury trains in Europe, often featuring restored Pullman carriages. His trains on the ECML had warm-hued interiors and liveries created by design professionals, as opposed to the man with a paint pot who seems to have been kept so busy during privatisation. GNER was the last operator of restaurant cars on the route. Its carriages were emblazoned with the words 'The Route of the Flying Scotsman', and the 10 a.m. services once again operated under that name. But GNER ran into financial trouble, leading to the suspicion among rail fans that the East Coast franchise was skewed against any operator supplying anything more than the most utilitarian service. Then again, the next operator, the much more prosaic National Express East Coast – which dropped the *Flying Scotsman* service – was also forced to relinquish the franchise in 2009, whereon the government stepped in, operating the line under the brand name of East Coast, and establishing a precedent that opponents of privatisation hoped would be followed elsewhere. Why not 'de-privatise' by letting all the privatised franchises fall back into the government basket at the end of their terms? But the East Coast franchise will soon be in private hands once again.

East Coast revived the *Flying Scotsman* as a named service. At the time of writing, it runs on weekday mornings at 5.40 a.m. from Edinburgh to London, stopping only once on the way, at Newcastle. There is no balancing service in the opposite direction.

THE CROSS

The one-directional nature of the modern-day *Scotsman* raises north–south issues. The implication is that the significant journey is from north to south, which is the very thing that worries opponents of High Speed 2: that the line will increase the magnetic power of London. One opponent of HS2 said he didn't think many people would be getting on the train to see a Gilbert & Sullivan at the Birmingham Hippodrome, whereas northerners certainly would use it to spend more time, and therefore money, in the ever more dominant capital. A friend of mine who lives near Sunderland says rather bitterly that 'It's a longer journey from London to the north than it is from the north to London.' He means a bigger cultural leap, London being so much the centre of gravity of the nation.

In the heyday of the *Scotsman* the nation was more balanced, and this was reflected in the set-up at King's Cross. Yes, the station was in London, but it served the Great Northern Railway – the middle word being the important one – and had been very beautifully built, by William and Joseph Cubitt, who were from Norfolk but applied to the building a severity and plainness that seem northern. Mr Gradgrind, if he'd had an aesthetic bone in his body, might have come up with this station, whereby the two simple, arched engine sheds are unambiguously indicated by the two giant, semicircular windows of a façade unadorned except by a smallish Italianate clock – and a clock is hardly a luxury when it is attached to a railway station. A chippy northerner might complain that what seems at a casual glance like a four-faceted clock actually had no *north* face, but then the station itself is in the way, so no one would be able to read the time from that direction, and the clock hasn't done anything as southern and frivolous as chime since 1927.

The façade proclaimed 'Great Northern Railway', and then 'London & North Eastern', in which the name of the capital is outweighed by the other two elements. The conductors of buses approaching the station used to call out 'King's Cross for Scotland'. Northern-ness was perpetuated in that the road east of the station was called York Way, and there was a secondary station on that side called York Road, where 'up' or southbound suburban trains would call before delving into a smoky tunnel that took them towards an amplification of the underground Metropolitan Line, and so into the City of London, or even to the south of England. (Trains emerged from these Widened Lines on the other side of the main station by means of a tunnel coming from under the Great Northern Hotel and called Hotel Curve. The tunnel mouth was so smoky that a man with a lantern had to be in permanent attendance. I mention all this mainly in order to savour the terms 'Widened Lines' and 'Hotel Curve'.)

When I was catching trains from the Cross to York in the 1980s and early '90s, I would have a pre-train pint in a pub called the Duke of York on York Way. That was in the days before the Cross went all ciabatta-with-pesto-drizzled-over, and the pub had a black-and-white TV as late as about 1994, and whenever you lifted up your pint, the beer mat came with it. On the bar was a solitary pickled egg floating like a medical specimen in a jar of brown brine.

The bar existing at about the same time on the far west platform also had a northern name, in that it was called The Ridings. The west was traditionally the departure side of the station, and that was where the action was in the heyday of the *Scotsman*: a throng of parcel offices, booking offices, newspaper kiosks ('Take the *Yorkshire Post* With You', the poster used to urge), bathing and dressing rooms, refreshment and waiting rooms – one perplexingly billed as 'Ladies and General Waiting Room', in which any male loiterer might reply when challenged, 'I'm just generally waiting.' All this bustle suggested that the journey from south to *north* was the important one, and the Cross was famous for its departures rather than arrivals, whether it be the 10 a.m. *Flying*

Scotsman, the 10.15 Leeds Express, the Coronation at 4 p.m. or the Silver Jubilee at 5.30. And you could buy a booklet on the *Scotsman* called *On Either Side: Features of Interest To Be Seen from the Train: King's Cross to Scotland.* The underlining is mine.

King's Cross reflected a national balance in that, while it was famous for sending people to the north, it was equally famous for receiving goods *from* the north. The goods yard and goods station were located north of the first tunnel out King's Cross – Gasworks Tunnel, which carries the lines under the Regent's Canal – and south of the second, Copenhagen Tunnel, which carries the line under a lot of houses, including (in the eighteenth century) that of the Danish ambassador. (The two tunnels inhibited train movements but came into their own during the war, when they were used to shelter trains and engines from bombs.)

Grain, vegetables, potatoes and fish were among the principal cargoes brought to the Goods Yard, coal especially. In *King's Cross Station through Time*, John Christopher writes: 'It is said that each major station had its own distinctive smell, and for King's Cross that was the smell of coal.' Before the building of the station, coal had been brought to London by colliers sailing down the North Sea, then along the Thames. Some of the coal arriving at King's Cross – both before and after the building of the station – was used by the Gas Light & Coke Company to make coal gas, and that company was responsible for the gasometers at the Cross, one of which has been preserved as a monument. Gas production at King's Cross – which ceased in 1904 – is also commemorated in the name of that first tunnel. According to John Betjeman, in his book *London's Railway Stations*, the coal smell at King's Cross was particularly strong when the north wind was blowing, funnelling the fumes through the bores of Gasworks Tunnel. On 11 May 1902 these fumes, laden with coal dust, caused a fire on the forecourt of the station, which can be seen as significant in north–south terms ...

The forecourt of the station was for a long time a cluttered disgrace, ruining the elegance of the façade. In 1906 the Great Northern, Piccadilly & Brompton Railway (the Piccadilly Line of the Underground) built a dirty great oxblood-tiled tube station building on the forecourt. This was surrounded by a left luggage office, a cab shelter and an 'emigrants' transit shed'. A few years previously, a vendor of garden furniture, for use in the expanding north London suburbs, created a sort of garden centre in front of the station. The fire of 1902 burned this down, which – if we factor in that coal dust – might seem like the industrial north taking revenge on the burgeoning capital. But the promotion of suburban living in front of King's Cross, whose suburban station (an annexe west of the main one) was erected in 1875, continued, and in 1934 the building firm of Laing's erected a show house of the kind awaiting those moving to Hornsey, Barnet, Hadley Wood or similar. There was a dreamlike incongruity about this lone 1930s' villa in the early Victorian townscape.

The film The Ladykillers (1955) shows coal trains from the north flowing into King's Cross beneath the back yard of Mrs Wilberforce's house – which is propped on the top of Copenhagen Tunnel – like a continuous black river. Actually the house shifts around. When we see Mrs Wilberforce's point of view as she answers her front door, we are confronted by the Midland Grand Hotel, suggesting that the old dear is gravitating towards Bloomsbury. Within twenty years coal stopped coming into King's Cross, as domestic use of coal declined, and London began to be powered by a smaller number of power stations, fuelled by oil.

On a guided tour of the refurbished King's Cross, I was told there are very few people left alive who understand how the 'coal drops' of the Cross worked. In the redevelopment of what is called King's Cross Central, the coal drops are to become 'boutique retail'. The towering granary close by now houses the University of the Arts London, incorporating St Martin's School of Art. The superbly named Coal and Fish Offices, which were gutted by fire in the early '80s – and for years looked like the clichéd idea of a haunted house, presiding fittingly over what seemed to be a blackened graveyard – will now accommodate a restaurant and 'studio space'. The former goods yard will also house the European headquarters of Google, and it has been granted that touch of the fairy's wand that all ambitious redevelopments seek: Waitrose is coming.

The main feature of the redevelopment of the station itself is the new Western Concourse, whose roof is like a giant white mushroom, or half a mushroom. There is now a piazza at the front of the station, and the 'temporary' (for forty years) canopy has finally been removed and replaced by something more discreet that does not interfere with the elegance of the station front. The roof glass of the train shed itself has been replaced so that you can see the clock tower from down on the platforms. There is a new footbridge, and the whole train shed has been swept clean of grime ... but also of passengers, facilities, colour and atmosphere. In place of the apple-green engines and teak carriages of the LNER are the grey trains of East Coast. You now await your train while staring up at the departure board in the Western Concourse, as opposed to while drinking a pint in The Ridings and watching the racing on TV. You are surrounded by all the shops you can see on your high street. The train shed itself is protected by barriers. In fact, King's Cross is the most ferociously barricaded station in Britain, but I get the feeling that barriers are a fad whose time has passed. You can get through them by inserting a ticket for a nearby station, and then travel to a far one. In the case of the Cross, for instance, you could get through the barrier with a ticket for Stevenage, then go to Aberdeen, although you might have to contend with a ticket collector on the train.

On the once bustling departure platform there is now a bleak window for excess fares and not much else. You can see people eating in a Leon café, but that must be accessed from the Western concourse. The actual station is a place where you spend thirty seconds walking to or from your train. The *concourse* is where you are supposed to hang out. Imagine the owner of a beautiful mansion ... who spent all her time in the conservatory.

The best thing about the refurbished station is a pub called The Parcel Yard. It is accessed by stairs from the Western Concourse and overlooks both the main and suburban stations. It has been created out of the old parcels office and has the authentic feel of backstage BR or LNER. Everything is gratifyingly solid, big and underlit. There is what Martin Amis has called, in reference to railways, 'toilet glass', meaning frosted glass with wire mesh in it, intended to screen one level of officialdom from another, or from the public. The institutional feel is relieved by some pretty railway art, and colourful enamel signs, and the beer is well kept. I also like the ticket hall in the new concourse, partly because it too is not new. It is a former 'plant room', with a double- height ceiling, and an echo that I associate with old-fashioned railway rooms.

THE 5.40

I have begun with King's Cross because nothing will dislodge my idea of it as the starting place for the *Flying Scotsman*. But the modern-day, extant *Scotsman*, as opposed to the one of my dreams, starts at Edinburgh Waverley, a distinguished station in its own right, and the largest in physical area outside London. (The biggest in Britain, and the busiest, is Waterloo.)

Waverley was built in 1867 by the North British Railway. In 1902 the company added a grand hotel and called it after their railway. The hotel no longer has an entrance on the station and is now called the Balmoral, in spite of being nowhere near Balmoral, but it is still proud of its railway associations. Most people who travel by means other than car between London and Scotland do so by plane, but most guests at the Balmoral have arrived by train. Older guests still refer to the hotel by its railway name, the North British, and the hotel still keeps its clock tower clock three minutes fast 'so the people of Edinburgh will not be late for their trains'.

The rooms overlooking the station are often specially requested, and I checked into one of these myself. The station is where you would expect a river to be: that is, in the deep groove running through the middle of the city between the New Town and the Old. In fact, the groove was made by a glacier, and once accommodated the Nor Loch. The station – the subject most commonly depicted on LNER postcards – is oddly arranged. You could say it was – for the most part – one giant platform intercut by bays. It is roofed over by numerous glass apexes, and from my hotel window I seemed to be looking down on a sprawling collection of greenhouses – a garden centre, in fact. Blurred people, taxis and trains came and went beneath the glass, as though under water. Waverley is famous as the terminus of the East Coast Main Line, but it has always been served by connections to the West Coast Main Line. It is also, of course, an access point for 'further north', and cute little *Flying Scotsmen*, pulled by smaller engines, with smaller headboards on the front, would take portions of the train on to Aberdeen, Perth, Glasgow. Anybody not taking one of these, but disembarking from the *Scotsman* at Waverley, would – in the Golden Age – be arriving in time for a cocktail. The enjoyments of the train could be exchanged for the enjoyments of the town.

In my own case, in December 2013, it was more a case of hurrying to get out of the cold while feeling slightly hung over. When I descended the steps from hotel to train at 5.30, on a dark and freezing morning (recollecting that Waverley means 'windy corner'), I cursed the aeroplanes that have not only blighted Britain with their noise and pollution but also dictated the early start of the modern *Scotsman*. The train competes with the southbound planes in allowing a full working day in London. Actually, the train offers more than a full working day, in that you can work on board for four hours. Everyone in the first-class carriage I boarded was already emailing or texting. Most had the technological 'full house': laptop, tablet and smartphone. The ability of executives to work on a train has complicated the pitch for High Speed 2. The net effect of shaving fifteen minutes off the time between Birmingham and London might be to reduce rather than increase the productivity of passengers.

The inter-war *Flying Scotsman* was not a working train. It was a good way of wasting a day, with the aid of a long lunch, a cocktail and afternoon tea. But the idea of working on trains is not new. Anthony Trollope made himself 'a little tablet or writing slope', and found 'after a few days' practice that I could write as quickly in a railway carriage as I could at my desk'.

I learn from that historical goldmine the railway website called Turnip Rail that in 1910 the Birmingham–London 'City-to-City' express of the London & North Western

Railway offered an on-board typing service, in the shape of a Miss Tarrant, deputed from the Euston typing room. Miss Tarrant, who sat at a desk in a customised compartment, said of her first day on the job, 'I was kept busy all the way up. Twelve passengers dictated letters to me and only once, when we were passing through the Kilsby Tunnel, was the dictation interrupted.' The first letter, addressed to some office or other in London, seems to have been written by an official of the railway ...

> Dear Sirs,
> I am taking the liberty of forwarding to you this letter. It
> is the first typed on any railway train in the United
> Kingdom. This has been made possible by the energy,
> perseverance and up-to-date methods of the London &
> North Western Railway Company.

The letter, signed by a W. H. Davis, was headed 'Shorthand and typing room, London & NW City to City Express'. The scheme did not prosper, though. Unlike the mobile phone shouters of today, likely customers worried about lack of confidentiality.

Our *Flying Scotsman* was an electrical train: Class 91 power car and Mark 4 carriages. These were built on the assumption they would be running in tilting trains, which never came to pass. In order to tilt, they narrow towards the top. They are therefore more claustrophobic than the Mark 3s, but they rattle less. The seating was 2+2 on one side of the gangway, 1+1 on the other. I took my seat at a 1+1. I'd been at a 1+1 on the way to Edinburgh. That had been a Mark 3 carriage, and the small table had vibrated so violently whenever we were passed by another fast train that I had to keep my coffee cup on the floor. But then I had been sitting on the right in relation to the direction of travel: in other words, next to passing trains, since British trains go on the left, like our cars. I assumed – as it would turn out correctly – that my little table would not shake so badly on the way to London, what with the greater solidity of the Mark 4s and no trains running directly alongside me.

Whereas there had been one typist on that Birmingham-to-London train, our carriage was full of them and none looked up when the guard muttered, 'This is the 5.40 East Coast service to London King's Cross, calling at Newcastle and London King's Cross only.' No mention of the *Flying Scotsman*, although the name did appear on the window labels.

As we pulled away from the station into the darkness of what might as well have been midnight, I realised that the most scenic part of the East Coast route would be hidden from us. After the Calton South Tunnel, we began a drift coastwards, towards Prestonpans, from where, in daylight, I would have been able to see the hills of Fife across the Firth of Forth. There was no point looking out of the window. It was too early in the morning, I thought, to do *anything*. I do not have a smartphone or a tablet, and my laptop isn't very portable. I was too ashamed of my £10 mobile to take it out and play with it, and I was too tired to read, even though *The Times* was available free. If I'd been on the Golden Age *Scotsman* after dark (as would have been the case towards the end of the trip in midwinter), I might have been staring at the pictures in the carriage panels: a photograph of the front at Cleethorpes; a print of ships in gathering darkness: *Night Parade – Harwich for the Continent*. Or perhaps *Dinner Dance at the Royal Hotel York*, or an advertisement for line-side factory sites: 'Contact the Industrial Agent, King's Cross.' The latter two would only ever have been in first-class.

At Dunbar I realised that the black void immediately to

my left was the sea. The train is close to the sea for most of the 60 miles between here and the pretty coastal village of Alnmouth, in Northumberland. On a sunny day the proximity is exhilarating, sea and train alike seeming to be elemental forces of nature.

A female attendant came up to take my breakfast order. I opted for the Great British Breakfast. The attendant was charming, but I didn't care for the way she put a piece of A4 paper in front of me as a preliminary to the service of breakfast. This is a symbolic stand-in for a tablecloth, and I kept thinking of Golden Age *Scotsman* table linen, and the flowers on the table, the napkin furled inside a large wine glass. But my breakfast *was* served on a real plate with real cutlery. It was basically a bijou full-English with genteel touches such as sautée potatoes and cheese omelette, but it was too early for proper hunger, and the man opposite, evidently a regular on the train, declined the breakfast.

I did not want to interrupt this chap, who seemed, from the anxiety on his face, to be getting a lot of bad news via his tablet. I assumed he was engaged in some fraught early-morning negotiation by email. Perhaps the whole future of his business was at stake, but when, on getting up to go to the loo, I saw that he was playing a game in which you were supposed to balance one rock on top of another, I decided he could be interrupted. I asked why he didn't have breakfast, and he said, 'Oh, I always have the second serving, after Newcastle.' As we surveyed the bleary typists, I suggested that this was not a fun train. He agreed. Every other Tuesday (and this was a Tuesday) he travelled up to London on business; he returned on a Thursday evening train. 'Everyone has a drink on the Thursday train,' he said. 'For a while we had this thing called the Thursday Club.' I asked him if he always travelled up on the *Flying Scotsman*. 'Eh?' he said. It turned out that, yes, he always travelled on the *Scotsman*, but that he didn't know it *was* the *Scotsman*.

He went back to his game, and I squinted into the darkness to try to make out the decorative trackside sign that, 3 miles north of Berwick, pinpoints the Scottish border. I could not do so, but most people take the border to be at Berwick, where stands the Royal Border Bridge, a half-mile viaduct spanning the River Tweed, built by Robert Stephenson in 1847. It allows the passenger to examine the town – which it skirts on three sides – from a haughty perspective. In the darkness of the morning Berwick seemed all latent potential, like a town on the first page of storybook.

There were the first glimmerings of sunlight, and the Tweed had a slight luminosity redolent of the way it is shown in an LNER poster of the late '30s, showing the *Coronation* speeding over the Bridge at dusk. A group of people on the high riverbank look on with religious awe.

Soon after the commencement of the *Scotsman*'s non-stop runs, the LNER arranged a publicity stunt with Imperial Airways, whereby the well-known flier Captain Gordon Olley would take a party of journalists north in a plane scheduled to rendezvous with the train over the Royal Border Bridge. Radio messages would be exchanged. The journalists would then await the *Scotsman* at Waverley. Captain Olley was so confident of reaching the Bridge before the train that he behaved like the hare in *The Tortoise and the Hare*, flying over scenic parts of Britain on the way north and generally showing off. The train he actually met over the Royal Border bridge was the *Junior Scotsman*, which left King's Cross shortly after its more famous sibling. Olley then hurried on to Edinburgh, but the *Flying Scotsman* had got there first.

At Beal we passed Holy Island, whose mystical import seemed all the greater for being in silhouette. The Farne

Islands lay somewhere beyond. Ten miles later we passed
Lucker, a place of no significance to the modern train, but
Lucker was the site of one of the half-dozen water troughs
from which water would be scooped into the tender of whatever steam engine was doing the run. Water troughs were
indicated by trackside signs showing wavy lines.

The troughs at Lucker were 2,000 feet long and six inches
deep. The loco, going at 60 m.p.h., would lower its scoop for
a minute in order to pick up 2,000 gallons. If you were in the
carriage closest to the engine, you would be well advised to
make sure the window was closed.

A dozen miles later we crossed the Alne at Alnmouth,
where a level crossing is controlled by an actual man in an
actual crossing box. This is called 'visual oversight'. The
only manned boxes on the ECML control crossings, and the
number is in low single figures. There are no manned signal
boxes as such, and we will say more about signalling in a
minute.

At two minutes past seven we pulled into Newcastle, a station almost as airily beautiful as York, and the first where
round-arched ribs were used, pre-dating Paddington and
York. Like York, it is on a curve. In fact, the station – famous
as a staging post for the far north – is on an east–west axis, so
that if you approach it on the main line from the north, you
are in fact approaching it from the east, and if you approach
it from the south, you are in fact doing so from the west.
This – the latter – is the best way, because you have the full
drama of the diamond junction that, immediately after the
station, offers routes north in the direction of the main line,
or south over the High-Level Bridge (Robert Stephenson
again, with roadway beneath) across the Tyne, which once
served the south-of-Newcastle portion of the main line. In
1906 that role was taken over by the King Edward VII Bridge,

built 500 yards to the west. This allows main-line trains to flow through Newcastle without having to reverse, as used to be the case. Perhaps the simplest thing to say is: look at a map. It's also worth tracking down images of the diamond junction, preferably old ones, since it was much simplified in the 1980s. In Edwardian times it featured on many post-cards, captioned 'Biggest railway crossing in the world'. These show about eight lines going one way; another eight going the other way; but before the divergence they are all on top of each other. The lines diverged – and still diverge – either side of the keep of the New Castle, built by Henry II. In those Edwardian days the keep resembled a medieval Canute desperately trying to hold back the railway. It looks surer of itself now that there are fewer lines.

There was now enough light in the day to enjoy the crossing of the Tyne, which always looks to have hosted a bridge-building completion. In his description of the East Coast Main Line for his series of pamphlets called *Mile by Mile on Britain's Railways*, the enigmatic railway writer S. N. Pike refers to the area 30 miles north and south of Newcastle as follows: 'We are now approaching a highly industrial part of the country, and in the next few miles many single line railways will be seen branching away to right and left to serve the collieries, steel works and other heavy industries hereabout.'

He describes the scenery around Durham as 'a mixture of natural beauty and colliery rubbish heaps', and the railway companies couldn't seem to decide whether this landscape was beautiful or not. In 1924 the LMS produced a poster called *Coal* in their 'British Industries' series. It shows men leaving a colliery on the LMS side of the country and is at once melancholic and celebratory, the men looking sombre yet noble, like the landscape in which the colliery is set. In

1932 the LNER produced an equally un-ingratiating poster
showing a collier on the Tyne belching out black smoke.
'The Tyne,' ran the text, 'LNER docks are the largest for coal
exporting in the world.'

When the Deltics were thundering up and down the East
Coast Main Line in the early '60s, there were still about 1,300
deep-level coal mines in Britain. When the HSTs had got into
their stride in the early '80s, there were about 200. At the
time of writing there are three, two of them scheduled for
closure. Some coal is still moved up and down the line, but,
as mentioned, none of it goes to London, and most of it is
imported via the Tyne, typically travelling south to the power
stations of the Aire or Trent valleys in long containers,
usually bearing the logos of the haulage firms, such as DB
Schenker, Freightliner or Railfreight. They are open-topped,
but so designed that in order to see the coal inside you have
to be on a footbridge, directly above them. The lettering on
the side does not proclaim 'coal'. Until the '70s coal wagons were very obviously coal wagons – open-topped wooden
boxes with coal sticking out – and there were 600,000 of
them in Britain. They were the staple units of the British
economy, and whereas the modern coal wagons move en
masse in 'block loads', any one of the old coal wagons might
be part of, say, three successive trains in a journey across the
country, these trains being formed and broken up in smoky
marshalling yards such as no longer exist. Models of the
wagons were subjected to a similar rough-and-tumble on a
smaller scale, in that they were like the pawns of any boy's
model railway set, to be used as bargaining chips, derailed
for fun, pitched carelessly into the toy box when it was time
to pack up.

The day was fully illuminated as our version of the *Flying Scotsman* crossed the ten-arch railway viaduct that gives

the celebrated view of eleventh-century Durham Castle and twelfth-century Durham Cathedral on what is nearly an island created by a loop of the River Wear. A speed restriction applies on the viaduct. This is not so the view can be savoured, but it might as well be. My Plus One had finished his breakfast, and his knife and fork began to rattle on his plate as we came off the viaduct. The knives on the *Silver Jubilee* had flat handles so they wouldn't rattle.

A further word, incidentally, about S. N. Pike, whose interest in trains is somehow evident from his name alone. In 1947 he self-published pamphlets describing the main lines of three of the four main-line companies. He did not cover the Great Western. Nobody knows why not, or why he wrote the three he did or, as far as I can tell, what 'S. N.' stands for. Perhaps he wanted to chronicle the railways on the eve of their nationalisation, or the last days of Britain as 'workshop of the world'. His pamphlets, recently republished in book form, read as tear-jerkers. Whenever he writes the word 'factories' by the side of one of his line diagrams ... there are no factories today. It's possible he made his observations before the war. He certainly has that 1930s' obsession with speed, and every couple of pages the formula for calculating the speed of the engine by timing the passage between trackside mileposts is repeated, giving the reader no excuse for ignoring it:

> The exact speed of the train may be calculated over any distance from ¼ mile upwards by this simple formula. Convert the distance selected into ¼ mile units (3 miles would be 12 units). Then multiply the number of units by 900 and divide the result by the number of seconds it has taken to cover the distance. The answer will be mph.

The mile posts are still there, coloured bright yellow, for anyone who wants to try.

Just like the inter-war *Scotsman*, we bypassed Darlington on
its avoiding loop, thus depriving passengers of the chance to
see *Locomotion Number One* – the engine built for the Stockton
& Darlington Railway – which was displayed at Darlington
station between 1892 and 1975. The Stockton & Darlington
was the first public steam railway. It was opened it 1825, engineered by George Stephenson, and it was all about coal, which
it brought from collieries around Stockton inland to Darlington. The Stockton & Darlington, which was soon extended to
Middlesbrough for the purposes of coal exporting, bequeathed
200 miles of railway to the North Eastern Railway.

Before being put in Darlington station, *Locomotion Number One* had been displayed – from 1857 – at the Stockton &
Darlington Railway Workshops at Hopetown, outside Darlington, and so began railway preservation, barely a quarter
of a century after the start of railways. The engine is now
in the Darlington Railway Centre and Museum, located in
the old Darlington North Road station. It was not, by the
way, originally called *Locomotion Number One*, just as the First
World War was not called the First World War at the time.
The engine was christened *Active*.

Today the only intermediate stations between Darlington and York are at Northallerton and Thirsk. The Darlington–York stretch, being through flat fields – so flat that I
could see the North York Moors to the left, the Pennines to
the right – was always a 'racing ground' of the London &
North Eastern, and today rail fans go to Northallerton for the
pleasure of seeing it ignored by 125 m.p.h. expresses. It was
between Northallerton and Thirsk that a prototype of the
HST did 148 m.p.h. In the days of the *Scotsman* there were ten
other stations on the Darlington–York stretch, most leading

somewhere pretty, not that the *Scotsman* itself ever paid them the slightest attention. About 8 miles north of York, around Tollerton (which had a railway halt until the 1960s), the fresh footplate crew would have laid down their newspapers, put out their pipes and walked through the little corridor in the tender to relieve the first crew.

YORK

We ran through York, just as the non-stopping steam-age *Scotsman* would have done. As a native of the city I was affronted, but it was only by the arm-twisting of the disreputable George Hudson that the main line came to York in the first place.

Nobody looked out of the window, but even today York is served by half a dozen operators. In steam days York was a paradise for the railwayac. Many companies had a connection from their own territories, and York would accommodate their locomotives in the various sheds of the railway lands, always providing they stumped up the cost of bed and board for a locomotive, plus breakfast of coal and water. In his book *Rail Centres: York* (1983) Ken Hoole writes that in early twentieth century 'the usual charge' for stabling was £25, about £2,500 in today's money. You'd think that a man whose first name appears on the book jacket as 'Ken.' would be a stickler for particularity, but he doesn't say whether this £25 was per night, week, month, year or for ever. The companies thus accommodated included the London & North Western Railway, the Great Northern, Great Eastern, Great Central, Midland and the Lancashire & Yorkshire.

I wrote about York, and the decline of its railway hinterland, in the introduction. The discrepancy between the Golden Age and now might be summed up by saying that the chief railway features of the city have been swept up and put in the National Railway Museum, which opened in 1975. There had been a smaller railway museum on the railway lands since 1927. It was in a brick shed that could accommodate two old engines, but they were so close to the wall that as you climbed up or down from the footplates, you'd brush your anorak against the sooty brick. If I told my mother I was going there, she'd tell me to put old clothes on. The man in charge was not a qualified curator, to put it mildly. I was recently at a function at the NRM with my dad, who said, within earshot of the top brass, 'In my day the whole collection was looked after perfectly well by a Grade Four clerk.' (Grade Four wasn't very senior.)

On departure from York, we passed, on the left, a concrete rectangle with the letters Y-O-R-K cut out and filled with soil, awaiting spring and a floral spelling of the word. During LNER days, the staff at Inverbervie station in the northeast of Scotland moved three tons of white stones from the nearby beach to create the LNER logo. Presumably those three tons had to be returned to the beach during the war, when all such displays had to be dismantled.

As we left York behind, I was mindful of the words of Pike, '....we see the enormous signal box which controls the loco yard to the south of the station.' In his day there were various signal boxes in the vicinity of York, including the station signal box on the main 'up' platform, which is now a Costa Coffee. There were a couple of hundred signal boxes along the ECML. They were physically connected by cables – and not electrical cables – to the semaphore signals they controlled, and the trains were passed between the track sections overseen by each one, the signalmen genteelly offering and accepting the trains, like men passing the port, except that they communicated by bell codes.

In the '30's, semaphore signals began to be replaced electrical, coloured light signals. As on the roads, there are red,
amber and green lights, but these lights can be seen from a
mile away, and any red signal is long preceded by two sets
of amber warning signals. If any train passes a red signal,
it ought, eventually, to be stopped by one refinement or
another of the system of Automatic Train Control that had
been introduced by the Great Western in 1906.

The number of signal boxes has gradually been whittled
down, first, by the introduction of electrical 'power boxes'
in the 1930s. In the '80s came Integrated Electrical Control
Centres. They are deliberately self-effacing, in the hope that
terrorists won't notice them, or perhaps will be repelled by
the architecture. At the time of writing, the ECML is controlled by a dozen of these. The one at King's Cross is a
dreary grey box on the right-hand side as you head north.
The York one is a grim prefab behind barbed wire.

Today we have the prospect of all signalling in Britain
being controlled by a dozen Rail Operating Centres, known
as ROCs. These will communicate directly with the train
cabs; all line-side signalling will disappear, and trains will
be more efficiently managed, and so allowed to run closer
together. This must be the way. The express train drivers of
the future will be going too fast to read the signals. They were
almost going too fast in the heyday of the *Scotsman*. In 1932,
when the typographer Eric Gill was given his free ride, he
returned to London on the footplate of a night express. All he
could see along the line were the coloured lights revealed by
raised or lowered signal arms. He was amazed by the degree
of trust the driver put in the signals. 'If it seemed a foolhardy
proceeding to rush headlong into tunnels in the day time,
how much more foolhardy did it seem at night to career
along at 80 miles an hour in a black world with nothing to

help you but your memory of the road and a lot of flickering lights – lights often almost obliterated by smoke and rain.'

The East Coast main line will be controlled by one ROC – 'The Rock', as it is proudly called – being built at York. It is to the right as you leave the station towards London: a red brick building with the smug air of a sixth-form college, and surrounded by high-security fencing.

The Victorian signal boxes along the line have been demolished or sold off. Would any apparent signal box have a caravan outside if it were still owned by the railway? Would it be painted pink, like a former box south of Doncaster? The only manned boxes remaining control level crossings, as mentioned, and these are modern buildings. In short, the romantic appeal of the lonely signalman, in his lighthouse-on-the-land, with his crackling fire (fuelled by lumps of coal tossed out by well-disposed passing firemen), his bicycle propped against the box, the musicality of the tinkling bells, the wooden cross in the garden indicating the grave of his dog ... All that has gone, to be replaced by something tech-nologically impressive but ugly and incomprehensible to the lay observer. The net gain is the impossibility – we are told – of accidents.

YORK TO LONDON

After York, at Chaloners Whin Junction, the line used to bear left towards Selby, but in 1984 the line was diverted in a more southerly direction to avoid running over the mines of the newly exploited Selby coalfield – newly, and not long, exploited since it closed in 2004. If the line had continued on its old routes, trains would have been subjected to intervals of slow running, called – superbly, I think – 'pitfall slacks'. That old route (now a cycle track) would have been more interesting for close students of Andrew Martin, of whom, I suspect, I am the only one. It would have taken us past Ashfield Secondary Modern, my alma mater, to the right of the rangy, riverside village of Bishopthorpe, where my grandfather, and his grandfather was born, and where Jim Stringer, the main character of my series of novels featuring a railway detective, lives. The line crossed the River Ouse in the highly rural location of Naburn village. (The bridge survives, far too massive for its present-day job of carrying dog-walkers and cyclists over the increasingly green-shaded river.) After 10 miles through fields the old line crossed the River Aire in the middle of Selby, by means of a Heath Robinson-ish swing bridge, the procedure overlooked with disapproval by Selby Abbey.

Soon before or after York the steward, in black jacket with gold piping, would have walked along the corridors of the *Scotsman* announcing lunch. At 9 a.m. on the modern-day train, with breakfast recently digested, it was difficult to identify with the Golden Age railway gourmand.

He or she would have been rising and walking towards a four-course meal, at least, and alcohol would have been involved. An aperitif would have been pressed on them, whereas anyone who ordered wine on the present-day *Scotsman* would have been put down as an alcoholic. We can assume that a certain LNER poster of 1933 by Austin Cooper was aimed as much at partakers of luncheon as of dinner: it showed a waiter made of simple geometric shapes, and if that implied modernity, the message was distinctly Edwardian: 'In mixing cocktails and serving crusted port – regard for our passenger's eupeptic welfare – there are qualities that distinguish the LNER waiter.' The only actual *Flying Scotsman* menu I have been able to discover dates from 1962, when things may have been more restrained, and a Deltic may have been pulling the train. The starters were tomato juice or oxtail soup. Then came the fish course (whiting), followed by roast chicken with bread sauce, boiled and roast potatoes, peas and carrots vichy (that is, in butter and molasses). The sweet was fruit flan; then cheese and biscuits. The cost – excluding wine, but everyone would have had wine – was 13s. 6d. (about £17 today), or a shilling less if you declined cheese and biscuits and coffee.

Even if you weren't hungry, you'd eat – 'to pass the time', as Louis MacNeice writes in his neurotic poem of 1955, 'Restaurant Car':

> The water in the carafe
> Shakes its hips, both glass and soup-plate spill ...
> The waiters totter on the invisible tightrope ...

You'd finish a southbound *Flying Scotsman* lunch some time after Peterborough, by which time teas would be being served around you, and you'd probably go back to your compartment and, as MacNeice suggests, go to sleep.

In the brilliant and brutal crime film of 1971, *Get Carter*, Michael Caine plays Jack Carter, a Newcastle-born gangster resident in London, who heads north to learn the truth about the suspicious death of his brother. The opening credits suggest he travels on the *Scotsman* itself, hauled by a Deltic. He is shown reading a book (*Farewell My Lovely*) in a first-class Mark 2 compartment. He then eats lunch, beginning with soup, moving the spoon away from himself in the approved manner. He is then seen reading his book again, all remarkably genteel considering he will soon be throwing people off the multi-storey car park in Gateshead.

We came to Doncaster, a big junction, and the place where the mighty engines of the main line were built, including the

Flying Scotsman and the Gresley A4s. Nothing is built at the
modern, depleted works – which were always known as 'the
plant' – but repairs are carried on. At the time of writing the
red-brick former offices of the works (on the right-hand side
from London-bound trains) are emblazoned with a banner
reading 'To Let'. But there is still a big freight terminal at
Doncaster, even if part of its purpose is to transfer freight
from rail to road.

The executive sitting on the opposite side of the aisle was
embarking on what threatened to be a long phone call. What
I want to hear when people start a phone call on a train is
'I'm going to have to be quick because I'm on a train.' But
this caller said, 'OK, chaps can you all hear me? I'm on a
train, so if I cut out it'll be because I'm in a tunnel, but I'll
call you straight back.'

He was going to be making a conference call, and I was to
be included, albeit against my will, and with a non-speaking
role. 'Now the importance of this tool,' he began 'is three-
fold ...'. I had to get away from him. If I'd been on the Scotsman, I might have wondered whether there was enough
time before London for a haircut. No one ever stares at their
reflection in a carriage window without seeing something
that could be improved.

I walked the length of the train. There were ten carriages,
mostly quite full, so there were about seventy people per carriage. The Scotsman might have been a train of twelve carriages, but what with two restaurant cars, a buffet car, the
barber's, a retiring room, a brake carriage (part of any brake
car was given over to storage, and a large hand-brake to be
screwed down by the guard when the train came to a conclu-
sive stop), and what with compartment seating, as opposed
to open, there might only have been only 300 passengers
even on a fully loaded Scotsman.

In standard class, I could see remnants of the cooked breakfast. Standard-class passengers must collect it from the Foodbar, and theirs comes on a plastic plate with plastic cutlery. An on-line review of the *Flying Scotsman* standard-class breakfast features a photograph of the meal, the verdict 'freshly cooked and tasting great', but with the caveat 'Fork broke on ante-penultimate mouthful'. (The writer was an academic.)

Twenty miles after Doncaster comes Retford. There used to be a flat crossing here. That is to say: the line from Sheffield to Lincoln crossed the main line on the same level. It now goes underneath. At Newark North Gate, another 20 miles south, the *Nottingham* to Lincoln Line still does cross the main line on the same level, and there is no 'visual oversight', so we passengers have to trust the remote controllers of the junction, or hope the effects will be limited to the coffee trying to leap out of our cups. This is the only remaining flat crossing in England. There is another in Wales.

Three miles north of Grantham we went through the Peascliffe Tunnel, whose 967 yards put paid (temporarily) to my neighbour's conference call. Grantham is the junction for Nottingham. Crew and engine changes were sometimes made here, and there was a shed for big engines that drew trainspotters from miles around. Grantham wouldn't be Grantham were it not for the railways.

Four miles south of Grantham we entered Stoke Tunnel, which marks the beginning of the descent (from our direction) of Stoke Bank, where Mallard clocked up its record. You don't notice the descent today, and modern trains go up the Bank almost as fast as Mallard went down it. I once asked a venerable and patrician volunteer at the National Rail Museum why Stoke Bank was so called, because while it's on roughly the same latitude as Stoke-on-Trent, it's 70

12. The *Flying Scotsman* locomotive on the East Coast Main Line near Grantham in 1931. It is probably not hauling the *Flying Scotsman* train, since there is no headboard.

miles east. 'Young man,' he said (I was forty-seven at the time), 'there are at least a dozen Stokes in Britain. There is Stoke Poges, scene of Thomas Gray's poem, *Elegy in a Country Churchyard*. I myself went to school in Stockport, and what is that but Stoke Port?' He commanded his young assistant to look up the Stoke in question on the internet, and it transpired that Stoke Bank is named after the village of Stoke Rochford, which is 5 miles south of Grantham, and which in turn was named after a house that burned down in 2005. Another venerable volunteer was present as this was announced. He was a devotee of the LMS (most the older volunteers at the NRM have an allegiance to one or other of the Big Four), and he said, 'The mystery is not why it's called Stoke Bank, but why it's called Stoke *Bank*.' At a gradient of only 1 in 200, he didn't think it qualified as a bank, not compared to Shap Bank on 'his' railway.

We came to the major east–west and north–south junction of Peterborough, where *Rail* and *Steam Railway* magazines are based, and yet whose station resembles a horrible prefab, having been unlucky enough to have been re-designed in the '70s, 'the decade that taste forgot', as Martin Amis once wrote. Here is what S. N. Pike has to say about the environs of Peterborough: 'This is the greatest brick-producing district in the world, and for miles the vista is of tall chimneys, furnaces, little railways and their hundreds of tubs, and the enormous artificial lakes created where the raw material has been scraped from the ground.' Bricks from Peterborough were known as Fletton bricks, yet the old station at Peterborough and the Great Northern Hotel adjacent to it were built before the industry got going in Peterborough, so they are of London Stock Bricks, from London, Kent and Essex. King's Cross station is a masterpiece in London Stock. Whereas Fletton bricks came in a range of colours, often a

13. The *Flying Scotsman* train, as proclaimed by the headboard, designed by Eric Gill, for which he received a free footplate ride. The train is near Potters Bar in 1937. The engine is A4 class *Dominion of New Zealand*.

fairly depressing purple that I associate with northern council estates, London Stock bricks were yellow, which quickly
became black with soot – which helped preserve them. Britain still makes, as well as imports, bricks, and London stocks
are still produced in Kent. Rather fewer Fletton bricks are
made. The clay used has a high carbon content. This makes
it cheap to bake the bricks, but the process gives off emis-
sions that have made Flettons politically incorrect. When I
go past Peterborough on the train, I see lonely-looking men
fishing in ponds, but these are not usually brick ponds, most
of which were filled in during the '70s.

For the 40 miles of fenland south of Peterborough I am
always in a dream world, suspended between north and
south, unable to concentrate on the enormous, flat fields
beyond the window. John Betjeman believed that the train
made a different noise between Fletton and Holme (immediately south of Peterborough), the line having been laid – in
this waterlogged ground – on bundles of reeds and rushes.
I doubt I would have been able to tell, even if the conference
call had not been resumed.

As we approached Stevenage, the guard announced that,
owing to a signalling problem at Potters Bar, we would be
diverted onto the 'loop line', by which he meant 'the Hertford Loop' as many people in the carriage did seem to know,
because the news was quickly relayed like a multiple echo
into a dozen mobile phones. 'We're coming in via Hertford,
so my ETA's changed', etc. The Hertford Loop is the more
usual territory of the electrical multiple units of First Capital
Connect. As we went from Cuffley to Crews Hill, I reflected
that it was here – in the days before the M25 went overhead hereabouts – that Pauline Johnson walked along the
footboards of the Flying Scotsman in high heels at 40 m.p.h.
In that context 40 m.p.h. was fast. We were doing 40 on

our modern *Scotsman*, and in this context it was a very slow speed that was prompting further updating from the mobile phoners, all very confident that the people they would be meeting in London were anxious to see them as quickly as possible.

I thought about what we were missing by avoiding the main line: the two tunnels north of Welwyn Garden City; also the Digswell Viaduct, considered a bottleneck but beautiful in itself, and affording a good view of the Garden City.

We came off the Loop (the Loop having come to an end) at Alexandra Palace. Then came the Bounds Green depot, where the electric trains of the ECML are maintained. The diesels are maintained at Edinburgh. There's another 'train care depot', as railway works are now called, as though trains were remedial cases, at Hornsey, this one used by First Capital Connect. We passed Finsbury Park, where the Piccadilly Line of the Underground used to terminate. The Great Northern railway and its successor, the LNER – tenants of Finsbury Park – were determined the Piccadilly would never extend any further north, since they wanted all the suburban traffic for themselves. They lost that battle in the early '30s after Frank Pick, number two on the Underground, sent a man up to Finsbury Park to photograph the chaos as suburbanites who didn't happen to live near one of the existing railway stations fought to board trams.

We passed the old Arsenal football ground on the left, which was always my signal to put on my coat and brace myself for whatever was in store in London. It still is, even though it's now flats in the shape of a football stadium. Then comes its replacement, the Emirates Stadium, with its Stalinist social-realist images of giant footballers.

We went through Copenhagen Tunnel with its mournful black turrets, under Mrs Wilberforce's House so to

speak ... but it was only a mock-up. Before the redevelopment of King's Cross, a man kept two shire horses on the
waste ground above the tunnel, and he seemed to light a lot
of fires up there. The conference caller to my right, having
been broken off somewhere around Hitchin, had attempted
to re-start proceedings just as we entered the tunnel: 'Hello
guys, can you still hear me?' They evidently could not. But
the guard could make himself heard in the tunnel: 'We will
shortly be arriving at London King's Cross, where this train
terminates. Please remember to take ...'

Need I go on? On the old *Scotsman* passengers had to
remember to take all their personal belongings with them
without being told. We arrived at King's Cross at 10.05, twenty-
five minutes late. Even so, we, unlike the passengers on the
old *Scotsman*, were in time to do nearly a full day's work in the
capital. Which is a good thing, I suppose.

FIVE

THE
CALEDONIAN
SLEEPER

THE CALEDONIAN SLEEPER

THE DARK LINE

The East Coast Main Line looks pretty skimpy in comparison with the West Coast Main Line, which is not so much a line as a network connecting London to the north-west, the west Midlands, north Wales and Scotland. After the grouping it was served by the London, Midland & Scottish Railway, which was the largest private company in the world. The LMS comprised, among others, the Midland Railway and the London & North Western Railway, which had been the biggest private company in its own time. The West Coast Main Line of today is essentially the heir of the LNWR. The core of the line – the main line of the main line – is the route from Euston to Glasgow via Watford, Rugby, Crewe, Preston and Carlisle ... in which case, we have to think of the connections to Birmingham, Holyhead, Manchester and Liverpool as mere branches.

As the slogan of the LNWR had it, this is 'The Premier Line', serving a population of 25 million, but anyone seeking a detailed discussion of its routes will have to look elsewhere, and they won't find it in those books called things like *Britain's Most Beautiful Railway Journeys*. The line offers branches – if no longer through trains – to some pretty spots such as Southport, Morecambe and Windermere, and it traverses the moorland of Shap on the way to Carlisle, which is the great outdoors even if not so operatically magnificent as the approach over the Settle–Carlisle line.

But the WCML was a scruffy, industrial railway, a 400-mile tradesman's entrance, and it is less secure in its identity now that so many of the line-side factories have been replaced by line-side Tescos, scrapyards or car parks. Many of its stations – Birmingham New Street, Manchester Piccadilly, Stafford, Coventry, Euston – were modernised when the line was electrified in the '60s, and they have that motorway service station blankness. Travelling along the WCML can be akin to a motorway experience, and I am sometimes disinclined to look out of the window. When I do look out, I am seeking out the history.

The line grew in the 1830s out of the linkage at Birmingham of Britain's first trunk railway, the London & Birmingham, with that the industrial line par excellence, the Grand Junction, which connected Liverpool, Manchester, Birmingham and Crewe. At one time, the interest for the window-gazer would have lain in what Orwell called the 'sinister magnificence' of industrial landscapes: chimneys, pitheads, smouldering slagheaps, infernal skies, corrupted sunsets and sunrises. In *Hard Times* Dickens evokes Coketown, essentially that midway point on the WCML, Preston: 'It was a town of red brick, or of brick that would have been red if the smoke and ashes had allowed it; but as matters stood it was a town of unnatural red and black like the painted face of a savage.' (Northern clays are more likely than southern clays to produce red bricks.)

In 1936 W. H. Auden, a great watcher from trains of industrial landscapes, wrote the poem Night Mail, evoking the
journey of the West Coast Postal, the LMS Travelling Post Office
train from Euston to Glasgow and Aberdeen, for a documentary by the GPO Film Unit. The poem describes 'the fields of
apparatus, the furnaces/ Set on the dark plain like gigantic
chessmen'. The commentary of the film, to which the reci-
tation of the poem forms the climax, speaks of 'the mines
of Wigan ... steelworks of Warrington ... machine shops of
Preston'. We are very far from the Cornish Riviera, and such
natural beauty as is seen from the WCML cannot be enjoyed
without guilt. Auden had written a line describing passing
hills as being 'heaped like slaughtered horses'. It was too
strong for the GPO and was cut, but Auden didn't mind.

He wrote the poem, stopwatch in hand to get the timings
right (almost as if he were a railwayman himself), in a back-
room of the GPO offices in Soho Square, surrounded by the
comings and goings of young post office messengers, rough
diamonds all. If a line was deemed not right, Auden just
crumpled it up and wrote another. The film, like the poem,
is compellingly austere and strange. At one point footage
of the speeding train is accompanied by a man apparently
bellowing from the bottom of a well: 'Four million miles
every year! Five hundred million letters every year!' But for
all its stylisation, the authentic tone of the mail sorters on
the train is captured in many aggrieved remarks, like 'Give
us a chance' or 'Here, what's your game?', and the same tone
is in a signalman's peeved instruction to a colleague: 'You'll
have to shunt the local, I've got the Postal on.'

Anyone needing to be reminded how good Night Mail was
should watch the BFI documentary of 1954 about another
train: the Elizabethan, an express that ran from King's Cross
to Edinburgh for ten years from 1952. It too has a versified

commentary, but an embarrassingly patronising one. As the train crew clock in at King's Cross's Top Shed, it runs:

> Bob Marable, top-link train driver
> Who's always a punctual arriver
> Wears boots of footplate size
> Has colour-light eyes
> And engine oil in his saliva.

For that last line the narrator abandons 'received pronunciation' in favour of an excruciating attempt at cockney.

My edition of the *Night Mail* DVD comes with a companion piece, *Night Mail 2*, a documentary of 1986, with a poem by Blake Morrison. That's about the mail being carried north by aeroplane from Gatwick. Morrison gracefully admitted that he was 'on a hiding into nothing' in being charged with capturing the much less pungent atmosphere of the north in the '80s. His own poem speaks of 'this grey milltown lying under a duvet,/ Its shuttles stopped, its chimneys empty/ A town sleeping in now there's nothing to get up for', the scene appearing 'in the daze of morning ... like a steamed-up windscreen slowly clearing'. Morrison used the opportunity to dust off Auden's line about the slaughtered horses.

Post Offices no longer travel. Yes, there is today a big plastic Royal Mail crest stuck on the grey tin wall that forms the east side of the Euston station train shed, but that denotes a local delivery office. A man serving at the counter disclaimed any connection with the station: 'It all goes by road these days.'

Most freight on Britain's railways travelled by night. There are fewer passenger trains at night, and passengers have had priority for a long time. Anyone travelling late on the WCML forty years ago would have been sharing the tracks with those regular nocturnal trundlers: coal, milk, newspapers, letters. (In my boyhood the generic name for any late passenger train was 'the milk train', although a more accurate name, given the befuddled state of the passengers, would have been 'the beer train'.) Of those commodities only coal will be seen today, or more likely not seen but heard coming down from Liverpool or Hunterston, or from the open-cast mines of East Ayrshire, to the Yorkshire power stations, or to Fiddlers Ferry power station at Warrington, or Rugeley, near Stafford. Coal is classed as 'bulk heavy haul' along with other minerals, such as limestone and cement. There is also 'container traffic': lighter stuff – say, Australian wine in bags in vans – perhaps brought up from Southampton docks and taken around the western edge of London, then to the north-west by Freightliner, one of our half-dozen freight operators, and the direct descendant of the BR freight operation.

I do think of the WCML as being dark, a stick of liquorice. Perhaps I am taking my cue subconsciously from a memory of industrial landscape, the blackness of atmosphere associated with the great junctions like Willesden, Rugby, Crewe; or it might be from the 'blackberry black' engines of the London & North Western Railway, or the blackness of the Black Fives, those rangy workhorses that were among the most famous engines built (between the '30s and '50s) at Crewe. The darkness might be metaphorical; the decay of that industrial landscape ... or the five-train smash that occurred at in 1915 at Quintinshill, on the Scottish border. Two negligent signalmen were to blame for the deaths by incineration – in an antiquated, fifteen-carriage gaslit train – of more than 200 members of the seventh battalion of the Royal Scots. The precise number was never ascertained, but it was certainly the worst rail disaster in Britain.

The line is nocturnal in that sleeper trains were pioneered

on it, and two of our three remaining sleepers run on the
WCML. We are about to board one of them, and we will be
doing so from the subterranean platforms of Euston station,
which has been described, by Richard Morrison in The Times,
as apparently designed by someone 'with a vampiric loath-
ing for sunlight'.

FIFTY SHADES OF GREY

Euston, opened by the London & Birmingham Railway in
1837, was the first London terminus, and just as the line it
served would become a network, so the station itself would
become a complex.

Whereas trains from King's Cross would go under the
annoying Regent's Canal (that old mode getting in the way
of the new one), the trains from Euston would go over it, and
in the early years they were required to be winched up the
resulting incline by a machine housed in Camden. (Sprawling and messy Euston operated in conjunction with facilities
in Camden and Willesden Junction.)

A year after the station opening, a sandstone arch or por-
tico or – still more correctly – propylaeum was built in front
of the station. It was 72 feet high, with four fluted columns 8
foot in diameter. It served no purpose except to celebrate the
arrival of the London & Birmingham Railway, but the Euston Arch would grow on people over the next hundred or so
years. Two stone lodges were built either side of it. Two further lodges were built at the south side of the Euston complex, almost on Euston Road, and these were inscribed with
the names of northern towns – destinations easily reachable
from Euston, supposedly, but some of the places named,
like Peterborough, Leicester and Swansea, were, as Alan A.
Jackson pointed out in London's Termini, 'to be reached much

14. The Euston Arch in 1919. It now lies in pieces in the River
Lea. Dan Cruickshank leads a campaign to have it rebuilt.

more expeditiously from other establishments up and down the road'.

Two railway hotels followed; then, in 1849, the Great Hall, a combined concourse and waiting-room that looks, from photographs, as though it ought to have been the centre-piece of something like the British Museum. Alan A. Jackson writes:

> Few other English buildings could offer anything to match the deeply-coffered ceiling of the Great Hall, embellished with massive curved consoles and plaster bas-reliefs in each corner, the whole beautifully lit by attic windows. The bas-reliefs ... were in pairs; with busty, long-thighed women and muscular men, they symbolised London, Birmingham, Northampton, Chester, Manchester, Carlisle, Lancaster and Liverpool.

Also inside the hall was a statue of Robert Stephenson, who had engineered the London & Birmingham, employing the 'straight through' doctrine: hence, for example, the deep cutting at Tring and the 1¼-mile Kilsby Tunnel south of Rugby, where the price of going straight through was twenty-six men's lives. He also laid out Euston station, although the architect was Philip Hardwick.

For a while, the arch framed a view of Hampstead Heath, but that disappeared as the Euston clutter grew. The station itself had started with two platforms, but burgeoned eventually to fifteen. The train shed had a series of pitched roofs of glass and iron. There was no dramatic train shed canopy, as at King's Cross or St Pancras, but the intricate lattice of steel that held up the glass was sufficiently interesting to grace the cover of *Railway Station Architecture*, by David Lloyd and Donald Insall. The book was published in 1968. The Euston

train shed had perhaps made the cover by virtue of a sympathy vote, because it had just been knocked down.

The new station was opened in 1968. Of the features of
Old Euston mentioned above, only the two mendacious
lodges and the statue of Robert Stephenson survive. He is
now on the piazza to the north of the station, immediately
outside All Bar One.

The arch had been demolished in 1963, before the new
station was built – all part of BR's attempt to redefine itself
as modern and therefore fit to compete with the motor car.
Aesthetic people assumed that the arch and the Great Hall
would somehow be accommodated within the new station, and if the reaction to their destruction was shock, this
became something more steely when St Pancras was also
threatened by the modernisers. It would be saved by the Victorian Society (which had been formed to campaign to save
the Euston Arch), and in particular by John Betjeman, who
described the new Euston station as 'disastrous and inhu-
mane'. The demolition contractor himself, a Mr Valori, disapproved of the demolition of the arch, and numbered all the
pieces of stone so it could be rebuilt. Most of it lies on the bed
of the River Lea. The campaign to resurrect it as 'an anchor
for the fragmented landscape around Euston' is fronted by
the broadcaster Dan Cruickshank. It can't be put back where
it was, because that site is taken by Platforms 8 and 11 of the
current station ... not unless the current station were itself
to be knocked down, which is not inconceivable, as we will
see in a moment. Either way, it could be put up on the patch
of unhealthy grass and blighted trees south of the piazza,
which is dignified with the name Euston Square Gardens. In
1962 a Canadian contractor had proposed to roll the arch on
wheels south to this position, but BR objected, saying this
would cost £190,000, whereas knocking it down would cost

£12,000. BR also said there was no room, but there plainly was, and is. A restored arch would fit neatly into the space in Euston Square Gardens between the two lodges, and the double-decker buses serving Euston would fit beneath the arch, which they would have to do, since it would straddle their access road to the station.

The new station hall is a simple rectangle in concrete and black marble. Its coffered ceiling may be intended as an echo the Great Hall. On a very sunny day you notice the strip of windows around the top. Otherwise, you forget about natural light as soon as you enter the Euston box, which seems to be illuminated by the garish light of the fast food outlets lining the walls. The station is about as tasteful as Blackpool, to which I am glad to say it will once more to be sending direct trains when this book is published, after many years of having to change at Preston. But it is not bracing like Blackpool. It is a headache incarnate. Euston is all about grab-bags of crisps, two-for-one on outsize chocolate bars, and the Britannia pub on the concourse ('Serving breakfast from 7.30 a.m.'); it is about risking a medium cappuccino – practically a bucket-full – and then not having 30 pence for the nightmarishly fluorescent Gentlemen's. The idea was always to combine the new station with retail, and in 1968 it accommodated such novelties as an off licence, a travel agents and betting shop. The shops seem to be in the station but not of it. A couple of years ago I was looking around the W. H. Smith's in Euston station, trying to find the national railway timetable. I thought I must be looking in the wrong place, so I asked the man at the till, 'Do you sell the timetable?' 'The timetable for *what*?' he replied testily. (On 23 September 1993 a Mr David Kane of Hope, Derbyshire, wrote to the *Daily Telegraph*: 'I spotted the new British Rail winter timetable, just published, in the "Puzzles and Comics" section of John Menzies bookshop at Manchester Piccadilly Railway Station.')

At Euston, waiting passengers do not commune with the trains, cannot even see them, because they are screened off and on a lower level. This is also true of Grand Central station in New York, but the concourse there is a mellow and romantic space. Grand Central is a true 'destination station', frequented by New Yorkers, who meet under the four-faceted clock or order a bowl of clam chowder with crusty bread and a glass of Chablis in the Oyster Bar. Nobody visits Euston unless they have to. The concourse is dominated by the departure screen, and people stand in front of it, waiting for their cue to bolt towards the trains. If they shift their gaze slightly to the left, they will see adverts projected onto a giant screen. If they shift their gaze slightly to the right, they will see another. The idea is that, by watching the indicator board, they are not congesting the platform entrances. For years, anyone arriving early and wanting a seat had to go and buy themselves a burger because there were no seats on the concourse itself. In his book of 1980, *Roaming the West Coast Rails*, Derek Cross records asking a station official why not: 'Well, sir, if we put seats here people would sit on them.' Today there are a few seats, but the station is still full of people sitting on the floor, like refugees. When the platform number of your train is flagged up on the indicator board, you make for the appropriate ramp leading down to your platform, and I usually find that everyone in the station turns out to have been waiting for the train that I want, a somehow humiliating experience.

The lesson of the new Euston is that glass, however dirty, is the correct covering for a train shed. Photographs of the old station show slightly befogged platforms with sudden, diagonal shafts of light. In *Roaming the West Coast Rails* Derek

15. The Great Hall of the old Euston. The statue of
Robert Stephenson now stands on the piazza north
of the modern station, outside All Bar One.

Cross writes, 'The old Euston was a fascinating place, dark, smoky and full of character ... Occasionally outgoing sleeping car expresses took a bit of finding ...', this presumably because the atmosphere had been thickening all day. In *Steam Up!* (1939) Eric Treacy, the railway bishop, mentions with approval 'the top-hatted stationmaster Turrill at Euston who likes to sing in his spare time'.

Surely nobody has so much as whistled on those twenty below-deck platforms at Euston. Talk about fifty shades of grey. The track ballast, platforms, walls, roof ... all grey. And the Virgin trains are grey, apart from a dash of red and yellow at the front, which may be meant to invoke the short-lived BR experiment with a 'blood and custard' livery, but somehow the tones are off, therefore reminiscent of a squeezed spot. In Euston I am always grateful for the green of the London Midland trains, which provide the suburban services on the WCML. A gateway for lorries on to Eversholt Street admits the only natural light to the undercroft, and this looks directly on to Euston Books ('Videos and Magazines').

The tracks lead into a great grey cutting, seen on their way by a great grey signal box, sited on the left immediately after the station and overlooked by the grey Euston Thistle Hotel. But while the platforms may be low down, the roadways beneath the station are lower still. (Betjeman spoke of the 'fume-ridden taxi rank'.) There is something sinister about this, as if the cars are biding their time underground while plotting a takeover.

Even those who argue that Euston is an efficient station do not seem to love it – I have never read an encomium to Euston. When I read in 2003 that a railway station had been voted Britain's second-biggest eyesore by readers of *County Life*, I assumed it would be Euston, but it was Euston's sibling Birmingham New Street, another product of the belated 'electric age' of BR. Birmingham New Street, like Euston, is subterranean, dark and depressing. It replaced a station of 1854 that, according to Derek Cross, was the *pièce de résistance* of the LNWR, featuring 'a remarkable iron arched roof with a maximum span of 211 feet, with a curving lattice framework under each of the ribs'. But Birmingham New Street is being rebuilt at the time of writing, and that precious – yet completely free – commodity, daylight, will be readmitted via a glass atrium. Euston may be in for a similar or, with luck, a worse fate. It is the favoured terminus for HS2, and, depending on which plan for the line comes to fruition, it might yet be flattened while the arch rises again.

THE GHOST OF BUCHAN

I started my journey in the Doric Arch pub on the piazza, which is a very good pub, easily the best thing on the Euston complex. It is full of railway memorabilia, including hardcore stuff, such as a signalling diagram for the Euston power box. I was introduced to it by Nicholas Whittaker, the author of *Platform Souls*, a very readable and eye-opening book about trainspotting. At 10 p.m. I drank a pint of stout in front of a poster showing the arch beneath a dark-blue starlit sky. The London & North Western Railway advertising copy ran: 'Sleeping saloons fitted with every modern convenience are attached to the Night Trains from London Euston to Holyhead (for Ireland), Liverpool and Manchester', a reminder that most night trains would have a combination of sleeper and non-sleeper carriages. There were also 'half-sleeper' carriages, combining sleeping berths and ordinary seats, and those in the latter presumably half-slept.

There were plenty of named sleepers and these were usually all-sleeper apart from the dining car. On the west coast,

from 1895, there was the Night Scot, which became, with electrification, the Night Limited. There was the Night Caledonian in
the '70s and '80s. It is strange, now, to think that King's Cross
once despatched sleepers, but it did, and there was the Night
Scotsman from 1927 until the mid-'80s. There was the Night
Capitals, which my father, who worked on sleeper costings,
had a hand in terminating, cars and planes having eaten into
the market, and trains undermining their own sleeper market by going faster. On the East and West Coast main lines in
the '80s there were the Nightrider services. The idea of a sort of
hotel room on wheels was beginning to seem comically lum-
bering, so these offered first-class reclining seats. The Night
Ferry we have already discussed, and we have mentioned the
Night Riviera, a train of clouded late nineteenth-century origins that still runs from Paddington to Cornwall.

   The Night Riviera is generally well patronised. It is always
fully booked on Fridays and Sundays (like the Caledonian, it
doesn't run on Saturday nights; that's when they work on the
line), and when fog prevents flights taking off from Newquay airport. It never made any money for its operator, First
Group, which also operates the Caledonian Sleeper. First did
little to advertise the service, and in 2005 they proposed its
discontinuation, but its regular users got up an 8,000-sig-
nature petition – the biggest ever railway protest. The Night
Riviera was saved, and benefited greatly from the publicity,
although I doubt it has gone into profit. At the time of the
protest, I spoke to a man who worked in one of the West
Country booking offices about the necessity of advertising
sleeper services. He said, 'For a time we displayed a model of
the sleeper train and bookings went up 20 per cent. When it
was taken away they fell by the same amount.' This reminded
me of a passage from Speak, Memory, the autobiography of
Vladimir Nabokov, which was published in 1951:

In the early years of this century, a travel agency on Nevski Avenue displayed a three-foot-long model of an oak brown international sleeping car. In delicate verisimilitude it completely outranked the painted tin of my clockwork trains. Unfortunately it was not for sale. One could make out the blue upholstery inside, the embossed leather lining of the compartment walls, their polished panels, inset mirrors, tulip-shaped reading lamps, and other maddening details.

I usually book my First Great Western trains by calling the company, which means I book with a person in Bombay. Having made a booking to Cornwall with a young man who told me his name was Mahantesh, I asked him whether he had ever visited England. He had not. Did he want to see the territory over which the company whose tickets he sold ran? He said, 'I will be very honest with you, Mr Martin, I would very much like to visit *Ireland*.' 'But that's nothing to do with First Great Western!' I expostulated. 'No, but my favourite band is from Ireland. It is called The Script.' I told him I had never heard of them. It was Mahantesh's turn to be appalled. 'You have never heard of their song, "If You Could See Me Now?"' It might be that a measure of guilt about having disclaimed any interest in visiting First Great Western country now kicked in. 'I have to tell you, Mr Martin, that another thing I would very much like to do is ride on the sleeper train from Paddington.'

'The *Night Riviera*?'

'Exactly.' He then considered the trains I was proposing to book. 'You are intending to come back from Penzance at four. Why not hang on for the sleeper? This is a very big chance for you!'

At 22.40 I finished my pint of stout at Euston and, realising

I still had an hour and ten minutes to go before train time, I ordered another. Part of the thrill of catching the *Caledonian Sleeper* is the lateness of the hour. It brings out the eight-year-old in me. I get to stay up late. Note, incidentally, my fluency in the twenty-four-hour clock, learned from train timetables. BR started to use it in the summer of 1965. Before that, '8.45' meant '8.45 a.m.', whereas '8/45' meant '8.45 p.m.'; and before that Bradshaw had written '8.45mrn' or '8.45aft'.

At 23.15 I crossed the concourse towards the train. The name *Caledonian Sleeper* was formally applied to the Euston–Scotland (and vice-versa) sleeper in 2004, although it had been used informally since BR days. At the time of writing, the train is operated by First Scotrail, which operates all the trains in Scotland, but the new franchise has just been awarded to the 'outsourcing' giant, Serco. Here is how the *Guardian*, which is not keen on outsourcing, reported the exciting news: 'Serco, the company dogged by scandals from overcharging for prisoner tagging to allegations of sexual assault at an immigration detention centre, is to run sleeper trains between London and Scotland.' Serco, which runs luxury trains in Australia (as well as having a share in Northern Rail), will be given a fifty million pound subsidy to build new trains for the service. The expectation is of an *Orient Express*-type experience, with the en suite bathrooms for sleeper cabins and other five star trappings long hankered after by a clientele that includes MPs, peers, royalty (apparently) and business people who want to finish the working day later or start earlier than the times permitted by airlines. But the new trains will not come until 2018.

The northbound *Caledonian Sleeper* is – and will remain – two trains. There is the Highland Train, departing at 21.15, calling at Crewe and Preston, then Edinburgh, where it divides into three for Aberdeen, Fort William and Inverness.

But I was heading towards the Lowland Train. This departs at 23.50, calls at Watford to pick up, Carlisle to set down, and divides at Carstairs, the rear going to Edinburgh, the front to Motherwell and Glasgow. In its *Encyclopaedia of Named Trains* the *Railway Magazine* agonises over whether the *Caledonian Sleeper* is a named train … or is it a brand, there being more than one train, like *Eurostar*, or the above-mentioned *Nightrider* … or the *Brighton Belle*? And there's the rub. You can't start banishing such a great train as the *Brighton Belle* from the lexicon of named trains on some technicality. The same goes for the *Caledonian Sleeper*, which is one of the last remaining outposts of British railway charisma.

Certainly, I was excited walking towards it – not as excited as I had been approaching the couchette carriages at the Gare de Lyon (along those platforms lined with palm trees planted in tubs) while jaunting with my father and the British Rail Touring Club, but very keen to board. The *Sleeper* offers first- and second-class berths and seated accommodation on reclining seats. I had paid £147.90 for a first-class one-way ticket to Glasgow. The First Group blue we have already bemoaned. But the train waiting on Platform 14 was thrillingly long: sixteen carriages, eight for Edinburgh, eight for Glasgow. That's why it has to leave from either Platform 14 or Platform 1, the longest ones at Euston. 'Mr Lockwood?' a great-coated and gratifyingly Scottish attendant was saying to a tweed-coated chap, and when he saw me he brought me into the fold, '… And Mr Martin, is it? Let me show you to your berths gentlemen.' I had the feeling of stepping into a John Buchan novel, and indeed I wore my own tweed coat, together with a scarf or – as Buchan would have said – a muffler, and stout boots, as being about right for a trip to Scotland on the brink of spring. 'It's a very long train,' I gushed gauchely. 'Aye, sir,' the attendant said, 'the second-longest sleeper train in Europe. The longest one, I think, runs from Paris to Madrid.'

We boarded a first-class berth carriage, which had been made from a BR Mark 3 carriage of late 1970s' vintage, and the attendant unlocked my berth. The pleasure lay in being reacquainted with all those railway amenities I'd been denied for forty years. We had a proper loco on the front – a twenty-five-year-old electric Class 90, more usually associated with freight trains – and I now stepped from a corridor into what was in effect a compartment. I beheld a dimmer switch! A window blind! A decent-sized sink with proper taps! A complimentary washbag! About ten years ago, I took my eldest son, then aged nine, on the *Night Riviera*, and the free washbag is what he took away – literally and metaphorically – from the experience. He is now at university, and when I told him I would be travelling on the *Caledonian Sleeper*, he said, 'You'll be getting a washbag!' But just as the football manager's dug-out is now the 'technical area', so the sleeper-train washbag is a 'passenger comfort kit'. As the attendant reassured me that he would be available throughout the night ('I've a wee pantry in the next carriage along'), I greedily inspected my haul: razor and shaving cream, body lotion (didn't see quite where that came in, given that there are no showers on the train), a flannel, a pair of earplugs, a pair of socks, collapsible toothbrush and an inch-long tube of toothpaste. I once interviewed a man who knew about train WCs. I had been regretting the demise of those small but pungent cakes of green soap: just the smell of them made you feel clean. 'But people used to steal them,' he said. 'So the modern mode became liquid soap. But now thieves take empty bottles into the lavatories and decant the liquid soap into them.'

Only in first-class do you get a comfort kit, but the main

benefit of first is that you have a berth to yourself guaranteed. The first-class berths are the same as standard-class berths, but with the upper bed folded against the wall. If you were travelling as a married couple and you wanted to sleep with your wife (because it doesn't necessarily follow), there would be no point paying for first. If you did travel in first as a couple, you would be put in two adjacent berths, and the attendant would offer to unlock the connecting doors that are fitted between all berths except the end ones. Again, it doesn't necessarily follow that you would agree.

My berth was predominantly light grey and pale blue, the least cosy colours. I recalled a description, in the *Railway Magazine* in the early '30s, of some nineteenth-century sleeping-car stock that had scandalously persisted on the ECML into the early 1920s: '... old gas-lighted clerestory cars of the nineties with their heavy red velvet upholstery and gloomy batswing burners in the corridors.' The side with the locked connecting door was some sort of grey laminate. On the bed side, the carpet continued up the wall. The *Newsnight* presenter Kirsty Wark is a regular on the *Caledonian Sleeper* and often writes about it. (She is, to quote the title of a famous spy novel with sleeping-car scenes by Maurice Dekobra, *La Madone des Sleepings*.) She's keen on the service, but in an article in the *New Statesman* she said it was 'pretty gross to have carpets up the walls'. From old photographs I'd say that carpets or cloth panelling against the wall on the bed side has been a consistent feature of British sleeper carriages. The duvet in my berth looked very well laundered, and there was an attractive purple and red travelling blanket, but there were patches of sand in the hard-to-clean corners of the floor carpet.

I last travelled on the *Caledonian Sleeper* in 2005, when it was on the brink of an earlier refurbishment. One feature promised at the time was 'more control over light levels', which I think meant 'blinds that worked', because on that journey my window blind didn't go all the way up. This one did, and I meant to keep it open throughout the night.

THE LOUNGE CAR

We moved away from Euston with the gentlest of lurches, and no whistle, perhaps out of consideration for anybody already asleep (because you can board the sleeper an hour before departure).

We swayed into the arc-lit grey cutting, which for all its greyness I would like to overlook from a big, stucco-fronted house on Mornington Terrace. We rattled over the iron bridge that takes the line over the Regent's Canal. The bridge seems very low. When I cycle along the towpath of the canal, I always duck my head when I come to it. Nonetheless it is the cause of the first stage of the climb of the tracks out of Euston, a climb that continues until Tring. The reverberation of the bridge allows the *Caledonian Sleeper* to be heard even where I live, in Highgate. You can recognise the bridge from the train by a blob of mauve graffiti to your right, but even though the sleeper is marshalled with the window berths facing right (away from such as one can make out of the sea on the WCML), I could not see anything at this late hour, and there was no moon to help.

The bridge is parallel to Gloucester Road NW1, and there's a pub near by called The Engineer. The sign shows a top-hatted cigar-smoking man who looks suspiciously like Brunel, which would be wrong. But it might be Robert Stephenson (which would be right), because he smoked cigars too. He built the next feature of the line, the Primrose Hill Tunnel, which has a handsome, castellated entrance, insisted on by Eton College, who own the land hereabouts. So began the entire genre of castellated tunnels. You can see the tunnel mouth if you prop your bike against the north wall of the footbridge running over the WCML between Primrose Hill and Chalk Farm, and stand on the pedal crank to see over. You can't see it from the *Caledonian Sleeper* at midnight.

We rolled through Willesden Junction. It has not had a platform on the WCML since 1962, but there is still the local station, the junction with the West London Line, and a sprawling traction maintenance depot. There is indeed a 'rough loveliness' about the place, as claimed by the artist Leon Kossoff, whose garden overlooks the Junction, and who has often painted it. We rattled through Harrow & Wealdstone, and past the famous Kodak factory, which still looks a big concern, although Kodak is now in the mysterious, miniaturised digital realm, which means they have relinquished part of the site, and I have no hope of understanding what goes on there.

We called at Watford – the station preceded by a giant illuminated Tesco sign – to pick up passengers only, although I don't suppose anyone could stop you from getting off. Watford is umbilically tied to Euston, being the main target of the electric suburban services that began in the 1920s.

We passed through Bletchley, where the WCML used to be crossed by the London Midland & Scottish Oxford-to-Cambridge line, which was known as the 'Varsity Line' or the 'Brain Line'. Passenger services were withdrawn west of Bletchley to Oxford in 1967, the year Milton Keynes, just 3½ miles north of Bletchley was arising and being designated a New Town. How's that for joined-up planning? Trains continue to run east from Bletchley to Bedford, but not beyond there to Cambridge. It seems likely that the line from Bletchley to Oxford at least will be re-opened before 2019.

A couple of years ago I asked a ticket clerk at Oxford station if I could get a train to Cambridge, knowing perfectly well I couldn't but wanting him to apologise for the fact. 'You certainly can!' he said. 'You change at London.' (He seemed to have forgotten that you can get from anywhere to anywhere if you change at London.) We passed Milton Keynes, which of course does not appear in S. N. Pike's chronicling of the WCML of 1947. He denotes the spot with the words 'footbridges', 'deep cutting', 'Denbigh Hall signal box'.

I walked through to the lounge car, the next carriage along. On the way, I stepped into the lavatory. One of the modern types of WC, with a wide, electronically controlled door for wheelchair access, had been jemmied into Mark 3 carriage. Once inside, I pressed the button to close the door. I then pressed the button to lock the door. It did not illuminate as it is supposed to do. Therefore I did not know whether the door was locked or not. I got rid of my two pints of stout, but would not have risked a more comprehensive ablution. When I turned to the sink, I saw that the words 'No Water' had been handwritten on white tape placed over the button I would have pressed to obtain the usual niggardly trickle if that tape had not been there.

To move from the berths to the lounge car is to step even further back in time, because the lounge car is a converted BR buffet car of Mark 2 stock (late '60s–early '70s). The main hatch of the serving kiosk is kept shut, and food and drink are doled out from the side door – lending an improvised feel. The colour scheme was grey and burnt orange, and here too the carpeting ran up the wall at one end. The lounge car features unsecured seats – very unusual, as noted in the case of the *Brighton Belle*. The individual seats are upholstered, with steel frames, like 1970s' office chairs. (As one blogger wrote of the *Caledonian Sleeper*, 'You almost expect to go to sleep and wake up in the Winter of Discontent.') There are also black leather sofas. These had been in the offing when I last travelled on the *Sleeper*, and I had been assured they were to be 'as used in the *Big Brother House*'. I can't verify this, never having watched *Big Brother*. The individual seats were transverse, facing tables; the sofas were longitudinal. There were three menus: one for food, one for drinks and one for whiskies exclusively. When she travels, Kirsty Wark chooses her 'malt of the night ... I used to be loyal to Bruichladdich, but for some reason the Islay distillery no longer supplies miniatures.' She also has a Macsween's haggis and red wine. The food on the *Sleeper* is generally well reviewed. It is microwaved snack food or sandwiches, but there is a wide selection, and most of it costs less than a tenner. There's also a better choice of wine than is normal on a train. I considered a half-bottle of Chablis, but in the end I went for a quarter-bottle of generic Chardonnay (which turned into two of them).

There were half a dozen customers in the lounge car, which is open to holders of first-class berth ticket-holders at all times, and standard-class berth ticket-holders if the train is not crowded. It was not crowded tonight. There were eight customers in the lounge car – all men, mostly prodding away at their mobile devices. One man was sipping a whisky with a bottle of pills next to it. Everybody had a nightcap quietly on the go: nobody was eating, it was too late in the day.

I got talking to the two men on the sofa opposite. They were in the transport business. One of them introduced himself as 'car park attendant', but that was a joke because he then mentioned private equity. They had something to do with building car parks for airports. In short, they were the enemy. But the car park attendant – I'll call him Nick – liked trains, whereas the other man hated them, and would far rather have flown from London to Scotland ('It's so tedious this way'). But as Nick explained, 'We couldn't have had our

business dinner in Mayfair this evening without this service.'
He was not without his criticisms, however. 'Do you think
you're getting a real first-class service?' He paused, and we
all listened to the train, which sounded like some clumsy
people having sex on a very old bed. At that very moment a
warning flashed up on my laptop to the effect that no wi-fi
networks had been detected.

'I'd say what you're getting was a premium economy
service,' Nick continued (and keep in mind that he was
speaking before the new franchisee had been announced).
He thought there should be a 'genuine first-class option',
with queen-sized beds and *en suites*. (Kirsty Wark too wants
en suites.) The next class down would offer very comfortable
recliners with top-notch at-seat service. 'Have you ever travelled Virgin Upper Class?' asked Nick, 'I mean, like that.'
(By a strange coincidence, I had travelled on Virgin Upper
Class accommodation, as a result of my first ever journalistic
freebie. It was in the early '90s. I recall flying to Miami while
lying almost horizontally, slurping champagne and listening
to Bon Jovi on earphones.) Nick thought people wouldn't
mind travelling in open accommodation if the service were
sufficiently good, and he cited the new Anglo-Scottish Meg-
abus sleeper bus service being offered by 'my good friend'
the transport entrepreneur Brian Souter.

I thought (wrongly, as it turned out) that Nick and his
friend might be interested in a little sleeping car history ...

In 1838 the London & Birmingham Railway provided one-
or more bed carriages, in which two facing seats could be
connected by a pull-out board. But the first genuine sleeping cars were introduced in 1873, on the Anglo-Scottish services. The beds were in berths, and they were longitudinal.
In other words, you did not sleep at right-angles to the direction of the train. The toilet facilities varied, but some of these

berths did have what we would call today *en suite* lavatories and sinks. The London & North Western built the fanciest sleepers. According to Denis Jenkinson in LNWR *Carriages, A Concise History*:

> Windows had old gold figured tapestry blinds on sprung rollers ... Upholstery was in crimson and brown saladin moquette with matching crimson silk laces. Floors were double thickness (and filled with hair felt for sound insulation) and covered with linoleum and Wilton carpets. Ceilings were finished with flock paper to a floral pattern, picked out in cream and gold. Outside the compartments, corridors were panelled in polished oak mahogany in a walnut framing above a dado of dark oak. The corridor ceiling was finished in polished sycamore panels while the central cross-vestibule, used as a smoking saloon, had a set of four revolving chairs and a set of flap tables. Lighting was electrical.

There were also open sleeper carriages (beds but no berths). This was the American Pullman model, and it was adopted in 1874 by the Midland Railway, going its own way as usual. Passengers gained a degree of privacy by closing the velvet curtains surrounding each of the bunks, which were arranged in two tiers. The topmost ones seem to have been suspended from – and were close to – the ceiling. I would have gone for one of the lower ones, aligned to the windows, and I would have lain on my side to watch, by the light of a convenient full moon, the passing moorland of the Settle–Carlisle stretch.

In 1877 that equally maverick outfit, the Great Western, introduced 'dormitory cars': essentially two rooms with a transverse corridor dividing. One held four beds for ladies,

the other seven beds for gents. Here too the beds were longitudinal. But in the 1890s the Great Western introduced transverse beds in single or double berths with a side corridor,
and this became the standard format in Britain, '... hence the
layout of the *Caledonian Sleeper*,' I concluded, at which point
Nick said, 'Well, I'm off to bed,' and his anti-rail friend followed, but not before showing me an email he was about to
send his wife. Attached was a picture of his berth, which did
look prison cell-like. 'This'll teach me to misbehave', ran the
message.

The lounge car was now empty apart from me and the
man with the whisky and pills. The darkness was so complete beyond the windows that I suspected we might be in the
notorious Kilsby Tunnel, south of Rugby. It is illuminated by
two giant light wells open to the sky, one of them 120 feet
deep, but they're no use to the traveller going through the
tunnel at night.

We came to Rugby, where a sign reading 'Alstom' stood
out. Alstom is the French-owned heavy engineering firm
that made and maintains the Virgin Pendolino trains. Most
of them were built in Italy, and Pendolino is Italian for 'pen-
dulum'. The trains can go fast over the many bends of the
WCML by tilting with the curve, and the tilting technology
used on the Pendolino was originally developed by Fiat.
The Pendolinos fulfil the tilting dream of the British Rail
Advanced Passenger Train, which was aborted in the 1980s.
The Pendolino fleet is served by half a dozen Alstom train
care depots along the WCML (including Crewe, Preston and
Carlisle), but the Alstom business at Rugby is to do with
thermal engineering.

In the early days of railways almost all northbound trains
from London went through Rugby, hence the high-hand-
edness of that tea lady towards Charles Dickens. The Great

Central railway – which ran from Marylebone to Chester in
the north-west and Grimsby in the north-east – was carried
over Rugby by the 'Birdcage Bridge', which queered a train
driver's view of a huge signalling gantry; therefore all the
signals on the gantry were duplicated at a higher level. The
gantry was called the 'Rugby bedstead'. The bridge and the
bedstead have gone, as has the Great Central, the only trunk
route closed by Beeching. Some say it should re-opened
instead of building HS2 ... trouble is, all the houses in the
way. But Rugby station itself survives in its graceful Victorian
form.

We next passed through the brutalist glorified bus shelter
that is Stafford railway station, which was built in 1962, and
makes me ashamed for 1962, even though it was the year of
my birth. Twenty-three miles later, at about 1.30 a.m., we
were approaching Crewe.

CREWE AND BEYOND

Of the approach to Crewe from the south, S. N. Pike writes:

For more than two miles this side of Crewe, enormous
marshalling yards dominate the landscape on the left.
Miles and miles of railway track lie in serried rows as far
as the eye can reach. Thousands of wagons are here
assembled in the process of being sorted out and shunted
to their different tracks, and 400 goods trains are dealt
with daily. Certainly this must be the busiest yard in the
world. Crewe station itself covers 25 acres, handling as
many as 500 passenger trains in 24 hours. Leaving the
station we see on the left the enormous engine and
carriage works covering nearly 200 acres.

Crewe remains an important junction – for Liverpool, Manchester, north Wales, the Midlands. It has also been granted an HS2 connection. You still see a lot of carriages and wagons on the approach. Freightliner have a distribution centre in Crewe, and trains are 'cared for' there, but, as of the past ten years, trains are no longer built at Crewe. The works at Crewe had a primal force: both engines and carriages were built, and the works made its own steel. The Class 90 pulling our sleeper was built at Crewe, as were the power cars for the HSTs and those for the electric trains on the ECML.

The platforms we trundled through were apparently empty, but they must have been crowded with ghosts. Crewe was akin to a kind of purgatory or limbo. Passengers changed at Crewe, *crews* changed at Crewe, engines changed at Crewe, perhaps an electric loco being exchanged for steam or vice versa. And there were always dozens, if not hundreds, of train watchers ... who became trainspotters.

Some time in the 1930s Eric Treacy spent an hour at Crewe on his way to 'preach at a very important service somewhere in the Midlands'. It was fifty-nine minutes before he looked at his watch, and then he had to run for his connection. How had the time fled by? He gives the answer in *Steam Up!* He watched some porters loading a van with live pigeons; then he 'tried to console three frightened looking calves', apparently abandoned on a platform, their heads sticking out of sacking. He observed 'a wheeltapper progressing wheel to wheel on a Plymouth-bound train. [Tapping the wheels to make sure they were sound; the note would not ring clear in the case of a crack.] Then I stood near one of the station's policemen and listened to some of the daft questions asked by the British public on the move.' He went to the refreshment room where 'I fell into conversation with a driver of the old school, complete with walrus moustache and a nose which might have been coloured by exposure to the elements – and perhaps by something else.' The driver complained about young firemen. All they thought of was girls and dancing. Sitting in the corner of the refreshment room were a young, recently married couple, 'still with confetti sticking to them, en route to their honeymoon'. The woman was in floods of tears ...

In August 1951 *The Guardian* published an article entitled 'The Allure of Train-Spotting: Search for an Explanation among the Addicts at Crewe'. In that year Ian Allan's Locospotters Club had a quarter of a million members. Ian Allan, a sometime publicity officer with the Southern Railway, formalised trainspotting by publishing lists of locos or carriages that could be ticked off. Essentially these were lists of numbers, looking rather like logarithm tables. The arithmomania that had been latent in the more dilettantish 'train watching' thus came to the fore, and trainspotters came to be seen as anal retentives.

Here, from *Platform Souls*, is the young Nicholas Whittaker, being vouchsafed his first glimpse of Crewe in 1964, while passing through on a train from Burton to Rhyl with his mum:

> Ambling in from the Derby line, the tracks suddenly came at us from all sides, switching, meshing ... weaving a tangled magic carpet. Here was absolute railwayness on all sides, rails below us, electric wires above. A sprawling soot-clouded depot slipped away to the left before I even had a chance to gasp.

He would go on to spend many Saturdays on Crewe station.

> Sometimes we'd take our own sandwiches, but we often

visited the buffet for a packet of crisps or a Cornish pasty. There were the machines too, of course. It's a truism that all drinks from machines are foul, but I rather liked the chicken soup. It looked like steaming urine with green tinsel floating in it ...

Ten years ago I was commissioned to write an article on the theme 'whither trainspotting?' Whereas the spotters used to be schoolboys, they are now men of a certain age (those schoolboys grown up). I tracked down a couple of them, Paul and David, both in their sixties, visiting London from Manchester and staying in West Hampstead, which they found convenient for Willesden Junction. They were members of the Lancashire Locomotive Society. 'As late as the '80s,' Paul told me, 'club trips to London required a fifty-two-seater coach. Now it's a minibus with twelve at most.'

They would also be going to King's Cross. 'In my head,' said Paul, 'it's still full of Atlantics. It's like it was in *The Ladykillers*.' They expected to have to put up with abuse. The worst place to spot trains, they told me, was any location where men in white vans might be driving past. '"Get a life, mate",' Paul said, 'I've had that lots of times.' Station officials were not necessarily on their side. Who's to say that the sixty-year-old man with a flask of tea and an Ian Allan ABC guide might not be a member of Al-Qaeda? David had been questioned recently by an official at Manchester station: 'Nothing came of it, but it was, you know, close questioning.'

Then again, trainspotters had always had their run-ins with authority. They may have been obsessives, but they were seldom wimps. In *Forget the Anorak (What Trainspotting Was Really Like)* Michael G. Harvey relates his trainspotting adventures of the '50s. On an expedition to Ebbw Junction at Newport he and his mates threw stones to distract the gateman's attention, then dashed in. Their reward: 126 steam locomotives 'on shed'.

I used to be a member of The Railway Club, described in *The Oxford Companion to British Railway History* as 'the oldest society of railway enthusiasts in the world'. The definite article marks it out as early, and it had been founded in 1899. A booklet, free to members, chronicled the history, recording the discontinuation in 1927 of musical entertainments at meetings; the installation, in 1932, of a cigarette machine dispensing Wills Gold Flake in the club premises at Victoria; a brake van trip of 1954 'along the Shipston-on-Stour branch (as far as Tiptree)'. In 2007 the club had eighty-five members, of whom I was the youngest at forty-five. Every year a Christmas dinner was held at a hotel near King's Cross. Grace was said, and the queen was toasted. The chairman would then give his review of the year. One new member might have joined, but two would have died and one resigned. The club was wound up in 2009.

Today 'ghost walks' are conducted at Crewe station, and I believe they make reference to Walter de la Mare's ghost story of the 1920s, *Crewe*. The narrator begins:

> When murky dust begins to settle over the railway station at Crewe its first class waiting room grows steadily more stagnant. Particularly if one is alone in it. The long grimed windows do little more than sift the failing light that slopes in on them from the glass roof outside and is too feeble to penetrate into the recesses beyond. And the grained massive black-leather furniture becomes less and less inviting.

The narrator is about to leave for the 'lights and joys of coloured bottles' of the refreshment room when a voice calls to him. 'It was an unusual voice, rapid, incoherent and inter-nal, like that of a man in a dream or under the influence of a drug.' This man tells the narrator a ghost story, set in the countryside in high summer. The waiting-room is employed as a banal counterpoint to the events of the ghost story, but it is the waiting-room that sticks in the mind. At one point the storyteller is interrupted by the arrival of a

> thickset vigorous young porter carrying a bucket of coals in one hand, and a stumpy torch of smouldering brown paper in the other. He mounted one of our chairs and with a tug of finger and thumb instantly flooded our dingy quarters with an almost intolerable glare. That done he raked out the ash-grey fire with a lump of iron that may once have been a poker, and flung all but the complete contents of his bucket of coal on it.

If ours had been a steam train, the crew might have changed at Preston because it's half-way to Glasgow. The *Caledonian Sleeper* stopped there to take on the breakfasts. I like Preston station, which is prettily lined out in red and green. As we pulled away, I fell into a doze, and so I am sorry to fans of Warrington Bank Quay station and Wigan stations, although I can't believe there are many of those. On the platform at Warrington a signs says 'Welcome to Warrington', accompanied by a picture of splendid country house open to the public and advertised as being only half an hour away. Meanwhile the Unilever chemical works tower over the station.

Even if I *had* been awake, the sea – theoretically in view between Lancaster and Oxenholme – would have been invis-ible, given the lateness of the hour. Even on a sunny day you have to keep a careful eye out. You are alerted to its presence

by an outbreak of caravans around Carnforth, which is where
Brief Encounter was filmed, in the days when the station was
on the main line, which it is no longer.

When we stopped at Carlisle, I woke up and looked out
at the empty, monastery-like station. It serves Edinburgh,
Glasgow, the Cumbrian coast and Leeds via the Settle–Carlisle Line. Such is the altitude on that line that you feel you
are flying, especially in low cloud, when your ears pop. It
is said that the wind on the Ribblehead viaduct could stop
a steam engine. The purpose of the Settle–Carlisle was to
enable the Midland railway to get to Scotland by the only
route left available, so it is a trunk route, but the Midland put
some stops on the way, as though absent-mindedly, for dec-
oration, naming them after the nearest village, which was
usually not very near at all but sheltering sensibly in the valley below. The station house at – or named after the village
of – Dent is available to rent, and I stayed there alone once.
It was a ghostly experience. Dent station is just south of the
Moorcock Tunnel, the highest point on the Settle–Carlisle.
Beyond the North End of Moorcock Tunnel a famous train
crash occurred on Christmas Eve 1910. An overworked signalman made an error resulting in a Scotland-bound express
smashing into two locomotives 'running light' (without carriages). The signalman responsible, a man called Sutton,
famously turned to a colleague in the signal box and said,
'Go to Bunce [the stationmaster at nearby Aisgill] and tell
him I'm afraid I have wrecked the Scotch express.'

Looking from the station house, I became very conscious of
the blackened railway sleepers placed upright in the ground a
hundred years earlier to protect the track from snowdrifts. As
the evening wore on, they seemed to be closing in on me, and
I had to keep them at bay with a bottle of red wine. I wouldn't
rent Dent station house on Christmas Eve.

After Carlisle I continued my dreams (to paraphrase *Night Mail*), and so missed our climb up the Shap Bank. In steam days I might have been jolted awake because a banker engine would have been attached to the rear to give us a push. I awoke again to watch the passing of Scottish border hills in a grey and queasy dawn.

Our train divided at Carstairs, 30 miles south of Glasgow, but there was no pronounced shunt, our front eight carriages simply being freed from the rear eight, which would be taken to Edinburgh by another Class 90 loco, brought south from Mossend Depot.

My breakfast was delivered to me by a friendly female attendant as we were going through Motherwell. No bread rolls had been put on at Preston, so I was given a 'croissant', although I don't think anyone French would have recognised it as such. This accompanied a microwaved package labelled 'Meat Breakfast' (and, sure enough, I had selected the non-vegetarian option the night before) with various scientific footnotes – including 'Frozen product store below –18° C' – that increased my sense of being on some sort of survival exercise rather than travelling in de-luxe comfort. The package contained a small sausage, approximately nineteen baked beans, a sliver of mushroom and a lump of scrambled egg. It was perfectly tasty, but it was only a nod in the direction of breakfast. The coffee was instant, but OK. I drank it as we rumbled through Motherwell in gentle rain. Graffiti on a wall near the station urged 'Save Scottish Steel'. Motherwell was once Scotland's 'Steelopolis', but the Ravenscraig steel works closed in 1992.

We pulled into Glasgow Central dead on time, at 7.20. In his amusing book *Eleven Minutes Late* Matthew Engel describes Glasgow Central as 'My favourite station in Britain. It is full of rich old wood and rounded corners, and an

air of familiarity: the windows on the bridge over Argyle
Street are almost Parisian in their jollity ... the flower stall is
in the middle of the concourse, and the smell of lilies filled
the air.' It is a very handsome station, built by the Caledonian Railway in 1879 and rebuilt in Edwardian times. The
old wood and rounded corners belong to the booking office
and station retail outlets, which resemble big boats that have
moored on the concourse. Even the fast food outlets have
been elegantly accommodated within these structures, and
the words 'Burger King' look almost dignified when written
in brass capitals on old wood.

I had never been to Glasgow before, but I have been to
Chicago and I was reminded of that city by the scruffy barren-
ness of some of the outskirts, the wide, grid-pattern streets,
the architectural riches of the busy centre with the frequent
outbreaks of Art Nouveau ... and the entirely different way
with the English language. Many ships and even more locomotives used to be built in Glasgow. Today no locomotives
and few ships are built, but the city does not have the time-
worn air of the *Caledonian Sleeper*.

TERMINATION

I returned to London on a Virgin Pendolino. I used not to
like these trains, which were introduced in 2002. You feel
as though you've been swallowed by a very narrow snake.
The carriages taper towards the roof. This is because they are
designed to tilt at speed, and at least they do tilt, unlike the
Class 4 carriages on the ECML. It's depressing nonetheless
to see one passenger after another trying to stow their bag
on the luggage rack, only to realise there's room for nothing bigger than the smallest handbag. To compensate, floor-
to-ceiling luggage stands are fitted into the carriages, and

these always seem to have windows to themselves, whereas the seat I'd been allocated – B61 – was next to a wall of solid plastic.

There is a persistent flippancy in the 'customer-facing' language of Virgin Trains that I do not think sits well with the dark satanic gravitas of the WCML. Richard Branson apparently loves it 'when signs or announcements show a little sense of humour'. So the coffee is served in cups inscribed, 'Hey there hot stuff fancy a brew?' A notice in the lavatories reads: 'Please do not flush sanitary towels, napkins, old mobile phones, unpaid bills, your ex's jumper, hopes dreams or goldfish down this toilet.' The toilet walls are decorated with pictures of one of Richard Branson's hot-air balloons. I don't know why he doesn't decorate his trains with a wraparound transfer of himself lying on a beach on the Virgin Islands, which is where he lives, thereby disqualifying himself, I suggest, from promoting any increase in aircraft movements over the homes of Londoners.

The doors on his trains beep for a long time before they close, and the trains are generally plagued by electronic noise nuisance. I have never once travelled on a Pendolino without hearing what sounds like the chirping of a demented cuckoo, followed by the words, 'Attention train crew. Passenger emergency alarm operated.' This occurs because the passenger emergency alarm is located where you expect the toilet flush button to be, whereas the flush button itself is well hidden.

But on my journey back from Glasgow I began to warm to the train. I had complained to the guard about my seat, and he said, 'Tell you what sir, head along to carriage "U". You'll probably find yourself the only one in it.' I thought he was making a surreal joke, but sure enough, the standard carriages on a Pendolino go from A to F, then U. There was one other person in carriage U. I sat down at a window seat, and I was impressed by the way the hurtling train leaned into the curves of the track through the sunlit Scottish borders, like a fast motorcyclist. The motion was especially grace-ful when the track curve matched the curvature of a hill or river. The other man in the carriage then began watching a recording of a football match on his iPhone without using headphones, and I had to go over and tell him to turn the damn thing down. He acquiesced, but I was out of sorts for the next couple of hundred miles. Beyond Rugby, I was back in the groove. It was the best time to be going north–south on one of the main lines: late afternoon, when the low sun makes the fields bright green. I re-tuned into the electric note of the train, which would intensify as it accelerated, which it seemed to want to do at every opportunity. We were veritably bounding towards Euston.

I closed my eyes against the low sun. I was tired in a pleas-ant way, and railway dreams may well have been in store: the *Royal Scot* pounding past on the 'down' line; a menu pre-sented at my table, featuring mock turtle soup, halibut with sauce *fines herbes*, roast beef, fruit tart, cheese and coffee; the glittering sea appearing unexpectedly after Milton Keynes, bringing the smell of ozone through the open window; then a compartment suddenly enclosing me; a man in an astra-khan coat, sitting opposite, the clack of jointed rails, like the ticking of a clock as the gaslight guttered ... but he is merely offering a packet of Aspros, since it appears from the motion of the carriage that we are now actually on the sea.

Instead there came a deafening electronic chime, and an over-amplified voice: 'Ladies and gentlemen, this is Tony in the shop, just letting you know that we are now closing the shop for stock-taking prior to our arrival at London Eus-ton. Please await further announcements regarding arrival at Euston from your train manager.' There followed some crackling over the intercom, and it appeared that Tony had finished, but he had one more peroration in store: 'And now, ladies and gentlemen, please sit back, relax and enjoy the rest of your journey.'

ACKNOWLEDGEMENTS

I am particularly grateful to Bob Gwynne, Associate Curator of Rail Vehicles at the National Rail Museum, York. I am also greatly indebted to Russell Hollowood, assistant curator at the museum, and to David Monk-Steel, railway author, for talking to me about signalling and coal movements respectively.

I would also like to thank: Neil Marshall of the 5-Bel Trust; Nicholas Whittaker, author; Barry Doe, fares expert and Rail magazine columnist; Michael Smith, train driver; Michael Chapman and Alan Cox, of the Brick Society; Lauren Robertson, PR manager of the Balmoral Hotel; Terry Bye, editor of Pullman and CIWL News; and Joanna Hughes, Heritage Curator, EMI Group Archive Trust.

Press officers at Eurostar, East Coast, First Great Western and Southeastern Trains also kindly provided press tickets for travel on their services.

Niall Davitt and Peter Saxton offered many valuable suggestions for improving the manuscript. They also eliminated a good many mistakes; any remaining are my responsibility.

... And, yes, I know the signals at the chapter heads are of a kind more commonly associated with America, but they look pretty.